# Sir Garnet Wolseley

# Sir Garnet Wolseley

## Soldier of Empire

Stephen Manning

To Jack,
The 'LAST ONE'!
Thanks for all your
help & encouragement
during my writing/publishing
adventure.
Best wishes
[signature]
"Doc"

Pen & Sword
MILITARY

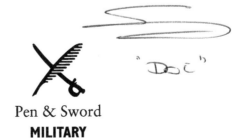

First published in Great Britain in 2023 by
Pen & Sword Military
An imprint of Pen & Sword Books Limited
Yorkshire – Philadelphia



ISBN 978 1 39907 244 1



A CIP catalogue record for this book is
available from the British Library



Typeset by Mac Style
Printed in the UK by CPI Group (UK) Ltd, Croydon, CR0 4YY.

MIX
Paper | Supporting
responsible forestry
FSC
www.fsc.org
FSC® C013604

Pen & Sword Books Limited incorporates the imprints of After
the Battle, Atlas, Archaeology, Aviation, Discovery, Family History,
Fiction, History, Maritime, Military, Military Classics, Politics,
Select, Transport, True Crime, Air World, Frontline Publishing, Leo
Cooper, Remember When, Seaforth Publishing, The Praetorian Press,
Wharncliffe Local History, Wharncliffe Transport, Wharncliffe True
Crime and White Owl.

For a complete list of Pen & Sword titles please contact

PEN & SWORD BOOKS LIMITED
47 Church Street, Barnsley, South Yorkshire, S70 2AS, England
E-mail: enquiries@pen-and-sword.co.uk
Website: www.pen-and-sword.co.uk
or
PEN AND SWORD BOOKS
1950 Lawrence Rd, Havertown, PA 19083, USA
E-mail: uspen-and-sword@casematepublishers.com
Website: www.penandswordbooks.com

To Dr Alison Hodgetts for her happiness and smiles which are infectious and whose support and encouragement have been so welcome.

# Contents

# List of Plates

1. A miniature of Ensign Wolseley before he departed for Burma.
2. British troops lift the Siege of Lucknow. This painting illustrates the brutal nature of the fighting in which Wolseley was engaged.
3. Lieutenant-Colonel Wolseley serving in China in 1860.
4. A picture of Lady Wolseley, circa 1870.
5. Colonel Wolseley at the time of the Red River Expedition of 1870.
6. Wolseley and his Staff at the Prah River Camp before the invasion of Asante territory.
7. A *Vanity Fair* print of Wolseley after his success in the Asante Expedition of 1873–4.
8. 'The Double Perambulator and the Nurse for all our South African Babies'. Wolseley takes care of Generals Chelmsford and Crealock, *Fun Magazine*, 11 June 1879.
9. Wolseley accepts the surrender of Zulu chiefs at Ulundi on 1 September 1879 and imposes his own settlement upon the Zulu nation.
10. Wolseley presents the Victoria Cross to Major Chard at the end of the Zulu War.
11. Wolseley cheers on the Swazi warriors as they assault Sekhukune's stronghold on the morning of 28 November 1879.
12. Wolseley in 1879 in South Africa.
13. A portrait of Wolseley by the artist Paul Albert Besnard, 1880, upon Wolseley's return from South Africa.
14. Brigadier Sir Baker C. Russell, who served under Wolseley in the Asante Campaign of 1873–4, the assault upon King Sekhukhune's stronghold in November 1879 and in the Egyptian War of 1882.
15. General Sir Evelyn Wood VC, who served under Wolseley in the Asante Campaign, in the Egyptian War and during the Gordon Relief Expedition. This photograph was taken in 1880 on Wood's return from South Africa.
16. General Sir Redvers Buller VC, who served under Wolseley in Canada, on the Asante Expedition and in Egypt and Sudan.
17. Lieutenant-General Sir Gerald Graham, VC, long-term friend of Wolseley. Both men fought together in the Crimean War, in the China

# Acknowledgements

To Dr Alison Hodgetts and Will Churcher for their proof-reading skills and encouragement throughout the writing of this book. Thanks also to the librarians of both Exeter Central Library and the University of Exeter Special Collections.

Thanks too to the Staff of the National Army Museum in Chelsea, The National Archives in Kew, and the Devon Heritage Centre in Exeter, whose assistance during my research was invaluable and much appreciated.

Finally, thanks to my sons, Alexander, and Dominic, for allowing me to bore them with talk of my research and the book's progress.

# Abbreviations

| | |
|---|---|
| DCLI | Duke of Cornwall's Light Infantry |
| DHC | Devon Heritage Centre |
| HBC | Hudson Bay Company |
| HLI | Highland Light Infantry |
| NA | National Archives |
| NAM | National Army Museum |
| RAM | Royal Artillery Museum |
| RMLI | Royal Marines Light Infantry |
| TNA | The National Archives |
| WO | War Office |

# Maps

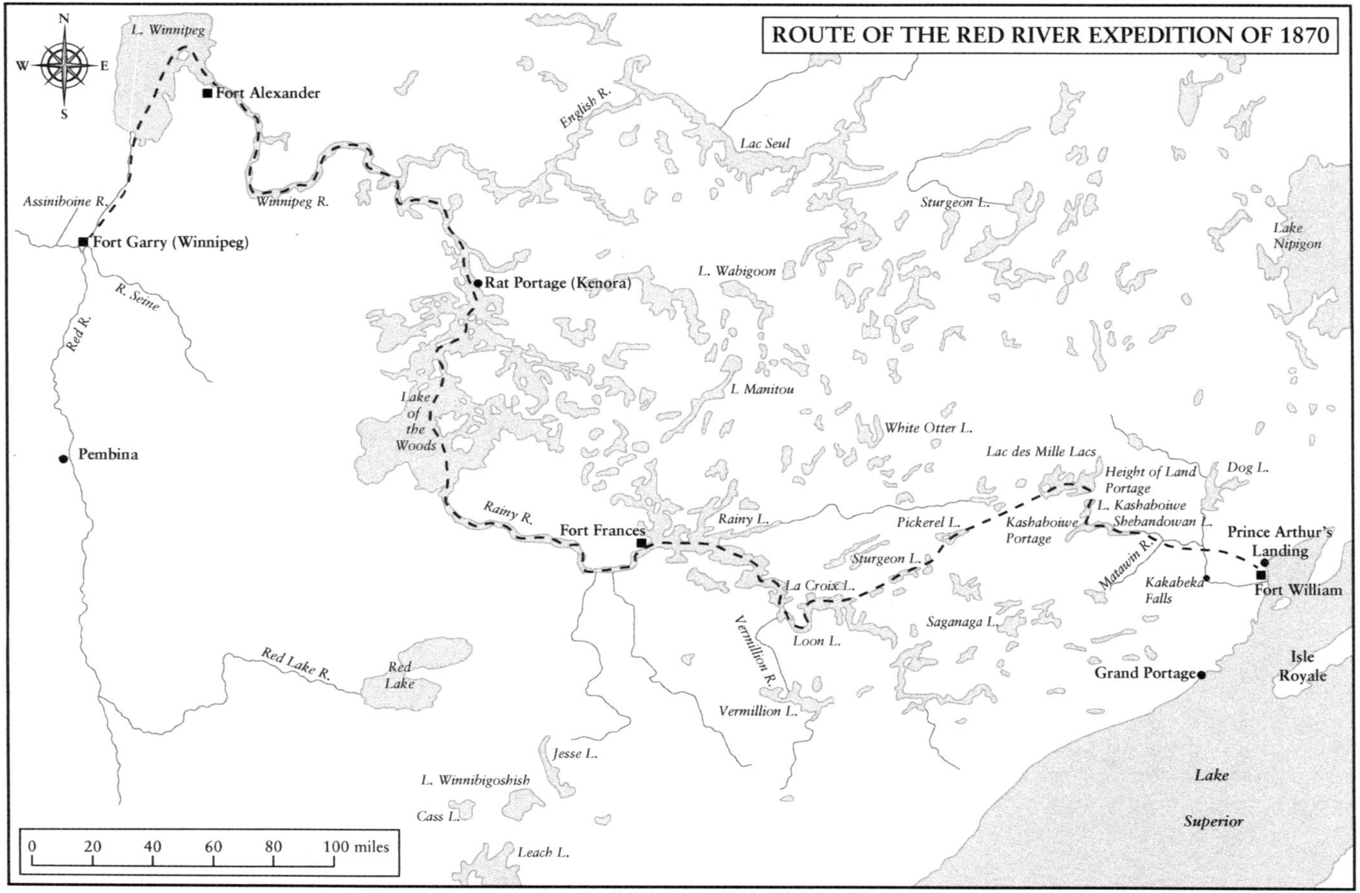
ROUTE OF THE RED RIVER EXPEDITION OF 1870
N
W
E
S
L. Winnipeg
Fort Alexander
Winnipeg R.
Assiniboine R.
Fort Garry (Winnipeg)
R. Seine
Red R.
Pembina
English R.
Lac Seul
Sturgeon L.
Lake Nipigon
L. Wabigoon
Rat Portage (Kenora)
L Manitou
Lake of the Woods
White Otter L.
Lac des Mille Lacs
Height of Land Portage
Dog L.
L. Kashaboiwe
Shebandowan L.
Kashaboiwe Portage
Pickerel L.
Rainy L.
Rainy R.
Fort Frances
Sturgeon L.
La Croix L.
Loon L.
Vermillion R.
Vermillion L.
Saganaga L.
Matawin R.
Kakabeka Falls
Prince Arthur's Landing
Fort William
Isle Royale
Grand Portage
Lake Superior
Red Lake R.
Red Lake
Jesse L.
L. Winnibigoshish
Cass L.
Leach L.
0
20
40
60
80
100 miles

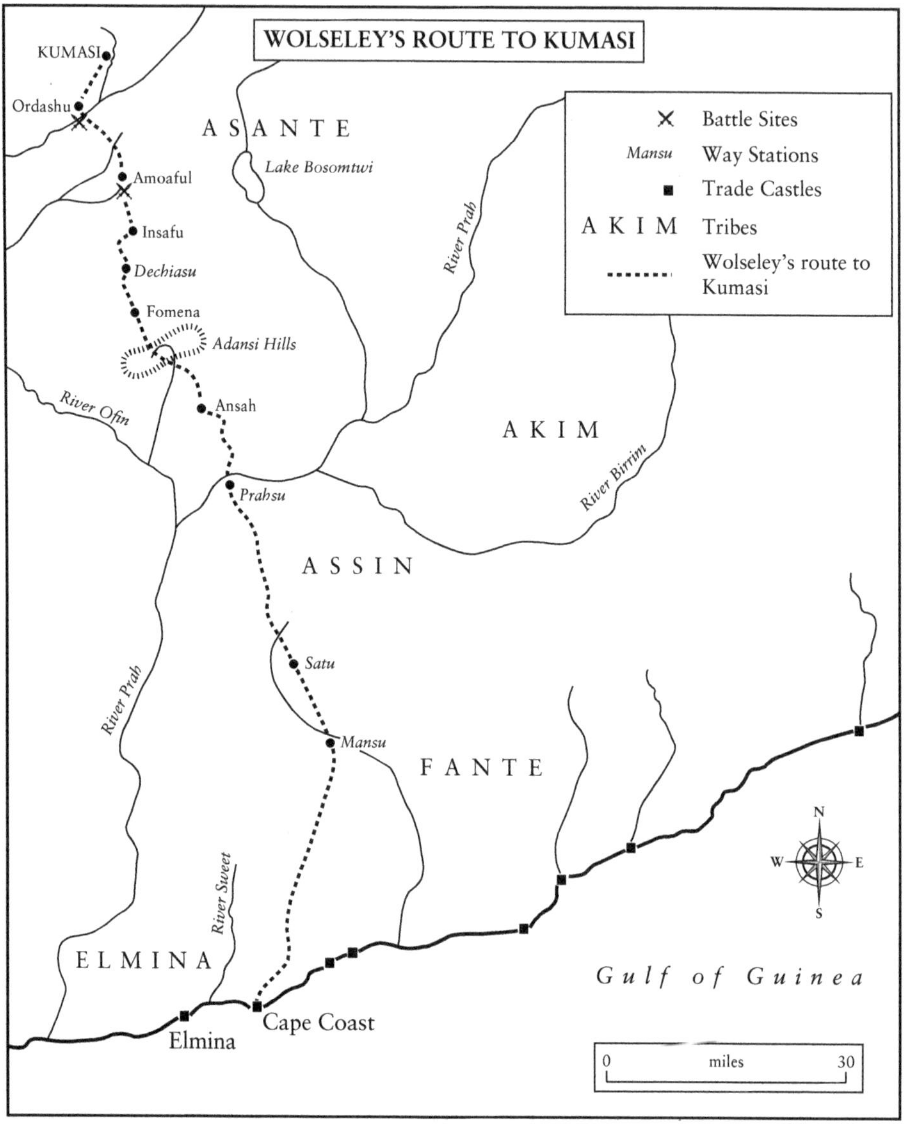

## WOLSELEY'S ROUTE TO KUMASI

KUMASI

Ordashu

A S \ A N T E

Lake Bosomtwi

Amoaful

Insafu

*Dechiasu*

Fomena

*Adansi Hills*

Ansah

*River Ofin*

*Prahsu*

A S S I N

*River Prah*

*Satu*

*Mansu*

F A N T E

*River Sweet*

E L M I N A

Elmina

Cape Coast

*River Prah*

A K I M

*River Birrim*

Gulf  of  Guinea

N
W · E
S

| ✕ | Battle Sites |
| *Mansu* | Way Stations |
| ■ | Trade Castles |
| A K I M | Tribes |
| ...... | Wolseley's route to Kumasi |

0      miles      30

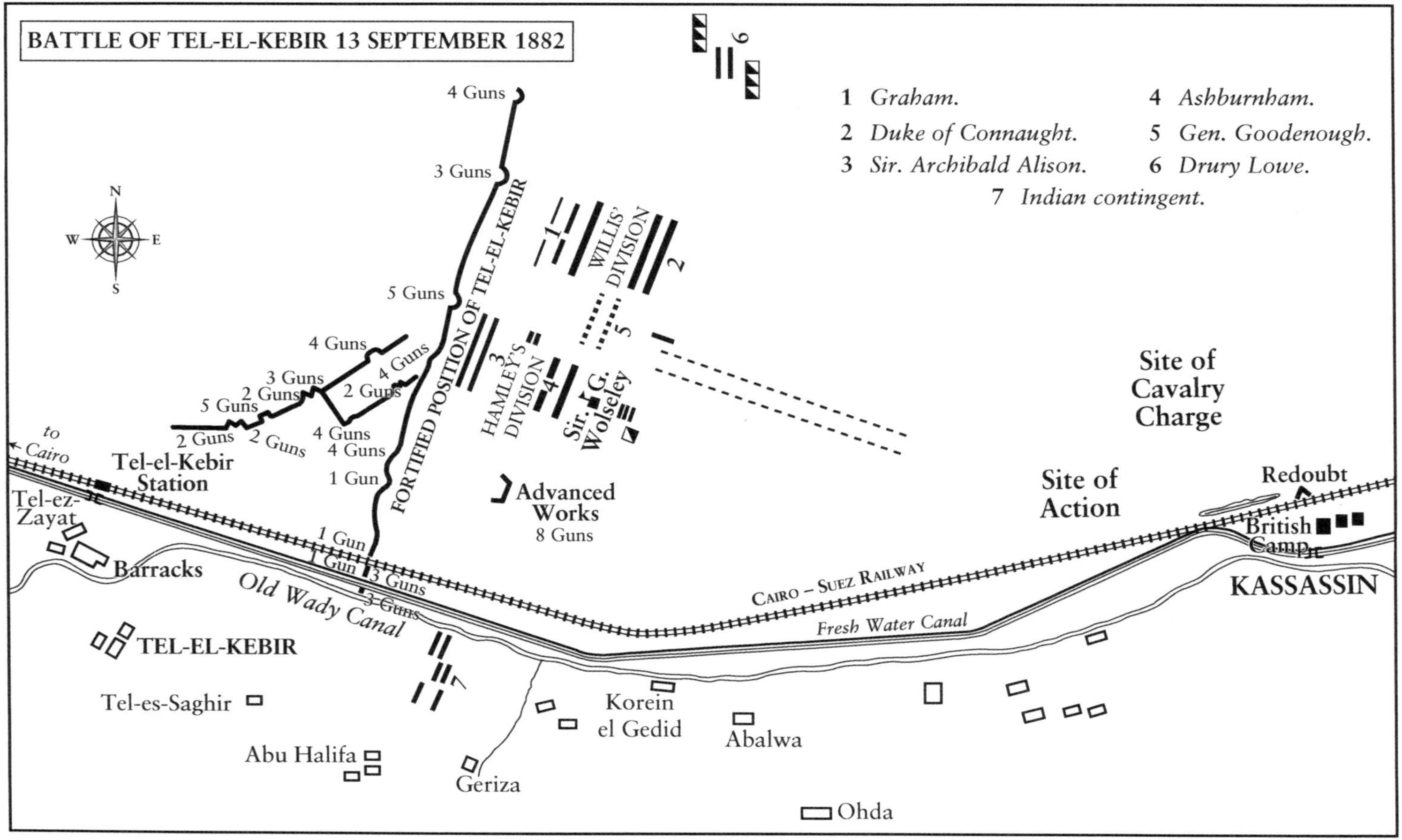
BATTLE OF TEL-EL-KEBIR 13 SEPTEMBER 1882
1 Graham.
2 Duke of Connaught.
3 Sir. Archibald Alison.
4 Ashburnham.
5 Gen. Goodenough.
6 Drury Lowe.
7 Indian contingent.
N
W
E
S
4 Guns
3 Guns
5 Guns
4 Guns
3 Guns
2 Guns
5 Guns
2 Guns
2 Guns
4 Guns
2 Guns
4 Guns
4 Guns
1 Gun
1 Gun
1 Gun
3 Guns
3 Guns
FORTIFIED POSITION OF TEL-EL-KEBIR
WILLIS' DIVISION
HAMLEY'S DIVISION
Sir. G. Wolseley
Advanced Works
8 Guns
Site of Cavalry Charge
Site of Action
Redoubt
British Camp
KASSASSIN
CAIRO – SUEZ RAILWAY
Fresh Water Canal
Old Wady Canal
to Cairo
Tel-el-Kebir Station
Tel-ez-Zayat
Barracks
TEL-EL-KEBIR
Tel-es-Saghir
Abu Halifa
Geriza
Korein el Gedid
Abalwa
Ohda

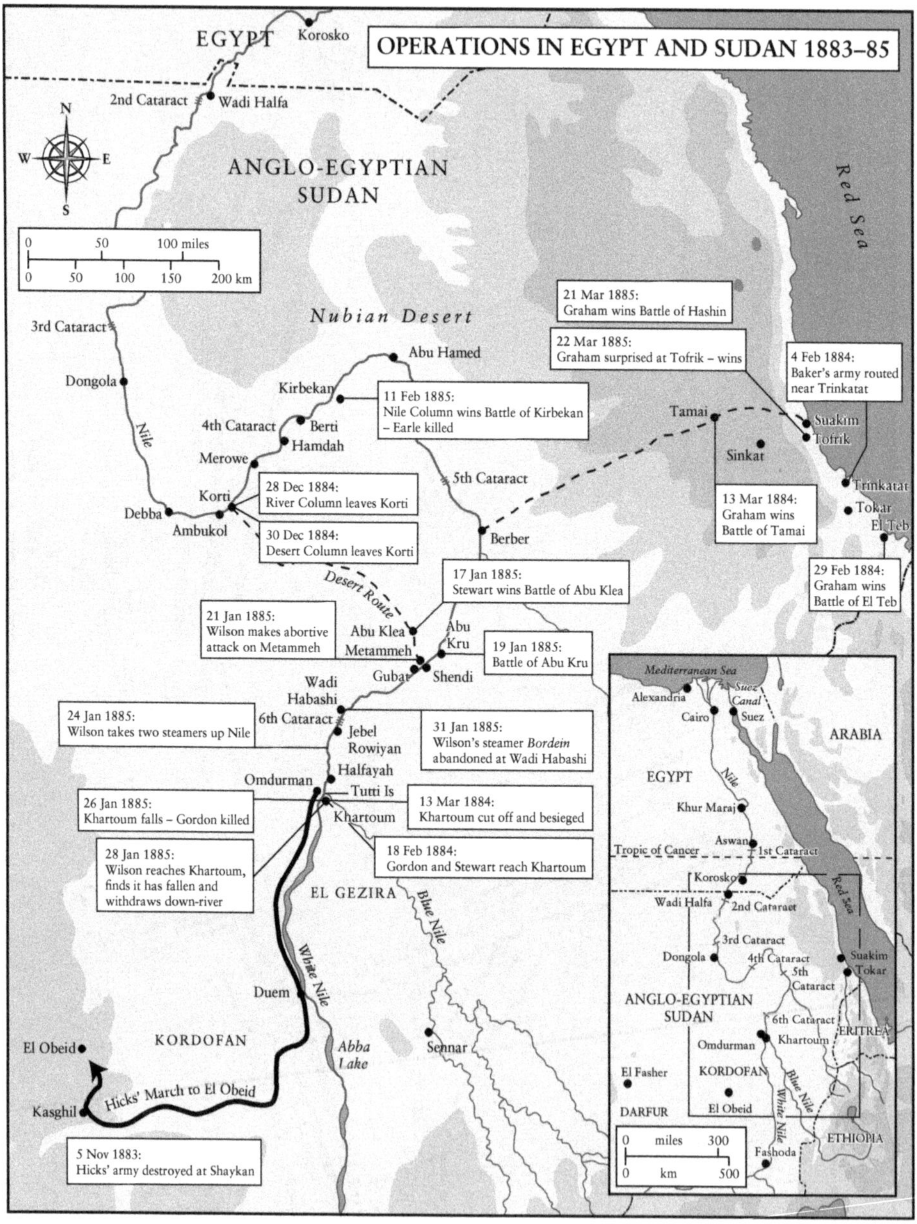

OPERATIONS IN EGYPT AND SUDAN 1883–85
EGYPT
Korosko
2nd Cataract
Wadi Halfa
N
W
E
S
ANGLO-EGYPTIAN
SUDAN
Red Sea
0 50 100 miles
0 50 100 150 200 km
Nubian Desert
3rd Cataract
21 Mar 1885: Graham wins Battle of Hashin
22 Mar 1885: Graham surprised at Tofrik – wins
4 Feb 1884: Baker's army routed near Trinkatat
Abu Hamed
Dongola
Kirbekan
11 Feb 1885: Nile Column wins Battle of Kirbekan – Earle killed
Tamai
Suakim
Tofrik
4th Cataract
Berti
Hamdah
Sinkat
Nile
Merowe
5th Cataract
Trinkatat
Korti
28 Dec 1884: River Column leaves Korti
13 Mar 1884: Graham wins Battle of Tamai
Tokar
Debba
El Teb
Ambukol
30 Dec 1884: Desert Column leaves Korti
Berber
Desert Route
17 Jan 1885: Stewart wins Battle of Abu Klea
29 Feb 1884: Graham wins Battle of El Teb
21 Jan 1885: Wilson makes abortive attack on Metammeh
Abu Klea
Abu Kru
Metammeh
19 Jan 1885: Battle of Abu Kru
Gubat
Shendi
Wadi Habashi
24 Jan 1885: Wilson takes two steamers up Nile
6th Cataract
Jebel Rowiyan
31 Jan 1885: Wilson's steamer *Bordein* abandoned at Wadi Habashi
Halfayah
Omdurman
Tutti Is
26 Jan 1885: Khartoum falls – Gordon killed
13 Mar 1884: Khartoum cut off and besieged
Khartoum
18 Feb 1884: Gordon and Stewart reach Khartoum
28 Jan 1885: Wilson reaches Khartoum, finds it has fallen and withdraws down-river
EL GEZIRA
Blue Nile
White Nile
Duem
El Obeid
KORDOFAN
Abba Lake
Sennar
Hicks' March to El Obeid
Kasghil
5 Nov 1883: Hicks' army destroyed at Shaykan
Mediterranean Sea
Alexandria
Suez Canal
Cairo
Suez
ARABIA
EGYPT
Nile
Khur Maraj
Aswan
Tropic of Cancer
1st Cataract
Korosko
Red Sea
Wadi Halfa
2nd Cataract
3rd Cataract
Dongola
4th Cataract
5th Cataract
Suakim
Tokar
ANGLO-EGYPTIAN SUDAN
6th Cataract
ERITREA
Omdurman
Khartoum
El Fasher
KORDOFAN
Blue Nile
White Nile
DARFUR
El Obeid
ETHIOPIA
0 miles 300
0 km 500
Fashoda

# Introduction

History is ever changing, never static. Morals alter, and the way society views historical events and the characters involved can move radically. Heroes of one century are villains in another, as the recent fate of Edward Colston testifies. Individuals who once possessed worldwide prestige are now long forgotten. In Victorian Britain, an age of imperial expansion, those who reached senior ranks in the military acquired notoriety, honours, wealth and above all fame. Men such as Evelyn Wood, Redvers Buller, Frederick Roberts and Garnet Wolseley were as much celebrities in their times as top footballers, performers or social media gurus are today. It is difficult to imagine how famous these commanders and many others of their profession were, as few of us today have heard of these generals who have been largely forgotten.

Sir Garnet Wolseley was arguably the most famous of Victoria's generals. At the height of his fame, after the 1882 Anglo-Egyptian War, his likeness could be found hanging in parlours across the country and whilst those generals who had been seen to have blundered, such as Lord Chelmsford in his handling of the Anglo-Zulu War, were abused in music hall ditties, Wolseley received the accolade of having the character of 'The Modern Major-General' in Gilbert and Sullivan's comic opera, *The Pirates of Penzance*, based on him and his exploits. Prime Minister Disraeli was said to have described Wolseley as 'Our Only General' and in the decades of the 1870s and into the 1880s Wolseley was certainly viewed as the man to resolve conflicts across the Empire, from Canada to the Sudan. He could be viewed today as something of a trouble-shooter – the man to 'get things done'.

Yet for all his years of military success, which finally came to an end in the failed attempt to rescue his friend Charles Gordon from Khartoum, he was an expert self-publicist who cleverly manipulated both politicians and the public into believing in an image of a man which was not quite as it appeared. Years of private correspondence between Wolseley and his wife, Lady Louisa, show him to be a man who was sometimes vindictive and callous towards his contemporaries and colleagues and, even by the standards of the day, a racist. His private journals written whilst serving in South Africa and the Sudan show a man who was critical of virtually everyone he met, and it is clear he was a conceited, arrogant man. Adrian Preston, editor of both of these journals, noted that the 'decisive, iron-willed, charming and tactful' general loved by his subordinates, 'stands in almost incredible contrast to the apprehensive, querulous, bombastic, vain and uncharitable'[1] individual who lived in his confidential writings. Like many great individuals of history, their greatness frequently came from a place of self-importance and self-projection and Wolseley certainly fits this stereotype.

During his years of service at the War Office he could, and on occasions had to be, cunning in his handling of both politicians and his military colleagues, especially the Queen's cousin the Duke of Cambridge, who for much of Wolseley's career was Commander-in-Chief of the British Army. The Queen herself never truly took to or trusted Wolseley and on occasions remarked 'are there no other generals in the British Army', when Wolseley was once more appointed to command an expedition.

The year 1900 saw the publication of a book entitled *Celebrities of the Army*, which was edited by Commander Chas Robinson, of the Royal Navy. It is a rather sycophantic volume which provides clipped biographies of the senior commanders who had any involvement in the then Boer War of 1899–1902, along with colour plate portraits. Although it can be seen as something of a propaganda tool, it also highlights how senior army officers of the time were very much viewed as celebrities. The entry for Sir Garnet Wolseley, by then Lord Wolseley, Baron Wolseley of Cairo, is particularly fulsome in its praise for the Commander-in-Chief of the British Army. Yet within the words of admiration there's the odd indication of some of the controversies that rested upon Wolseley's shoulders and that are still with us today. For example, Robinson wrote of Wolseley that, 'One of his prominent characteristics has been the faculty of inspiring either undiscriminating admiration or blind animosity'. Writing further, Robinson claimed that in 'fifty years hence, Wolseley should be a commanding figure. Gallant man, earnest soldier, level-headed, cautious commander, strong industrious administrator, he will, by virtue of sheer distinction, rank with Wellington and Von Moltke as one of the greatest military products of the Nineteenth Century.'[2]

Unlike either Wellington or Von Moltke, Wolseley never faced a Continental foe but served to facilitate the enlargement of the British Empire, increasing Britain's prestige at a time when such things were vital to a nation's self-belief, in a world of international competition. This manifested itself most clearly in the so-called 'Scramble for Africa' in the 1880s and 1890s. This is perhaps why, unlike the 'Iron Duke', Wolseley's fame has waned. In modern times the thought of a British Empire raises many emotions, many of them rightly negative, and again this might be a consideration in Wolseley's historic demise amongst the general British population.

I do not pretend that this work can be considered a biography. The last work in that genre was by Halik Kochanski in 1999 and having read that book, and several other biographies of Wolseley written over many decades, I must admit the thought of another biography simply did not appeal to me. Yet, I was driven to write this work as a reassessment of Wolseley's military achievements and by doing so cut through some of the legends surrounding the man, some of which he engineered himself. One point as to military titles in this book; Wolseley rapidly rose through the officer ranks to reach the pinnacle of Commander-in-Chief and I felt that to constantly bombard the reader with Wolseley's rank at specific moments might slow the narrative somewhat, so I have decided to note his rank where essential and appropriate and at other times refer to him as either simply 'Wolseley' or 'Sir Garnet'. If this frustrates some readers, I offer my apologies, but I hope it will please the majority. Again, as in my previous works, I hope you enjoy reading this book as much as I have enjoyed writing it.

Dr Stephen Manning
Exeter, 2023

# Chapter 1
# Death or Glory

According to Wolseley, writing in later life, if a young officer wanted to progress in his career in Victoria's army, he should do his best to get killed, and this was certainly his own personal approach in the early campaigns in which he served. There is no doubt that Wolseley possessed immense bravery and an intense drive, but there seems little doubt that the wounds he endured in his early years of campaigning were 'won' as he tried to battle through the promotion system then in place for British officers. Advancement could be achieved on the bases of conspicuous acts of bravery, seniority, or money. Wolseley was blessed with plenty of the former, but hardly any of the latter.

Wolseley was very much a product of his family background. Although from humble origins his descendants had a long history of service to the British monarchy, and Wolseley would continue this family tradition. He would describe himself in later life as Victoria's 'most faithful soldier and subject',[1] and he was most certainly a true patriot and Empire-builder. Garnet Joseph Wolseley, named after his father, was born on 4 June 1833 in Golden Bridge House near Dublin. Although when he was born Wolseley's father was a Dublin shopkeeper, he had previously served in the King's Own Borderers, predominantly in the West Indies, where, after 29 years' service, he reached the rank of Major. Unable to progress further via the purchase system he sold his commission and settled in Ireland where he married Frances Ann Smith, the daughter of a fervent Protestant; Wolseley's mother's faith would influence him throughout his life. The military historian John Keegan, writing in *Who's Who in Military History*, stated that '... a more unpromising start in life for a Victorian soldier with a career to make could not have been wished on him by the hardest of fairies'.[2]

Yet Keegan's curious words fail to convey that a military life and Royal service had been a long tradition in the Wolseley family. This, combined with the death of his father, when Wolseley was just seven years of age, seems to have predestined Garnet to a career in the army. His family roots could be traced back to the reign of King Edgar (reigned 959–975) who bestowed one of England's oldest estates at Rugely in Staffordshire upon the Wolseley clan. Other descendants included Sewardus, Lord Wisele (a corrupted version of

Wolseley), and a Robert, Lord of Wolseley was recorded in 1281, whilst Ralph Wolseley was a Baron of the Exchequer during the reign of Edward IV (1442–83). Further royal patronage came in the form of a baronetcy from Charles I in 1628. The second Baronet, Sir Charles Wolseley, represented the County of Staffordshire in the Parliaments of both Charles I and Charles II.

Later in the century Colonel William Wolseley, the youngest of the second Baronet's sons, led a troop of Protestants across the countryside of Ireland plundering the lands and homes of Jacobites as well as relieving the hard-pressed Protestant garrison at Enniskillen in July 1689. The following year the Colonel was at the head of 'Wolseley's Horse' and rode side by side with William of Orange as the King cemented his new position on the throne with a crushing victory over James II at the Battle of the Boyne (1 July 1690). Family legend had it that William promised Colonel Wolseley lands in Ireland as a gesture of thanks for his loyalty and support, but when William Wolseley's nephew, Richard, journeyed to Ireland to claim the land he failed to secure legal title. Undeterred, Richard remained and settled on confiscated land in County Carlow which the family seemed to obtain via 'squatter's rights' and in 1744 he was created baronet of Mount Wolseley of Carlow. The following years were not without violence and in 1798 Irish Catholics burned the family home in Tullow and desecrated the Wolseley family burial plot. Yet, the 'Irish Wolseleys' were not to be intimidated and remained in Ireland and it was from this Irish branch that Garnet Wolseley descended.

The Protestant Irish Wolseleys continued to follow a path of military service. One of Garnet's great-uncles was in the 8th Hussars whilst his grandfather, Richard's youngest son, served in the Seven Years War (1756–63), also in the 8th Hussars. He reached the rank of Captain, and, of course, his father served in the British Army for nearly three decades. Yet despite this military family legacy it was perhaps the death of his father, when Garnet was just seven years of age, that was the biggest factor in his decision to join the army. At this tender age he found himself the oldest of seven children, four boys and three girls, and it seems that even then he took the responsibility for his siblings' welfare upon himself. Throughout his life his family would remain a financial burden on Garnet, and this maybe have contributed to his drive and determination to succeed.

Writing in the first volume of his autobiography, *A Soldier's Life*, Wolseley wrote with huge affection of his mother who was a major influence upon his education and outlook on life, describing her as ' pure in heart' and 'very clever, capable, tactful, of sound judgement' as well as 'beautiful, gracious, tall and stately woman, full of love and tenderness for all about her'.[3] The death of Wolseley's father sunk the family into poverty and Garnet could not be sent to England for his education, which would have been the norm for the eldest son of an Anglo-Irish Protestant family. Instead, his mother spent many hours teaching him the Bible and about nature. These informal lessons were clearly very influential in Wolseley's later life for this instilled in him a strong Protestant work ethic and outlook. His mother was just able to send the young Wolseley to a local day school but sometimes she could not afford more than one day a week attendance.

Despite his limited education, Wolseley was clearly an intelligent child with a love of reading and mathematics. He particularly devoured military history texts, such as Napier's volumes on the Peninsular War. Away from lessons, Wolseley was a very active youngster who enjoyed outdoors pursuits, such as shooting and rowing, as well as boxing. What formal education Wolseley received ended when he was 14 years of age, for the financial straits his family suffered forced Wolseley to seek work to bring some extra money into the home. He obtained a position in a land surveyor's office in Dublin, and he excelled at the work. The methodical nature of the job, with its need for attention to detail, proved to offer an excellent training which would serve him well in his future army career, as was the knowledge he obtained of the pocket sextant, prismatic compass, and technical drawing.

Although he seemed almost predestined to an army career, Wolseley at first considered a career in the church, but at this time a clerical living, unless in the most improvised parish, required an initial purchase into the church. Without either a wealthy patron or the finance behind him this idea had to be abandoned. The option of a life as an army officer had similar financial constraints for the most likely way to obtain a commission was by purchase. The purchase system had begun in 1683, during the reign of Charles II, and had initially been viewed as a cash bond for ensuring good behaviour. In the event of gross misbehaviour, cowardice or desertion, the purchase price of the commission, or bond, would be forfeited and the monies given to the army's cashiers. Over time the purchase system evolved into one by which a commission as an officer could initially be secured. Later still the system changed into one where, as vacancies became available for more senior ranks, these could also be purchased from the individual officer who was either being promoted himself or retiring, thus avoiding the need to wait to be promoted by merit or seniority.

As the cost of purchase was high it contributed to the social exclusivity of the officer class and there is little doubt this also reduce the pool of talent into the Army and resulted in uniformity of thinking and even mediocrity. Yet, one benefit was that it did provide retiring officers with a direct source of capital for upon leaving the service they were able to sell their commission to another officer who wished to assume their rank, and this, of course is what Wolseley's father had done when he retired as a Major. This had the benefit to the Crown of reducing the liability to provide either any or a reduced pension for the retiring officer. When Wolseley was considering the army as a career the regulation cost of purchasing a commission in a regiment of the line was £400 (around £58,000 today) although it was common for commissions to sell for double or more of the amount set by law. In addition to this initial outlay there would have been the cost of uniforms and mess bills. An alternative was to gain a commission by attending and graduating from the officer cadet school at Sandhurst but the fees demanded by Sandhurst were beyond Wolseley's means.

The only other means of obtaining a commission, and the only one open to Wolseley, was to gain a nomination by the Commander-in-Chief of the British Army, then the Duke of Wellington. Wolseley first appealed to the Duke in 1847, when he was just 14 years of age. Wellington constantly received petitions from the impoverished sons of former officers, but Wolseley stressed his father's long and meritorious service, and this, along with the fact that like the Duke, Wolseley came from an Anglo-Irish background at least meant that Wellington did not dismiss Wolseley's approach out of hand. Wellington promised Wolseley that he would be considered for a commission when he reached the age of 16.

So encouraged, Wolseley used the years available to him wisely and in between his hours working in the land survey office he improved his French and Latin, as well as algebra and further studied field fortifications, history, and geography, all with the aim of meeting the educational requirements for a commission. At the age of 17, when he felt confident that he would reach the desired standard, he again wrote to Wellington, but this time he was to be disappointed for months went by and neither a negative nor positive response was received. Wolseley now turned to Lord Raglan, Wellington's Military Secretary, in the hope his appeal would once more be placed before the Duke, but again he was met with silence. In desperation, Wolseley's mother decided to act and in September 1851 she wrote a heartfelt plea to Wellington which stressed that she was a poor widow of a former officer and asked the Duke to personally intervene and consider her son as he had promised four years before. Again, months went by, and the family must have given up hope, but their emotions turned to joy when Garnet Wolseley was gazetted as an ensign in the 12th Foot on 12 March 1852. He was 18 years of age, and his long and illustrious career was about to begin.

Although Wolseley had successfully circumvented the purchase system and had acquired his commission without the need for a large, and in his family's case unrealistic, financial outlay, money, or the lack of it, would continue to hamper Wolseley's options. The pay for officers was relatively low and certainly did not cover the demands of the mess, uniforms, horses, and the need to maintain a social standing. Such costs were way above Wolseley's means, especially for those regiments stationed in Britain. In addition, future promotion for home-based officers was based solely on the ability to purchase a higher rank. Wolseley had to turn to the only option available to him not only for advancement but to also to be able to live within his means. That option was to be India.

Not only was India a much cheaper cost-of-living option, but it also offered a chance for war and war provided an opportunity for glory and advancement, as well as of course the risk of death or injury. Yet, for a young officer in Wolseley's position he had no other choice. With war in Burma, Wolseley reacted quickly and secured an immediate transfer to the 80th Foot who were then serving in the Second Burmese War. In June 1852 Ensign Wolseley journeyed to Chatham, the depot for men waiting to be sent to India and Burma. Even in these early weeks of service Wolseley quickly developed his critical eye for his contemporaries which was to be such a part of his judging personality throughout his life. In his memoirs Wolseley described his fellow Ensigns as 'wanting in good breeding' and 'all seemed badly educated'.[4] Fortunately for both Wolseley and, probably, his comrades he seems to have associated little with them in the ten days he spent at Chatham before embarking in the East Indiaman *Maidstone*, which sailed at the end of June.

Before the opening of the Suez Canal the voyage from Britain to India could take over five months, although three was the norm. Such travel was renowned for being uncomfortable and tedious. Wolseley, in his usual driven manner, used the time productively to learn Hindustani and he maintained his fitness by daily climbing the ship's rigging. A stopover in Cape Town broke the monotony and finally the *Maidstone* neared Calcutta at the end of September. Crew and passengers were alarmed to be greeted by the minute gun sounding from Fort William for this traditionally was fired to announce the passing of someone important. This was indeed the case for once ashore Wolseley and his fellow travellers were informed that the Duke of Wellington had died on 14 September. Wellington had been more than just the head of the British Army, he was its heart too and the end of his era would eventually result in a modernising of both weaponry, tactics and thinking. Wolseley, who had benefitted from Wellington's support, become one of the chief drivers in efforts to make the British Army more able to face the challenges of the latter part of Victoria's reign.

Wolseley was to be initially frustrated in his efforts to join the fighting in Burma for the ensigns were first despatched to the depot at Chinsura, which was where officers were sent before being dispersed to their individual postings. Life at Chinsura was dull, and Wolseley began to fear that the War would be over before he could join his new regiment. Finally, Wolseley was called forward and, joining other members of the new draft for the 80th, he sailed in a steamer to Rangoon. However, on arriving in Burma, in January 1852, Wolseley, discovered, much to his disappointment, that the war had been brought to a rapid and victorious conclusion. It appeared that all the immediate future offered him was drill and picket-duty.

Fortunately for Ensign Wolseley the conclusion of the war had not brought a total end to hostilities for Mya-htoon, a local criminal, or robber-chief, with his own army of supporters, continued to operate against the British, for his own personal gain. He was threatening supplies being transported along the Irrawaddy, between Rangoon to the British forward camp at Prome. Although little more than an irritant to the British, such banditry could not be tolerated by Major General Henry Godwin, the commander of British forces in Burma. In February 1853, Godwin gave command of an expedition to take Mya-htoon's base deep in the jungle to Captain Lock RN. Unfortunately, once away from the Irrawaddy the naval captain was militarily out of his depth, making several elementary errors which resulted in his force being ambushed. Lock and twelve of his men were killed in the engagement and the survivors were forced to make an ignominious retreat. Godwin was furious when he heard news of the reverse and immediately ordered a military expedition, under the command of Brigadier-General Sir John Cheape, to be assembled to avenge the British deaths. Wolseley, much to his delight, was ordered to take a detachment of the 80th to the village of Donabew from where Cheape was basing his operations against Mya-htoon.

Wolseley was to learn many lessons from his first combat experience, but perhaps the most significant was an appreciation of, and the need to fully understand, the terrain and climate in which the army operated. The British were fighting not just a determined and dangerous foe, but also the jungle and Wolseley soon discovered how ill-prepared he and his comrades were to face the latter. As Wolseley noted in his memoirs, 'The Queen's Army took an idiotic pride in dressing in India [and in Burma] as nearly as possible in the same clothing they wore at home ... We wore our ordinary cloth shell jackets buttoned up to the chin, and the usual white buck-skin gloves. Could any costume short of steel armour be more absurd in such a latitude?'[5] Naturally both Wolseley and his comrades suffered intolerable discomfort in such uniforms and Wolseley would take note of the importance of suitable clothing for his troops when he led them in such later campaigns as Asante (1873–4) and the Nile Expedition (1884–5). Although sometimes contemptuous of his men, Wolseley did show, throughout his career, a compassion for their suffering and many of his later reforms were undertaken to improve their well-being.

It was not just the heat and humidity of the jungle that Cheape's force had to deal with, but they also had great difficulty negotiating their way along narrow and sometimes ill-defined paths, led by guides who either through fear of reprisals, incompetence or deceit, frequently hindered rather than assisted the British advance. Yet despite these hardships the greatest danger to Wolseley and his comrades was not the jungle or even a Burmese bullet, but the risk of cholera. This dreadful disease, which inflicted upon its victims a cruel, painful, if, mercifully quick death, struck Cheape's column a few days after the 1,200 troops, half European and half Indian sepoys, marched away from the Irrawaddy. Departing on 6 March 1852 the force soon came under desultory fire from a hidden enemy, reportedly up to 4,000 strong. Fortunately for the British, Mya-htoon and his followers showed a great reluctance to engage in close-quarters fighting for the British presented a vulnerable target and the rebels may well have decimated the British if they had shown more determination.

Each day as the slow march inched towards its destination, cholera took a greater and greater toll. Wolseley was frequently on night sentry duty, and after grabbing just a few hours' sleep each night he was awoken by his Sergeant, a man named Quinn. The first question Wolseley directed towards Quinn was to ask how many men had died of cholera during the night and how many more were dying, and the young ensign must have wondered if his turn to endure an agonizing end might come. In just a few days over 100 men, out of the total force of 1,200, had been claimed by cholera. Cheape must surely have contemplated that the expedition might be forced to retire before reaching its target, for not only men were being lost to cholera, but the remainder were suffering a terrible ordeal as the commissariat began to fail and the troops were forced to accept reduced rations. With no tents carried, the men were also struggling with exhaustion inflicted by the terrain, climate, and lack of sleep as few managed to gain any rest on the damp jungle floor. Indeed, Cheape was forced to call a halt to the advance after seven days to allow his men to rest and for food and supplies to reach his men from the base at Donabew.

Yet despite all these hardships, after a 12-day ordeal Cheape had led his force to within striking distance of Mya-htoon's stronghold at Kyault Azein. Cheape resolved that his men would attack the main stockade on the following morning, 19 March. Much to his surprise Wolseley was informed that he would be leading the advance party and despite a mixture of both fear and excitement he slept soundly that night. As the first streaks of light appeared Wolseley was up rousing his men from their slumbers. The morning, like most in the jungle, was shrouded in a heavy dense fog, which normally took several hours to disperse and had previously hampered the British advance. However, Wolseley used this to his advantage and was able to approach to within 100m of the stockade with his party of four men. Here the group managed to conceal themselves as they kept a watch on the Burmese camp as it stirred itself awake. Wolseley was able to report back to his commanding officer, Major Holdich, that the enemy had not posted any pickets, even though they must have been aware of the nearby presence of the main British force. In addition, Wolseley and his men had noticed that the main stockade was surrounded by a deep riverbed, or nullah, that had clearly been diverted to enhance the defences which seemed impregnable to assault and certainly could not be outflanked without attracting fire from its defenders. Yet Wolseley was able to return to the main body and he informed Cheape that his reconnaissance had discovered that the nullah narrowed at one point and here the water was shallower and, in his opinion, might be vulnerable to a sudden rush assault.

Cheape ordered a general advance upon the stockade and the first assault resulted in some confusion with units, both European and Indian become intermixed, and Cheape summoned his forces back. He now resolved to rely on just his imperial troops and the men of the 80th and 18th Royal Irish were once again sent forward, with the 4th Sikhs in support. In addition, Cheape's sappers were able to clear a path for the artillery to unleash shell and rocket fire upon the stockade. Despite the damage inflicted, the Burmese defenders were able to respond with a heavy fire that wounded many in the assault, including Majors Wigston and Armstrong. With the assault stalling Lieutenant Allan Johnson of the 4th Sikhs and Ensign Wolseley rallied those around them, and the two officers charged forward at the head of this small force. In later life Wolseley was to write of this first charge and of the exhilaration and intense pleasure that flooded through him as he led his men forward. He stated, '… for the moment your whole existence, soul and body, seems to revel in a true sense of glory. The feeling is catching, it flies through a mob of soldiers and makes them, whilst the fit is on them, absolutely reckless of all consequences. The blood seems to boil, the brain is on fire.'[6]

Fortunately for both Wolseley and posterity his own personal charge was cut short within 20 yards of the enemy's stockade for when leading the charge, the ground suddenly opened underneath him and he fell into a *trou-de-loup*, or pit, constructed by the Burmese defenders, which had sharp stakes point up driven into the ground. Miraculously, although momentarily knocked out by the fall, Wolseley had managed to avoid the stakes and it was only his pride that had been bruised. Cautiously he emerged to discover that the others in his charging party had either been killed, wounded, or had retreated and that he was all alone with the enemy approaching his position. With only his sword with which to defend himself, for he had lost his pistol in the fall, Wolseley felt that his only hope of survival was to jump out of the pit and run back to the British lines. He waited for the enemy to let off a volley and then whilst they reloaded, he took his chance and fled to safety.

After such an ignominious first assault Wolseley was keen to redeem himself and when Cheape came forward with more artillery and reinforcements Wolseley pressed himself to the fore and requested that he once again be allowed to lead another assault. Cheape consented and with another volunteer, Lieutenant Taylor of the Madras Native Infantry, Wolseley collected all the men of the 80th he could find in the confusion and the two officers charged forward under a well-sustained fire from the enemy's battlements. When the two officers reached the pit into which Wolseley had so recently fallen, Taylor went to its left and Wolseley to the right. Suddenly Wolseley witnessed Taylor stumble forward, shot in the thigh and within seconds Wolseley too fell, also with a wound to his thigh. He somersaulted from the impact of the Burmese slug which was described as big as a plover's egg. Sergeant Quinn stopped and detailed men to remove Wolseley to the rear. Recovering his senses Wolseley yelled, 'Leave me alone; get into the stockade before they can reload'.[7] Now helpless on his back, Wolseley managed to wave his sword in support, and he cheered Quinn and the men of the 80th forward as they successfully took the stockade with the bayonet.

Assistant-Surgeon Murphy hurried forward and with the aid of a tourniquet was able to stem the flow of blood from Wolseley's wound. The ensign was indeed fortunately for although the wound was large the femoral artery had not been severed. Taylor was not so lucky, and Wolseley watched as his fellow officer bled to death in front of him. One of Wolseley's biographers, and a contemporary, Charles Rathbone Low, wrote in 1878 that if the Victoria Cross had been in existence in 1852 then surely Wolseley would have been awarded the medal for his actions at Kyault Azein.

Wolseley was now to endure a wretched few weeks at the hands of the Army doctors. It was only his young age and strong physical constitution that saw him survive the rather brutal treatments, which including starvation to supposedly reduce inflammation in his wounded leg, and the transportation of the wounded down the Irrawaddy. Although Wolseley's strength gradually improved, he was sent home to England as an invalid, and it took many months for his wound to heal. He would always suffer with discomfort and pain from his leg, but in his mind all the trials and tribulations he had suffered in Burma had been worth it. Not only did Cheape mention Wolseley in despatches, which was an extremely rare occurrence for an ensign in his first engagement, but later in the year Wolseley's bravery earnt him a promotion to lieutenant, without the need for purchase. Exposing himself to death had certainly benefitted the young Wolseley.

Wolseley's promotion saw him transfer to the 90th Regiment who were then based close to Dublin Castle and he spent some time there improving his drill. He found life dull for his financial position did not allow him to hunt and his wounded leg prevented him from dancing and fully enjoying the social scene of a recently promoted lieutenant. However, his time in Ireland was not to last long for in March 1854 France and Britain declared war on Russia and the Crimean War began. Although the 90th were due for service in India, the high casualties in the early battles of the war, such as at the Alma (20 September 1854), saw the regiment transferred in November to the seat of war. Once again, Wolseley could seek glory.

Wolseley landed in the Crimea in December 1854 and was disappointed to discover that he and his regiment had missed the bloody battles of Balaclava (25 October 1854) and Inkerman (5 November 1854). The war was to now enter something of a stalemate as Russian forces found themselves besieged behind the walls of Sebastopol by the Allies. For Wolseley his experiences of the Crimea were to leave him disillusioned with many aspects of the British Army. Not only was the Army's logistics found to be wanting, with both food and material supplies lacking, but he was to be appalled by the failings of the senior commanders, and his fellow officers who Wolseley thought were too concerned with their own comfort to show any real interest in their military craft. One exception to this rule was Charles Gordon with whom Wolseley would strike up a 30-year friendship and whose lives and careers would be intertwined. Of the senior officers, Wolseley had little respect for the British commander-in-chief, Lord Raglan who he felt had made basic command errors which had allowed the enemy to retreat behind the walls of Sebastopol, but his greatest wrath was directed at General John Burgoyne, who was responsible for the siege of the Russian naval port. Wolseley, with his training as a land surveyor and natural eye for terrain, strongly felt that Burgoyne had fatally directed forces towards the city's better-defended southern walls rather than focusing on the weaker northern defences. Over the next months Wolseley would play a prominent role in the siege and would once more gain plaudits and promotion.

Initially Wolseley served with his regiment, with his role restricted to leading his men on early morning and night-time patrols and picket duties. His company commander was a man of little original thinking except when it came to shirking his own work and responsibilities. This load naturally fell upon Wolseley's shoulders, and he rose to the challenge so effectively that within just a few weeks of his arrival he was gazetted to the rank of captain. He was to be outraged two weeks later when he was informed that at only 21, he was too young to assume such a rank. Wolseley's temper, for which he was to become notorious particularly when faced with what he considered incompetency or inefficiency, was quickly unleashed and on threat of his resignation his captaincy was restored. Yet this was still not enough for the newly-promoted captain, for he was soon bored with his regimental duties. With his experience as a land surveyor, he managed to obtain a transfer to the Royal Engineers who were particularly short of officers, and he was appointed as an assistant-engineer.

In this new role as a sapper, or combat engineer, Wolseley was at the forefront of danger in the most advanced Allied positions. He worked mainly at night, repairing defences that had been bombarded by the Russian guns in the day and on occasion using the cover of darkness to extend the British trenches. Wolseley would often be on duty for 24 hours and this combined with the stress and exertions of the position meant that he frequently fell exhausted into his bed, grabbing a few much-needed hours of rest before returning to his dangerous new role.

Wolseley was frequently under fire from both Russian shell and snipers. Despite many close shaves, he displayed a calmness and cheerfulness under fire that reassured his men and this he was to display throughout his career. Over the next six months Wolseley was to lead a charmed life but on 6 June 1854 his luck finally ran out when he was hit in the thigh and although the bullet did not penetrate it did cause heavy bruising. Despite the pain he refused to go to the rear. The action was part of an infantry assault by the British to take the Russian position known as the Quarries and Wolseley's role had been to extend the British trenches to reduce the threat to the infantry advance. Although the attack failed Wolseley and his fellow sappers were kept busy as the enemy respond with a fierce bombardment that severally weaken the British position. Fearing a Russian counter-attack, he was to continue to work frantically for over 36 hours to restore the British trenches. Finally, he was able to collapse into a 24-hour sleep. For his bravery and example, he was again Mentioned in Despatches.

Despite his latest wound Wolseley continued to serve in the front line from where he witnessed the failed and rather botched Allied assaults on the Russian positions of the Redan, the Malakoff and the Mamelon on 18 June. He was appalled by the reckless and futile attacks which resulted in so many lives being lost. The Russians, with their supply lines to Sebastopol now cut, attempted one last breakout, and attacked the Allied lines at Tchernaya on 16 August. Although the British lines were pulverized the Russians were beaten back, and the surrender of the besieged Sebastopol now seemed inevitable. The Russian artillery still fired defiantly, and on 30 August, it claimed yet more victims. On this day Wolseley led a working party of sappers forward to repair some of the damage done to the Allied defences in the earlier battle. The party came under heavy fire and soon twelve of his men were casualties. Wolseley though was undeterred and leading a sergeant and two sappers further forward the group was targeted by a Russian shell. The two sappers were killed instantly, and stones and pebbles smashed into Wolseley's face and body, knocking him unconscious. Remarkably the sergeant was untouched, and he was able to support Wolseley back through the trenches to seek medical attention.

On first examination the surgeon pronounced Wolseley 'a dead'un'.[8] Although Wolseley was able to assure the surgeon that he was very much alive, his head and body had been badly smashed, and his appearance was not distinguishable. Fragments of stone were embedded in his face, and his left cheek had been almost torn away. The surgeon probed this wound and removed a large stone lodged in his jawbone. Both eyes were so swollen that they were closed shut and it was later discovered that he had permanently lost his sight in his right eye. He had also sustained numerous wounds to his torso as well as damage to his right shin, and this injury would continue to cause him pain for nearly 10 years until it was operated on again. The surgeon stitched Wolseley's cheek and he was taken to St. George's Monastery near Balaklava to recuperate. He was later transferred to a nearby cave for his eyes were so badly damaged that for weeks he could not tolerate light and here he spent several weeks during which he suffered badly from melancholy.

Wolseley had constantly exposed himself to danger throughout his time in the engineers. He had worked in the most advanced positions for many months, directing the working parties and the work of the engineers was viewed as probably the most dangerous of all the ranks. This is reflected in the casualty rate for the engineers and sappers for by the time the Allies had taken Sebastopol on 8 September: 935 officers and men had served of which 218 had been killed and a further 119 had become casualties of the conflict. For his bravery Captain Wolseley was again recommended for promotion to the Secretary of State for War, the Duke of Newcastle. Wolseley was to hear in October, in a letter from the Military Secretary to the Commander-in-Chief, Viscount Hardinge, that his recommended promotion to the rank of major had been declined as he had only served three years and seven months in the army. Although naturally disappointed, Wolseley knew that he was beginning to gain a very positive reputation amongst senior officers.

Upon hearing the news of the surrender of Sebastopol Wolseley resigned his position of assistant-engineer. His eyes were causing so much concern that he was now ordered to return to London, yet before he could board a returning ship the sight in his left eye improved significantly and, resolved as he was that his right eyesight could not be saved, he decided to remain in the Crimea. He was offered a position on the Quartermaster-General's staff and his first role was that of a surveyor to Allied forces deployed in the Belbac valley, on the left flank of the Russian forces, for although Sebastopol had fallen the war continued. Here, whilst undertaking his surveying work, he had several close encounters with Russian cavalry who objected to Wolseley working so close to their lines. With the approach of winter, the Allies fell back from the Belbac valley and Wolseley was appointed Deputy Assistant-Quartermaster-General to the Light Division, under the command of Lord Paulet. Peace was finally agreed between Russia and the Allies by the Treaty of Paris of 30 March 1856 and Wolseley now worked under Colonel Hallowell at Balaklava to supervise the despatch of returning troops. The last regiment to embark, the 50th, handed over Sebastopol on 12 July 1856, to a unit of Cossacks and Wolseley was one of the last British soldiers to step from Russian soil. He returned to England and re-joined the 90th at Aldershot.

In early 1857 Wolseley received the news that he was to accompany the 90th Regiment to China where war looked imminent. In April, with most of the men already despatched, Wolseley left with the last remaining three companies on the HM Troopship *Transit*. The voyage was eventful, for the vessel underwent running repairs to maintain its seaworthiness which much delayed the journey. Arriving at The Cape the troops and crew were met with a rumour that they had been a rebellion amongst the Indian sepoys and that India was in uproar. Whilst most could not believe the news Wolseley was inclined to think that the *Transit* and her passengers might be soon diverted to a new seat of war. Fate intervened for when entering the Straits of Bangka, between Sumatra and the islands of Bangka, the unfortunate ship hit a rock and began to sink by the stern. Luck was with Wolseley and those onboard for the vessel sunk slowly which enabled all to be ferried via the ship's boats to a coral reef close to the foundering *Transit*. The following morning the men were able to use the boats to reach the nearby island of Bangka where fresh water was available. Here all were to wait for 10 days until a British gunboat arrived with confirmation that a massive rebellion had broken out in India and that Wolseley and the men of the 90th would be taken there where their presence was urgently needed.

The Indian Revolt began in May 1857, and it first ignited in the city of Meerut. Its origins had many complex roots and for many years it was thought that the uprising had been caused by the introduction of a new cartridge for the army-issue Enfield rifle which it was believed was greased by a blend of pork and beef fat, thus offending the religious sensibilities of both Muslim and Hindu recruits. Yet although the cartridge did lead to serious disquiet it was fundamentally opposition to British rule that resulted in the rebellion which was exploited by Indian nationalist leaders, such as Bahadur Shah. Within the Bengal Army poor terms of service and pensions, bad pay, lack of promotion, and increased cultural and racial insensitivity from British officers all contributed to the feelings of discontent among the 135,000 Indian soldiers. Fortunately for the British the revolt was largely restricted to the Bengal Army and those troops of the Madras and Bombay Armies were relatively unaffected whilst other Indian units, including Sikhs, Punjabi Muslims and Gurkhas, supported the British. Yet with only 35,000 British soldiers within the whole subcontinent, reinforcements were urgently needed. Troops were sent from garrison in such places as Mauritius and of course troops were diverted from service in China, Wolseley being one of them.

Following the outbreak at Meerut, uprisings occurred across northern and central India. The early weeks of the conflict were characterized by extreme brutality by the sepoys towards Europeans, both soldiers and civilians, whilst later, as the British gained the ascendency on the battlefield, retribution and revenge against the rebels became equally as brutal. The main centres of rebellion were Delhi, Cawnpore, Lucknow, Jhansi and Gwalior. Delhi fell quickly to the rebels and at both Cawnpore and Lucknow British troops and civilians were under siege and atrocities and massacres were experienced there and across northern India. Whilst Wolseley arrived too late in India to take part in the retaking of Delhi he was involved in the aftermath of Cawnpore and relief of Lucknow and in the latter, he would again distinguish himself.

After disembarking at Calcutta, Wolseley once again found himself in Chinsura where the three companies of the 90th from the ill-fated *Transit* were re-supplied. There would be many months of hard fighting ahead before these men were reunited with the rest of the battalion. Most of the troops, Wolseley included, had lost their possessions when their transport ship foundered and although they were given new Enfield rifles, uniforms were lacking. The three companies entered the campaign wearing a collection of ill-matched and often ill-fitting outfits. It is worth considering what these men and thousands of other troops, the 'Soldiers of the Queen', had to endure not just in this campaign but in the many others during Victoria's reign and, of course, Wolseley would frequently be at the heart of these operations. Diseases such as cholera, typhoid and dysentery would not only affect men on the line of march but often in their unsanitary barracks. Food there and on campaign was frequently poor both in terms of quality and quantity and this added to the deprivations they faced. British troops suffered from sunstroke in large numbers during the many Victorian campaigns and in their efforts to quell the Indian rebellion it was a significant killer, particularly amongst newly arrived reinforcements who had not yet acclimatized to India's oppressive heat. In May 1858 alone over 1,000 British troops died of sunstroke, fatigue and disease; a truly staggering figure.[9] Although Wolseley was a young man, he had suffered severely in both of his earlier campaigns, enduring hardships and physical injury, yet he, and many of his comrades would now rise to the demands placed upon them. The sense of revenge and retribution and the need to rescue those besieged by the rebels certainly spurred Wolseley and his comrades to endure incredible physical hardships as they fought to reclaim what they believed to be part of the Empire by right. Indeed, Wolseley was to write to his brother Dick that 'My sword is thirsty for the blood of these [the rebels] cursed women slayers'.[10]

Wolseley's personal Indian campaign began on 29 August 1857 when he was ordered to take his company to Cawnpore, which had been the site of an infamous massacre of British residents. At Chinsura station Wolseley had to use his initiative to load an accompanying 6-pounder artillery piece onto the train. The doors of the railway station were too narrow to allow for the passage of the gun onto the platform and with howls of protest from the station staff Wolseley had his men enlarge the doorway, causing significant damage in the process. Wolseley half-expected to receive a claim for compensation from the railway but it was not forthcoming, and he was able to embark both his men and the cannon onto the awaiting train which took them the 112 miles to terminus of the line at Raneegunge. From here Wolseley was forced to lead his men on foot for the remainder of the journey.

This march was one fraught with danger for the three companies from the 90th were the first British troops since the outbreak of the rebellion to march along what was known as the 'Grand Trunk Road', which was then a military highway or artery joining Calcutta and Delhi. Not only did the troops had to deal with the anxiety of not knowing what they might face in terms of opposition, but they also had to cope with heavy rains which swelled rivers and streams and turned tracks into muddy quagmires. As the men neared Cawnpore so the destruction inflicted by the rebels increased. Wolseley maintained a cheerful, encouraging disposition towards his men, although he was constantly on edge, fearing an ambush at any moment. Despite the hardship of the march the men of the 90th averaged over 20 miles a day and by 13 September they had reached Allahabad, before reaching Futteepore, just 40 miles from Cawnpore. Here the three companies were reunited, for they had become detached whilst on the march, and Major Roger Barnston took overall command. The force remained at Futteepore for a few weeks until their commander, General Havelock, moved forward to relieve Lucknow and ordered the 90th to Cawnpore. Here Wolseley and his comrades were able to witness the dreadful aftermath and sights of the recent June massacre of 120 women and children by rebels, led by Nana Sahib, including the infamous well in which many victims had been thrown. Blood splattered the walls of the various buildings near where Wolseley was forced to bivouac with his men.

The British senior command ensured that any troops who had to pass through Cawnpore at this time were made to visit the sites of the massacre and this was designed to generate a sense of hatred and revenge towards the rebels if it had not already existed. Wolseley wrote of his own experiences of Cawnpore, 'Upon entering those blood-stained rooms the heart seemed to stop. The horror of the scene was appalling and called up our worst angry passions ... it awoke in us, the countrymen of those helpless victims, a fiendish craving for the blood of the cowardly murderers who had ordered the massacre and of the brutes who had perpetrated it.'[11] Wolseley and his men would soon have the opportunity to reap their revenge.

Havelock's relief of Lucknow had not gone to plan. Although he had been able to break through the besiegers ranks and into the Residency, where British troops and civilians had been trapped, Havelock's command was insufficient to withdraw with the wounded, sick and able bodied. The relieving force now joined the ranks of the besieged and would need their own relief force. Sir Colin Campbell led his men, including Wolseley and the 90th, towards Lucknow and by the end of October Wolseley found himself at Alum Bagh, a palace on the outskirts of Lucknow, having escorted a convoy of baggage there. Here he spent a very dull week or so before Campbell arrived with his main force. At Alum Bagh Wolseley was under the direct command of a Major Duncan McIntyre and the two frequently clashed for the Major was no warrior and put a firm end to any hopes that Wolseley had of leading the occasional sally on the enemy positions which were only a few hundred metres away.

By 16 November Campbell was able to launch his own relief of Lucknow and Wolseley was given the honour of leading his company as the advanced guard in the initial attack. Wolseley and his men were to be closely followed by the 9th Lancers and the 93rd Highlanders, Campbell's own regiment which had so distinguished itself at the Battle of Balaclava. Campbell had earlier given a speech to the men of his command in which he had advised them to be ready to use the bayonet as much as possible against the enemy in the narrow streets of Lucknow. No one, including Wolseley, could have been under any illusion as to the bloody and brutal task that they now faced.

The first formidable obstacle the advancing column faced was Sekunder Bagh, formerly the garden of Alexander the Great, which was surrounded by strong walls, 20ft high, with turrets on each of the four corners. Campbell knew this area would be heavily and strongly defended and that his advance could be stalled here unless his men could get the supporting artillery into action quickly. With the British just 80m from the walls, Wolseley and his men helped the artillerymen drag their heavy guns across uneven ground and up over a deep hollow onto a level position from which to fire. At such close range a hole was soon blasted in the formidable walls and through the gap the 93rd and Wolseley and his men poured. The fighting was brief and bloody, and later Wolseley counted over 2,000 sepoy victims of British vengeance.

The British were now able to turn their attention onto the next target, the Shah Najif Mosque. Although Wolseley and Major Barnston were able to gain some cover from the enemy's fire in the ruins of native buildings near the mosque, here they and the men of the 90th were hit by British shells which began to fall short of their intended target. As hot splinters flew through the air, Major Barnston received a wound in his thigh which would prove to be fatal. Now effectively in command and angered by the damage done by the British guns upon his comrades, Wolseley led his men forward in an attempt to force their way into the mosque. However, without scaling ladders their efforts proved futile. Again, artillery was brought forward and after a bombardment of three hours the mosque was finally taken. This proved to be the last action of the day and Wolseley managed a few hours' sleep before awaking the next morning with the smell of burning flesh filling his nostrils, for a dead sepoy was hanging across a wall, his coat on fire, again the result of British vengefulness. By the end of the following day Wolseley was to witness even more grisly sights.

Wolseley was to play a major part in the action of 17 November, a day in which the siege would be finally lifted. Campbell again turned to his artillery to soften up the defences of the rebels and for three hours Captain Peel of the Royal Navy directed his guns at the turreted Khoorsheyd Munzil, or Happy Palace, which was built in the style of a miniature castle, with a moat and drawbridge. This had been converted into a regimental mess hall by the British before the rebellion. Campbell now assembled a storming party which comprised the companies of the 90th, along with some men of the 53rd and the Sikhs of the 4th Punjab Rifles. Wolseley was given the honour of leading the assault. Campbell provided Wolseley with clear instructions; he was to fight his way to the ditch surrounding the Palace and place his men in a secure position whilst he obtained details of the remaining defences which he was to then relay back to Campbell. The only latitude Wolseley was given was that if he saw an opportunity to break into the Palace grounds, he should take it. Finally, Campbell promised Wolseley that he would recommend him for the Victoria Cross if the assault was a success.

Thus fired up with emotion, pride, adrenaline and fear, Wolseley led around fifty of his men of the 90th in the initial charge to the moat. The enemy's fire was intense but although men fell around him Wolseley seemed to be living a charmed life. On reaching his target he noticed that the blasts of Peel's gun had filled the moat with rubble and that by scampering over the debris he could lead a force to secure the drawbridge. Wolseley did not hesitate and now joined by the Irishmen of the 53rd and the Sikhs he charged on. Campbell could hardly believe his eyes as Wolseley's command poured into the Palace grounds and the sounds of fighting now filled the air. Many rebel muskets were directed towards Wolseley but amazingly he remained unscathed. The rebels were unable to lower the rear drawbridge to affect their escape and were thus caught in a trap and slaughtered to a man. Campbell now ordered a young Lieutenant Roberts, who in later years would be Wolseley's main rival for senior office, to run forward with regimental colours to place them on the Palace walls to signify to those still besieged that their relief was now imminent and assured.

With Wolseley's success Campbell was now determined that his own regiment, the 93rd Highlanders, should lead the way forward to the Residency and be the first to make contact with the British troops and civilians there. Wolseley though had a different plan. He saw an opportunity to continue the charge. Three hundred metres ahead was the Motee Mahul, or Pearl of Palaces, which was the last obstacle to the relieving forces and as such the rebels had attempted to make it impregnable. An extra defending wall had been built out from the main defences and it had been loopholed to command a field of fire. All other entrances to the Palace had been bricked up and the rebels must have been confident that their defences could repel any attack. Wolseley realized that momentum was now with him and his men and ignoring Campbell's orders he used his own initiative and led his men forward.

Not only were the defenders able to fire from the Motee Mahul but they also held the surrounding buildings from which a determined hail of bullets was directed upon Wolseley and his men. Yet the wild rush of men, maddened by fury and led by the determined Wolseley, enabled this small force to get within yards of the loopholed defences and here, in an archway the men were able to gain some respite from the defender's fire. Breathing heavily, Wolseley took a moment to assess the situation and realized that the loopholes actually presented the attackers with an opportunity, along with the fact that the enemy had failed to dig a ditch around their new defensive wall. He waited for the rebels to unleash a volley and whilst they pulled back the barrels of their muskets to reload Wolseley led his men in another rush and they were able to safely reach the loopholed defences. Now followed a brutal fight in which the British troops and the sepoys fired at each other through the loopholes. After some minutes, the British fire gained the ascendency and the defenders melted away from the walls. Despite this success Wolseley and his men were still unable to breach the walls but calling for entrenching tools and crowbars his men set about undermining the newly constructed brickwork. During this period a Private Andrews, one of Wolseley's most devoted men, was shot whilst out in the open, beckoning for troops to come forward. Wolseley immediately ran out to drag Andrews to safety and the enemy directed their fire towards him. Fortunately, Wolseley miraculously avoided being hit but Andrews was again wounded before his Captain could bring him to relative safety. Andrews survived to collect his army pension.

Whilst the men of the 90th continued to try and undermine the defences Wolseley moved around the walls in an unsuccessful attempt to locate another way in. On his return he found Ensign Haig had managed to open a hole wide enough for him to wriggle through. Wolseley must have expected the Ensign to be killed at any moment but to his relief Haig crawled through the gap and was quickly joined by his comrades from the 90th, who were soon ably supported by the men of the 53rd and the Sikhs. Again, Wolseley was at the front of the assault which turned into a bloody pursuit of the sepoys from room to room in the Palace. Here the slaughter was even more intense and when the defender's resistance finally broke, and the survivors tried to flee by swimming across the Gomti river Wolseley and his men 'had capital practice at them in the water'.[12] The British were interrupted in his brutal act by an explosion at the west wall of the Palace's courtyard. Not knowing what to expect Wolseley prepared his men for another assault, but as the smoke and dust cleared a company of the besieged garrison emerged to greet their saviours. In a twist of fate Wolseley was now able to reach out and grab the hand of Captain William Tingling, also of the 90th. Not only were the men of the 90th now reunited, but Lucknow had been relieved, and Wolseley had gained the distinction of being the first of Campbell's force to reach the besieged garrison.

Whilst Campbell rushed forward to greet his fellow senior officers, Havelock and Outram, Wolseley was relieved to shake the hands of his comrades from the 90th but he was unsettled by how the siege had affected them physically. Indeed, Wolseley struggled to even recognize some of his fellow officers, such was the toll taken on them by the siege and he learned of the sad death of the regiment's commanding officer, Colonel Campbell, who had succumbed to disease only four days before the relief. The hearts of all were raised though as Wolseley distributed both tobacco and rum amongst them.

Captain Wolseley had done enough during the assaults of both 16 and 17 November to win the Victoria Cross several times over, but the award was never granted, for Wolseley would have had to be recommended by his commanding officer and Campbell was never to make such a recommendation. Indeed, he was furious with the young, brave Captain for overstepping his orders and denying his own men of the 93rd the distinction and honour of relieving the beleaguered garrison. Wolseley's expectation of praise and honours for his bravery and initiative were shattered when he was greeted by Brigadier Adrian Hope with the news that Campbell was incensed with rage towards Wolseley for disobeying his orders and Hope advised the exhausted, and disappointed, Captain to avoid Campbell at all costs.

That evening Wolseley slept on the roadside by the Shah Najif Mosque but was awoke by the arrival of a latecomer who stood on the prone Captain. Wolseley directed an oath into the night towards the perpetrator. However, in the morning Wolseley rose to discover that the latecomer was Campbell himself. There was no escape and Campbell bitterly accused Wolseley of ignoring his orders. Yet there was a wry smile on Campbell's face and although Wolseley received a long and torturous lecture on the error of being overzealous the old warrior clearly recognized that Wolseley was an exceptionally brave and talented leader of men. Wolseley was promised a promotion, but there was to be no further mention of the award of the Victoria Cross. Over subsequent years of senior service Wolseley was to pin this prestigious award to the chest of numerous recipients, many of whom he described as unworthy, and this was particularly the case in the aftermath of the Anglo-Zulu War of 1879. After his own exploits of exceptional bravery this clearly left a bitter taste for Wolseley.

Although Campbell had broken the siege, he was now faced with a two-fold dilemma. The sepoy contingent at Gwalior had rebelled and had used the absence of a large British force in Cawnpore to retake that city. In addition, Campbell had to escort 1,000 sick and wounded and 500 women and children from Lucknow to safety. Although his decision would later receive some criticism, the British commander felt, in these circumstances, that he had no choice but to now abandon the recently relieved Lucknow. Whilst Campbell returned to Cawnpore with the bulk of his force, General Outram remained at Alum Bagh with a force of 3,395 British troops and 1,047 loyal sepoys and Lucknow was once more in the hands of the rebels. It was estimated that Outram's division, of around 5,000 men, of which Wolseley was a part, was outnumbered by the rebellious sepoys in the immediate region by around twenty to one.

Wolseley was to remain at Alum Bagh from November 1857 to March 1858, when Campbell returned with the main force, having retaken Cawnpore. This period was largely a time of tedium for Wolseley, but he was able to rest and regain his strength after the exertions and privations of the earlier campaign. Although the rebels used the time to shore up their defences at Lucknow, they never threatened Outram's command, and this must be viewed as something of a lost opportunity by them.

On his return with around 10,000 troops, including reinforcements recently arrived from Britain, Campbell wasted no time in attacking the 90,000 rebels now defending Lucknow. Campbell's intelligence sources indicated that the defenders had rebuilt the original defences and that every building had been loopholed in the expectation that any British attack would result in street fighting, which had characterized the November assault. Campbell realized that a similar assault would result in a high 'butcher's bill' of British dead, so, with the advice of his chief engineer, Colonel Robert Napier, the British commander devised a two-pronged assault. He returned to his earlier reliance on artillery to blast rebel positions and to keep the defenders pinned down. At the same time Campbell ordered Outram to take the majority of his command across the Gomti river on newly-built pontoon bridges, and once across open an enfilading fire into the rear and sides of the main rebel force thus making the strongest defences in front of Campbell untenable for the rebels to hold.

The attack was launched on 5 March 1858, with a reliance on the use of British troops fresh from England. Although Wolseley recalled that the sight of mixed units, such as the Rifles and the Queen's Bays, as well as the Bengal Fusiliers, made for a colourful spectacle, he was bitter that the 90th were placed in the rear of the advance. This does not appear to have been a slight towards them by Campbell but was probably a recognition by the senior command that Wolseley and his men had already earnt their spurs. The British took just over a week to retake Lucknow and although brief the fighting was bitter and furious. As each position was taken back, Campbell ordered his artillery forward to pound the next strong point in the way to reoccupying the Residency. Wolseley followed in the wake of the advance and was thus witness to the aftermath of battle, both sight and smell, of which the latter he found particularly repulsive. No prisoners were taken by either side and there was considerable brutality. Wolseley was also appalled by the amount of looting undertaken by the recently-arrived British troops, of which their officers seemed blind to.

Campbell's brilliant assault was crowned by perhaps the worse pun in British military history for at its successful conclusion an aide-de-camp to the General was able to issue a proclamation of victory which read '*Nunc fortunatus sum*' or 'I am in luck now!' Lucknow had been the last sizeable city held by the rebels and with its fall those remaining in the fight scattered into smaller groups into the countryside. The British naturally adapted their own tactics to those of pursuit and Campbell's force was divided into field forces which spread out across the countryside. Sir Hope Grant was given the command of one such column, named the Lucknow Field Force. Wolseley had been actively seeking a staff appointment and Campbell, true to his earlier promise of promotion, put Wolseley forward for the position of deputy-assistant quartermaster-general when the then current incumbent, Lieutenant Frederick Roberts, was forced to return to England on sick-leave. Wolseley was delighted and a few days after his appointment he was even more thrilled to receive a promotion to the local rank of brevet major.

Wolseley was incredibly fortunate in that he now began a relationship, and indeed friendship, with Sir Hope Grant which would last until the latter's death in 1875. For one who was frequently critical of senior officers, as well as his contemporaries, Wolseley came to respect and like Hope Grant for his work rate, his clear ability, and his knowledge of soldiering. In later life Wolseley was to describe Hope Grant as having '... all the best instincts of a soldier, and was a brave daring man that no amount of work could tire ... He was liked by every good man who knew him, and all those with whom he was intimate loved him. I never met a man with a higher sense of duty.'[13] Wolseley certainly learnt a great deal from his mentor which he would take into his own senior career. Based at Lucknow, Hope Grant despatched his forces in any direction across the Oudh region where he knew rebels to be, and Wolseley was certainly kept extremely busy. His role included the compiling of intelligence reports, the drawing of maps for the advancing forces, for none existed of the Oudh area at this time, as well as assigning quarters as troops moved across the countryside and supervising transport.

Throughout the various pursuits, the British, Wolseley included, had to cope with the worst of the Indian heat, which frequently top 50 degrees Celsius in the shade! Such temperatures claimed numerous sunstroke victims. For Wolseley, he soon appreciated the need to reduce the men's suffering and became a firm advocate for the use of mounted infantry which he would deploy in his own later campaigns. Wolseley was involved in one particularly sharp action in this period when on 13 April, whilst leading a mounted reconnaissance patrol, he encountered a strong force of enemy cavalry. With only five troopers by his side Wolseley was forced to turn his horse around and gallop back to the advance guard, which included two artillery pieces. There was just time for the guns to unlimbered, and a round of canister fired, before the enemy cavalry descended upon the small British force. Fierce hand-to-hand fighting ensured, and Wolseley was forced to draw his sword. The arrival of Hope Grant with the main body of the army guaranteed that the rebels swiftly retired but the British suffered several casualties.

Apart from this one moment of extreme danger the pursuit was largely tiresome and sometimes tedious. It continued for many months, and it was not until 23 May 1859 that the last engagement was fought, fully two years from the start of the rebellion, which was now officially declared over. The Lucknow Field Force retired back to Lucknow on 4 June 1859, which coincidently was Wolseley's 26th birthday. Here he was greeted with the news that he was to receive the local rank of brevet lieutenant-colonel and he became the youngest colonel in the British Army. This promotion so soon after his move to major owed much to Wolseley's abilities, for he was mentioned several times in despatch whilst serving on the staff, but also Hope Grant's patronage. Wolseley could take huge pride in his rapid rise and even more so because he had achieved all through his own merit and bravery with none of his promotions via the purchase system.

Wolseley retained his position as a quartermaster and spent the next few months applying his recently gained experience in quartering troops into the construction of a new cantonment in Lucknow. Although with his accelerated rank he was a draw to many of the English ladies who journeyed to England in search of a suitable husband, Wolseley concluded at this time that matrimony was not a good mix with a soldier's life. However, it seems he began a relationship with a local lady, who became his housekeeper and mistress. Writing to his brother Richard on 7 August 1859 Wolseley stated that, 'I manage to console myself with an Eastern Princess and find she answers all the purposes of a wife without giving any of the bother'.[14] Indian life seems to have suited Wolseley and he was certainly happy to consider a longer career in India, but after just five months he was ripped away from this new domestic bliss by the announcement that Sir Hope Grant was to command a large expeditionary force to go to North China and naturally the general wanted the newly-appointed Colonel Wolseley to join him.

This latest conflict with the Imperial Government of China was, like so many colonial wars of the nineteenth century, centred on previous disputes. Throughout the century Britain had been attempting to impose their economic will on China, especially in the control of the opium trade which proved to be particularly lucrative to British merchants and tax collectors. Although this trade was centred on Hong Kong and Canton, the British wanted to expand their economic presence away from these cities. This had resulted in earlier Opium Wars in 1842 which had seen the British claim Hong Kong and in 1856 there was further conflict. This began with the seizure of a supposedly British-registered schooner, the *Arrow*, by the Chinese authorities on spurious grounds. Sir John Bowring, who commanded the Far East Station, saw this incident as an opportunity to inflame tensions, and with the Imperial Chinese government in no mood to accept Bowring's demands, diplomacy quickly moved towards confrontation.

Initial conflict centred upon Canton which after a prolonged attack was taken by the British. The war now moved north and once more the British were successful, taking the Taku Forts, which were seen as the gateway to moving onto Peking itself. Peace negotiations now began, but the Chinese used the withdrawal of British forces to reoccupy the forts and strengthen their defences. When diplomacy again failed the British relaunched their attack on the forts, but on this occasion the attack was ill-conceived, the Chinese resolute in their defence and on 24 June 1858 the British were defeated in their assault. Repulsed, the British returned to Hong Kong to lick their wounds. The outbreak of revolt in India placed huge strain on British military resources and their plans in China were forced onto the back burner. Once operations in India were concluded the British government, now with the support of the French who were also keen to open trade, turned their attention back to China. Under the pretext of ensuring that the Chinese government honour their commitment signed in the Treaty of Tientsin, of June 1858, that allowed for the British, French, American and Russian governments to expand their trade with Chinese ports, as well as allowing for foreign legations in Peking and for missionary activity to be permitted in China, the British and French decided to focus their forces upon Peking once more. For the British it was also an opportunity to gain revenge for their miliary setback outside of the walls of the Taku Forts. Wolseley was now to play an important part in this new conflict.

Hope Grant was keen that Colonel Wolseley would retain his post as Quartermaster-General whilst serving in China but Campbell, now following his battlefield successes ennobled as Lord Clyde, thought Wolseley too young and inexperienced for such an important Staff role. The position went to Colonel Kenneth Mackenzie of the Gordon Highlanders, with Colonel Robert Rose as his second-in-command. Wolseley had to settle for being the third member of the quartermaster team, a role that he seems to have accepted with grace and he was certainly still well placed to influence his own furtherment.

As soon as he had heard of his appointment, Wolseley scoured the bookshops of Calcutta and by the time Hope Grant and his Staff left India Wolseley had devoured as much information as he could on the history, geography and recent politics of Victoria's latest foe. He even used the transit time to learn some words of Chinese and by the time he and the rest of the Staff arrived in Hong Kong on 13 March 1860, Wolseley felt he had a reasonable appreciation of what now lay ahead of him. Throughout his career Wolseley would pride himself on his desire and ability to learn as much about the enemy he faced as he possibly could.

Wolseley was soon despatched to Kowloon to establish a camping ground for the ever-growing army and was certainly kept busy in this task. Much to his angst, and that of Hope Grant, the British force would, out of political necessity, fight alongside a French army commanded by General Montauban, a veteran of colonial fighting in Algeria. Hope Grant's command was very much one drawn from across the Empire. British troops had accompanied the Staff from India, but there were Indian units from Bombay and Madras and even muleteers recruited from the Philippines. The cosmopolitan nature of the expeditionary force was reflected in the numerous and diverse uniforms on display and the expanding camp at Kowloon must have been a mixture of colours.

The British and French governments had earlier issued an ultimatum to the Chinese Imperial government which demanded the right to land at the mouth of the Peiho river and travel to Peking for the ratification of the Treaty of Tientsin. After some procrastination the request was refused and thus the home governments ordered Hope Grant and Montauban to begin operations. These began with the unopposed occupation of the island of Chausan, which although of little military value did demonstrate that the expedition would try the patience of the Staff. For it was here that the allies became involved in a quarrel over the height of their respective flagpoles, with the French taking exception to the fact that, apparently inadvertently, the Union Jack was flying slightly higher than the Tricolour! Wolseley expressed the view of many of his colleagues on the staff that he had, '… always hated the French, and I see no likelihood of my feelings changing as regards them'. He later wrote that the whole expedition '… was hampered throughout its course by the French contingent we had to act with'.[15]

The main operations began in the middle of May with the 14,000-strong British contingent sailing north. It was comprised of a cavalry brigade, several battalions of infantry, as well as Royal Marine Light Infantry (RMLI) and the 99th Regiment of Foot, and four batteries of field artillery as well as a siege train of heavy artillery. With the French force of 7,000 troops unable to meet its own needs for transport and logistics, Hope Grant was later force to reduce his own numbers to 11,000 troops to be able to accommodate the French. The mumblings from the British staff, including Wolseley, would surely have been audible in Paris!

By 28 July the Allied force was anchored off the mouth of the Peiho river and there must have been some trepidation onboard the landing vessels as they edged passed the two forts built to protect the entrance, but fortunately the large cannons protruding from the walls were later discovered to be dummies and the expedition sailed on. The target of the Chinese capital lay less than 100 miles to the north-west. On 1 August the Allies made another unopposed landing at Peh-tang, the key to the formidable Taku Forts which had to be taken before the advance could continue.

At Peh-tang the Allies were welcomed by the locals, who had been terrorised by the Chinese imperial forces, particularly Tartar cavalry patrols who were an ever-present sight on the skyline. Yet the immediate obstacle to the advance was to be the mud flats that sucked at the troops as they attempted to reach the solid ground of a causeway. With the last mile too shallow for the landing craft, the troops had no alternative but to disembark and wade through the waist-deep mud and although the Tartar cavalry kept a wary eye on proceedings, they did nothing to oppose the comical advance. The air was wrought with both blasphemes and laughter as the troops struggled onwards. The correspondent of *The Times* recorded that, 'Nearly every man was disembarrassed of his lower integuments, and one gallant brigadier led on his men with no other garment than his shirt'.[16]

When Wolseley and his comrades finally reached solid ground and the village of Peh-tang they were depressed to find their bivouacs for the night to be squalid and filthy. Furthermore, the exertions of pulling themselves through the mud and their salted meat provisions meant that the pint of water that each soldier carried was soon consumed and a great thirst was suffered by all. Although surrounded by water it was found to be brackish and the need of a suitable, clean supply became the paramount concern for Hope Grant and his staff. In the morning Wolseley was tasked with riding ahead of the main body to firstly secure adequate water but also to reconnoitre the advance. This was to become his main role throughout the campaign, and it would frequently place him in danger. To reach the target of the Taku forts the allies would have to transverse eight miles of salt marsh and mud. The formidable and intimidating nature of the Chinese strong points was recorded by David Field Rennie in his work *The British Arms in North China*, '… Looking out for land I saw in the distant haze three dark masses, apparently equidistant from each other and of symmetrical shape, looming obscurely above the horizon. I looked at them through my glass and concluded they were the Taku forts.'[17]

Hope Grant's faith in Wolseley's abilities and daring saw the newly-appointed colonel command a reconnaissance force of 200 cavalry and 100 infantry and with these troops Wolseley moved ahead of the main army across unknown and unmapped ground. Apart from mapping out what lay in front of the advance Wolseley had to locate suitably firm ground over which the allies could traverse with their artillery, which included the addition of the new Armstrong 12-pounder breech-loading gun as well as heavier artillery. In the first serious engagement of the war, the Armstrongs demonstrated their effectiveness when they disrupted a charge of 2,000 Tartar cavalry which had emerged from the Chinese entrenchments outside of Sinho to launch an attack upon the 2nd Division as it advanced. Certainly, the allies had a technological advantage over the enemy. Despite the fire of the Armstrongs, the bravery of the Tartars was clearly demonstrated, and it took a determined charge from both the Sikh cavalry and the King's Dragoon Guards to force the enemy back to Sinho. It appeared that the only obstacle now to an allied assault upon the formidable Taku forts was the fortified town of Tangku. Yet the following day, Wolseley again led a reconnaissance during which he discovered that Tangku had largely been abandoned with only a small enemy force remaining. Wolseley established that although Tangku, surrounded as it was by streams and canals, presented a formidable obstacle, the ground around was sufficiently hard to allow for the movement of artillery and on the morning of 14 August the Armstrong guns battered the fort and quickly silenced all opposition. Hope Grant could now plan his assault upon the Taku Forts.

Naturally, Wolseley was a big part of Hope Grant's plans. The Colonel was kept frantically busy both leading reconnaissance forays, as well as surveying and map making. The weather conditions were appalling with almost constant rainstorms, which meant that neither he or his comrades were ever able to get themselves or their belongings dry. Under such a workload Wolseley's one good eye suffered greatly from strain as he tried to create maps for the following days advance from candlelight in his wet tent. Despite these hardships, and lack of decent rations, he was able to write to his mother that he was '... jolly and well and enjoy my profession as much now as I did the day I first donned Her Majesty's Scarlet'.[18]

The Taku Forts, with the over fifty Chinese guns, might inflict severe damage upon any advancing force, but the allies could also not simply bypass the forts and leave a substantial enemy force to their rear. Hope Grant had to carefully plan his assault for no concealment was possible for any force approaching the forts. The low-lying nature of the terrain meant that the vantage from the strong walls of the forts was significant. In addition, the landscape of mud flats was inundated at high tide and crossed with deep ditches at low tide. To add to his difficulties, Hope Grant had to deal with General Montauban who would frequently take a contrary view to that offered by him and his Staff.

In his final plans for the assault Hope Grant was very reliant on advice from two engineers, Major Graham, V.C., and Sir Robert Napier who, although commanding a division in the attack, had used his previous engineering experience to good effect, as he had in the second assault upon Lucknow during the Indian Rebellion. Despite French protests, Hope Grant resolved to attack the forts on the northern bank from the rear, across the marshes and ditches. He surmised that if these were taken the southern forts would be untenable to hold and thus victory would be gained. Furthermore, Hope Grant realized that if the central of the three forts was taken first then he could use this position to concentrate his own fire upon the other two. It is not known if Wolseley was involved in the planning that revolved around the assault upon the forts, but it seems likely that with his engineering experience from the trenches outside of Sebastopol and his knowledge of the terrain gained whilst on reconnaissance that he would have been a part of the discussions.

After successfully taking Tangku, the British spent the next four days constructing pontoon bridges across the numerous muddy ditches, as well as a causeway to allow artillery pieces to be conveyed forward. It was dangerous work for the enemy directed fire from guns of the forts and the British suffered some casualties, with Major Graham receiving a wound in his arm. By 19 August the allies had reached the outer canals of the forts and under cover of darkness they advanced to within 800m of the forts. The following day, the allies tried to entice the Chinese to surrender but their pleas were met with a heavy fire from the walls of the forts and Hope Grant resolved to storm the forts the following day. The final assault was to be a bloody one in which the allied artillery was advanced closer and closer to breach the walls before a charge from the infantry.

By 4 am on the morning of 21 August 1860 men of the 44th and 67th Regiments, along with their comrades in the RMLI, filed out from their bivouacs to begin the assault upon the middle of the three north bank Taku forts. The early morning light enabled the British artillery to move forward under some cover and they began a bombardment of the battlements. Although there was one early success when a British shell detonated one of the Chinese powder magazines within the fort, generally the lighter artillery pieces made little impression upon the thick walls and 8in howitzers and 9-pounders had to be brought forward to the edge of the outer line of ditch defences. Both troops from the RMLI and the French brought forward pontoon bridges to span the ditches and elements of these troops were able to reach the base of the walls, but both storming parties had taking significant losses from the fire of the defenders and there were insufficient scaling ladders now within these groups to gain access to the fort. Wolseley had been with the advance parties and helped lay a pontoon bridge across one of the ditches. Again, providence was with him for the fire from the defenders was particularly heavy against the advancing troops and although men fell all around him, including Major Graham who was wounded in the leg, Wolseley was not harmed.

Napier later described the Chinese soldiers' resistance at this point of the battle as 'noble and vigorous' and he was forced to bring forward yet more artillery, which finally managed to make a partial breach in the walls, near to one of the gates. Through this hole men of the 67th and 44th squeezed through and bitter hand-to-hand fighting ensured in which the garrison were slaughtered by the sword and bayonet or died in their attempts to flee. Three Victoria Crosses were awarded in this bloody encounter. The fort was securely in allied hands by 8.30 am, and its surviving guns were now trained onto the other northern forts, along with the British artillery. By noon the remaining forts had surrendered without the need for further costly infantry assaults. The forts on the southern banks capitulated the following day. Hope Grant knew that the road to Peking was now open to the allies.

Wolseley had a moment to view the interior of the captured fort before he was again employed by Hope Grant in reconnoitring the route forward. Wolseley described what he had seen in the aftermath of battle:

> The scene within the works bespoke the manner in which our artillery had done its part, and the *debris* caused by the explosion of the magazine lay in heaps everywhere, intermingled with overturned cannon, broken gun-carriages, and the dead and wounded of the garrison. Never did the interior of any place testify more plainly to the noble manner in which it had been defended.[19]

Although Wolseley and most of the senior officers felt that with the taking of the Taku Forts the war was effectively won, there was still much work for the young colonel to undertake. Indeed, it was not until 27 August that he was able to write home to his mother with details of the assault upon the forts for he was constantly employed in surveying, drawing and map-making for the advancing allies. His description of his work and the risks he had to undertake must have been of huge concern for his mother. He wrote of one foray he had undertaken as

> … not a pleasant mission to be engaged on, for if you go up close you are safe to be shot in such a dead level country, where there is no cover

> whatever, and if you do not go up close you can see or learn next to nothing. Under such circumstances I always use my own discretion, and risk nothing more than I believe to be necessary for the due performance of my task.[20]

Hope Grant resolved to march his force to the city of Tientsin, a distance of nearly 70 miles, and once there he would allow Lord Elgin, as High Commissioner, to begin negotiations with the Imperial court. Whilst Hope Grant and the remainder of his Staff journeyed on the *Grenada* supported by gunboats, Wolseley was tasked with mapping and surveying for the army. The enemy offered no resistance and only the dreadful state of the roads impeded the march. Thankfully the monotony of the mud flats was soon left behind as the allies entered green fertile land, dotted with affluent-looking villages with an abundance of food. Wolseley found the country fascinating and although his workload was heavy, he clearly enjoyed the campaigning.

The allies spent eight days at Tientsin in fruitless negotiations with imperial envoys and in frustration Elgin and Hope Grant decided to renew the advance from 8 September. With winter now approaching Hope Grant knew that speed was essential whilst the Chinese tried every diplomatic trick to slow the advance. Wolseley was once again at the forefront of the advance and the closer the allies got to Peking the more difficult his job became, for not only was his forward reconnaissances being hampered and impeded by Tartar cavalry, but the locals became more and more reluctant to impart information or help. On 18 September, when enjoying the luxury of a late breakfast Wolseley received reports that enemy cavalry was trying to encircle his small command. He was forced to fall back to the main army and even had to hide in a field of tall maize to avoid the enemy. Wolseley was later to write that this incident had caused him the most concern in his career for many of his men were on foot and would have been an easy target for the Tartars.

The duplicity of the Chinese negotiators came to ahead in a most violent fashion. Lord Elgin had been in constant communications via both letter and through Sir Henry Smith Parkes, the official interpreter for the allies, and had agreed that his force would stop at a place called Chang-kia-wan and send only 1,000 troops forward to Tung-chow where the treaty of Tientsin would finally be ratified. Yet riding ahead with a small escort Parkes had been captured and it was soon apparent that a large Chinese army, under the command of a Tartar named Sankolinsin, had been assembled near Tung-chow and whilst Elgin and Parkes had been talking peace terms the Chinese had been bringing together a huge army to oppose the allies. A furious Hope Grant was now determined to push onto Peking. With only 4,000 troops at his disposal, against an estimated 20,000 of the enemy, Hope Grant did not hesitate to take the offensive and, utilizing his superiority in artillery to great effect, was able to weaken the extended Chinese line, four miles long, outside of the town of Changchiawan. Hope Grant then unleashed his Sikh cavalry and Punjab infantry upon the enemy's right flank whilst the French attacked the left in an attempt to enfilade the Chinese position. Whilst the right flank collapsed the French met strong resistance, particularly from Tartar cavalry units which allowed the bulk of Sankolinsin's army to escape the battlefield.

The Chinese army did not disintegrate and Sankolinsin was again able to confront the allies with a substantial force at Tungchow. Once more Hope Grant did not hesitate and on the morning of 21 September, he personally led out his forces to attack Tungchow. The plans for a two-pronged infantry assault by French troops to the right of the town and the British on the left, with a wide arcing cavalry movement to the rear of the enemy which was designed to entrap them, was largely abandoned when the Tartar cavalry unleashed a wild charge, which at one point threatened Hope Grant and his staff, including Wolseley. Fortunately, this charge was slowed by the use of canister shot fired from the Armstrong guns and disintegrated in the face of a determined stand by the allied cavalry units, which then counter-charged and drove the enemy from the battlefield. Wolseley joined the Sikh cavalry in the pursuit of the fleeing enemy, which retreated to the north of the city. The road to Peking was now completely open to the allies.

However, Hope Grant was in an awkward position for the Chinese held Parkes and his escort and he was concerned that these men might be murdered if he pushed on too rapidly. Furthermore, he was lacking his siege artillery which was a few days behind the main thrust. He resolved to wait whilst Elgin now began negotiations with Prince Kung, younger brother of the Emperor, the latter having fled the city. The Prince tried his best to deter the allies from entering Peking and endeavoured to use the hostages as a bargaining tool, yet Elgin insisted that he would not continue diplomacy until the prisoners were released. Elgin gave Prince Kung three days to respond, or the advance would continue. With no response forthcoming Hope Grant again moved forward. During this period of negotiations Wolseley continued to remain busy and had even led a reconnaissance to the very gates of Peking and on another he witnessed French troops looting the Imperial Summer Palace. Three days later it was the turn of British troops to recommence the looting. This also saw the destruction of parts of the Palace and its grounds. Whilst Wolseley certainly did not approve of the actions, he was not completely innocent for he did take possession of a French miniature enamel painting which in later life he discovered to be of some value.

Finally, Prince Kung relented, and the hostages, including Parkes, began to be released in small numbers, with all telling of torture and abuse from their captors. By 14 October Hope Grant had brought all his forces to the walls of Peking and Elgin was able to threaten Kung that unless the north-eastern entrance, the Anting Gate was opened by noon, so Elgin could safely enter to begin the surrender negotiations, then a bombardment would be unleashed upon the city. Hope Grant and Elgin were playing a game of bluff for although the siege artillery was in place the British were dangerous low on ammunition and in all probability had insufficient to breach the city walls. Yet the bluff worked for a just a few minutes before the noon deadline the gates were opened and 400 troops under Napier, Wolseley amongst them, marched in to take possession of the Imperial capital.

All, including Wolseley, were disappointed by what they found, especially after the grandeur of the Summer Palace, and Wolseley wrote that he found Peking a dirty city with black filth covering the streets. Whilst surrender terms were being agreed Wolseley continued his work and when surveying the west wall of the city, he encountered a party of Chinese who were pulling five carts. On each cart were stacked coffins containing the remains of the last prisoners captured outside Tung-chow. Wolseley passed his gruesome discovery onto Elgin and ensured that the bodies were buried with full military honours in the city's Russian cemetery. The bodies of two of the captives, Captain Brabazon, who was known to have been beheaded, and the French interpreter, Abbe de Luc, were never found.

The death of so many of the prisoners soured the negotiations but Elgin insisted that justice was seen to be done and in the final surrender document, the Chinese authorities agreed to a compensation payment of £100,000 to the families of those murdered, whilst Hope Grant ordered what remained of the Summer Palace to be destroyed in retribution for the death of the captives. On 24 October Wolseley led a detachment to cover the route Elgin would take to the Hall of Audience to ensure the High Commissioner's safety. Wolseley was then present as Elgin and Prince Kung signed the surrender document and ratified the Treaty of Tientsin which confirmed foreign access to Chinese ports. In the briefest of wars, the allies had successfully overcome both the terrain and superior enemy numbers to complete a stunning victory, in which Colonel Wolseley had played an important part. In later life, when delivering an address at Aldershot Wolseley stated, 'If I have attained any measure of military prosperity, my gratitude is due to one man, Sir Hope Grant'.[21] Certainly Wolseley had huge respect for the General, who was one of the few men in Wolseley's life from whom he would accept instruction, guidance and even criticism without taking offence. In return Hope Grant recognized the Colonel's ability, if not genius, and Wolseley was frequently mentioned in despatches throughout their time together.

At the end of the campaign, Hope Grant, along with twelve members of the Staff, Wolseley amongst them, hired a P & O Steamer and over the winter of 1860–1, this small party sailed to Japan. It was only six years since Commodore Perry of the United States Navy had used 'gunboat diplomacy' to force the Japanese Shogunate to open its ports to foreign trade and the group visited the treaty ports of Tokyo and Yokohoma. Japan must have seemed very alien to the party of British officers. Wolseley was clearly captivated by the country and his writings about his time there in the second volume of his autobiography are arguably some of the best written pages of the book, for his enthusiasm for his travels shines through. Like all tours his time in Japan came to an end and Wolseley was desperate to return to Ireland and enjoy some well-earnt leave. However, Hope Grant had one more task for him back in China.

Wolseley travelled to Shanghai and from there he sailed up the Yangtze River to Nanking, which had become the centre of Taiping resistance. His mission was to produce a report on the military strength and capabilities of the Taipings who had been in open rebellion against the Imperial government in Peking for 11 years. As Wolseley passed through the countryside, which had been ravage by war and occupation, he already began to conclude that the Taiping leadership were not the group that Britain or any of the Western powers should be considering as allies. Tales had been reaching the West of great brutality by the supporters of the rebels and Wolseley saw the results of some of the arbitrary violence that characterized the rebellion. Yet he was warmly received in Nanking and given complete freedom to prepare his report, which was illustrated with sketches of the environs. He concluded that the Taipings were both materially and military weak and stated their continued existence was more a reflection of the Imperial Government's weakness than the strength of the rebellion and that the western powers were right in concluding treaties with the administration in Peking. Indeed, under the leadership of Wolseley's dear friend Charles Gordon, who led the so-called 'Ever Victorious Army', the Taiping Rebellion was crushed in 1863. By then, the world was being rocked by conflict on a massive scale as civil war erupted in America. The events there would draw Wolseley to the Continent and ultimately to his first independent field command.

Yet first, after nearly nine years away on virtually constant active service, Wolseley was going home on leave to Ireland. He could look back at this period as one which had been fraught with danger but one of huge personal success. Not only had he avoided death but had achieved more glory in this short period than most of his contemporaries would in their whole careers. He was one of the youngest-ever colonels in the British Army and all this had been achieved through his own efforts, determination, and bravery and without a 'step-up' from the purchase system. As he boarded his ship in Shanghai to sail back to Britain, he must have done so with a sense of huge satisfaction at what he had achieved.

# Chapter 2
# Independent Command

After the exertions of the numerous campaigns he had endured, Wolseley was granted a substantial period of leave of 18 months. He spent some of this time in Paris improving his painting and language skills and enjoying the Parisian lifestyle, but he found that life in the French capital was expensive, and his officer's pay he had managed to save whilst in India and China began to diminish rapidly. In addition, his finances were impacted by family commitments, which would place a great burden upon Wolseley throughout his life. As the nominal head of the family his brothers would frequently and repeatedly approach Wolseley for 'loans'. Whilst Dick repaid his borrowings, George, and in particular Fred, seemed to have an ability to dream up madcap business ventures which became a constant drain on Garnet. Indeed, although naturally driven, Wolseley's need for rapid advancement in the Army was undoubtedly partly due to his financial support of his wider family.

After Paris Wolseley spent some weeks visiting friends and relations in England and Ireland and it was whilst staying with one of his married sisters in County Cork that he was to have his leave cut short. Naturally, Wolseley, like most of the country, had been keeping an eye on the events in America where the two opposing forces, the Union in the northern states and the Confederates of the southern states, had been engaged for over six months in bloody conflict. Although many expected the Union forces, with both their numerical and resource advantages, to quickly rout the Confederates, this was not to be the case and the Civil War would last for over four bloody years and see the deaths of over a million and half troops in battle and from disease. Indeed, as the year 1861 was drawing to a close the Confederates had been boosted by a number of battlefield successes including at the First Battle of Manassas (21 July 1861). Although Britain would manage to maintain a neutral position throughout the conflict, economically it benefitted by buying cotton from the Confederate States and selling military equipment, particularly the Enfield rifle. With British troops stationed in Canada, and Union politicians angered by Britain's economic links with the Southern States, tensions were frequently high. The commander of British forces in Canada, Lieutenant-General Fenwick Williams, was himself convinced that once the Civil War had been successfully concluded the Union would turn its army north for the conquest of Canada and the General frequently petitioned Horse Guards to increase the small garrison of 4,500 British troops.

It was to be the so-called 'Trent Incident' of November 1861 which would see a significant increase in British troop numbers in Canada and would lead ultimately to Wolseley's first independent command. The *Trent* was a British mail steamer which was intercepted by a Union frigate, the USS *San Jacinto* under the command of Captain Charles Wilkes. Onboard the British vessel were two Confederate envoys, John Slidell and James Murray Mason, who were travelling to Britain to try and press the government to not only recognize the Confederate States diplomatically but to also seek economic and military aid. The two men were seized from the *Trent* and imprisoned in Washington. Their seizure was greeted by many loyal to the Union as a patriotic act and Captain Wilkes was publicly lauded. The British government took a firm stance against the boarding of a British ship in international waters, seeing it as an act of aggression, and for a few tense weeks there was some concern in both Britain and in the administration of Abraham Lincoln that hostilities could result. Whilst the possibility of Britain becoming engaged in the conflict was always unlikely, there was a real chance that aid might be significantly increased to the Confederate States. While diplomats tried to resolve the dispute the British government was determined to show a defiant stance and General Williams finally got what he had been requesting, for around 15,000 additional troops were despatched to reinforce Canada.

Wolseley duly received a War Office telegram informing him that he was to embark in four days' time for Canada where he would serve as Assistant Quartermaster General. He left his sister and journeyed immediately to London where he met his superior, Colonel Kenneth Mackenzie, and the two men, along with most of the Staff officers boarded the steamship *Melbourne* for their transatlantic voyage. Unfortunately, the vessel was barely seaworthy, and Wolseley was to endure a slow and uncomfortable transit; it was not until 5 January 1862 that he finally stepped ashore in Halifax, after 30 days at sea. The voyage had taken nearly three weeks longer than the normal journey time. Here Wolseley and his colleagues were informed that the diplomatic and political crisis had been averted for Lincoln, not wishing to sully relations with Britain, had backed down and partly met the demands of the British government. The actions of Captain Wilkes in seizing the *Trent* were disavowed by Lincoln, the Confederate envoys were released and allowed to continue their mission to Britain. Crucially, the British had not insisted on an apology for Wilkes' actions thus removing a major obstacle to a diplomatic solution.

The late arrival of the *Melbourne* meant that the British reinforcements were ahead of the Staff and already on their way to Montreal. Furthermore the St. Lawrence River, which allowed for passage into the heart of Canada, was now frozen over and Wolseley and his colleagues had no alternative but to travel overland. At this time of year this was a potentially deadly journey and so the party decided to take the safer if underhand approach of travelling via Boston. With Anglo-American relations still fragile it was thought prudent for the group to remove all signs of their military background from their clothing and baggage before they stepped onto American shores. For Wolseley this diversion allowed him a brief opportunity to view some of the important sites from the American War of Independence, including the battlefield at Bunker Hill (17 June 1775), and provided him with some experience of travelling incognito in America, something which would later prove to be useful.

Once in Canada Wolseley was sent to Riviere de Loup, which at that point was the eastern terminus of the railway, to arrange accommodation for the troops as they journeyed to Montreal. Although Wolseley was kept busy for a few weeks once the final troops had passed through in March 1862, he escorted the last companies and joined his fellow Staff officers in Montreal. Here he was able to enjoy his new posting, which with the threat of war now nullified, offered amusements and little work. Wolseley spent time improving his skating skills with numerous expeditions into the surrounding countryside and enjoyed the plays that the garrison troops performed, but the greatest diversion was from the local female population. He wrote of his time in Montreal as '… an elysium of bliss for young officers, the only trouble being to keep single'.[1] Wolseley, however, was already considering marriage for whilst visiting a friend's house in Ireland, before he departed for Canada, he '… fell most dreadfully in love, indeed by far the most serious affair of the heart that I have hitherto had'.[2] The lady concerned was the 18-year-old Louisa Erskine, who was considered attractive with a fair complexion and golden hair. Although Wolseley was smitten he confided in a letter to his sister Matilda that he would marry Louisa if he could but, '… you may all rest assured that I shall never marry to live in poverty and as that lady [Louisa] is as poor as I am there is not much chance of her being Mrs Garnet Junior'.[3] Yet despite his money problems Wolseley maintained a lengthy correspondence with Louisa, which once the pair were finally married would continue for the remainder of his career in the army, whether Wolseley was on campaign or working at Horse Guards. Their correspondence has survived and apart from being an interesting historical record of what Wolseley was thinking at specific moments they also show that the couple were as judgemental as each other when commenting on their friends and contemporaries. Indeed, for many reasons Garnet and Louisa were a perfect match.

Marriage was still a distant prospect; Wolseley's superior, Colonel Mackenzie, returned to England and for a period of several months Wolseley acted as Deputy Quartermaster-General until relieved in August by Colonel Lysons. He now had a short period of leave and decided that with civil war raging in America it was too good an opportunity not to witness for himself the largest clash of arms the world had seen since the Crimea War. Naturally, Wolseley as a serving British officer could not simply cross into America and risk a further diplomatic incident so he now set upon planning another great adventure.

For someone who would always display a high degree of rational thought when it came to his own advancement the decision by Wolseley to use his two months' leave to travel south to witness for himself the war seems an illogical one. For one who was always so judicious of army rules and authority, he had to keep his plans secret from his superiors. One of his friends in Montreal, William Muir, who was the chief medical officer and was central to Wolseley's plans, suggested that they should journey south together with one trying to join the headquarters of the Union forces whilst the other that of the Confederate army and afterwards they could compare notes. So bizarrely the pair decided to toss a coin to see who would make the first choice. Wolseley won and selected the Confederate forces. Such a choice naturally increased the risk of the enterprise for not only would the pair have to travel incognito, but Wolseley had the added danger of having to pass through Union troops to reach the front line before even trying to find the Confederate headquarters. If he was intercepted, he might be considered as a spy and even risk execution, with all that might follow from this at a time of political upheaval between England and America. Yet as a now senior serving British officer he was aware that whilst the British government had a reasonable understanding of the capabilities and resources of the Union forces comparatively little was known about the Confederate army. Consequently, Wolseley realized that although his expedition might be frowned upon by his immediate superiors, the government would probably secretly welcome his self-appointed 'mission'. He was later to discover that his exploits would attract interest in the publishing world too.

Despite all the risks Wolseley was determined to go south. Like many in the British army he was impressed by the performance of the Confederate forces and in awe of General Robert E. Lee, the senior commander. Also, he held a view that if the Confederates were successful and the Southern States were able to withdraw from the Union then American power would be significantly lessened and this could only benefit the Empire in its continued growth, both economically and territoriality.

In early September 1862 Wolseley and Muir headed south, with Wolseley armed with letters of introduction written for him by Confederate sympathizers in Canada. The pair reached Philadelphia where they decided to separate, and each continued their objectives of visiting and observing the opposing armies. Wolseley headed for New York, where he obtained further introductory letters and then onto Baltimore. Armed with these letters he was able to travel towards the banks of the Potomac River, the nominal border between the warring states, via overnight stops at the houses of Confederate supporters. In Baltimore Wolseley was fortunate enough to encounter Frank Lawley, the recently-arrived *Times* correspondent, and the two men agreed to travel south together. Lawley's presence added some much-needed gravitas and respectability to the expedition.

After days of travelling in a two-horse buggy, led by a 'rebel' sympathiser as Wolseley described him, the two men reached the banks of the Potomac. It was at this point the full magnitude of the potential danger the party was facing was brought vividly home, for the Union forces regularly guarded the riverbank and gunboats sailed up and down both night and day. Not only were the Union soldiers and sailors guarding the river to stop any possible Confederate incursion, but they were also trying to stop the lucrative smuggling of both people and goods. It took Lawley and Wolseley several days to find someone willing to take the risk of ferrying them across the Potomac and in this period, they spent most of their time in hiding. On one occasion a Union infantry patrol entered the cabin in which they were concealed. Whilst Lawley attempted to convince the officer in charge they were simple wild fowlers, and inquired as to how they might obtain a craft so as to take part in their sport, Wolseley charmed the same officer by offering him a cigar and engaging him in conversation about how they might travel to Washington by boat. This was a very close call and the same night, much to their relief, the pair were finally able to cross the river into Virginia. Following a walk of several miles, an interception by a Confederate cavalry patrol and a journey in a farmer's cart the men reached Beaverdam Station and from there they were able to catch a train to Richmond, the capital of the Confederate States. The train ride brought home, certainly to Lawley, the full scale and horror of the war, for the carriages were full of sick and wounded who were travelling from General Lee's army. Many of the troops had had limbs amputated and were in terrible pain and the smell of infection and death pervaded the nostrils of the two men. Both were relieved when the train finally arrived in Richmond.

Here Lawley and Wolseley were warmly welcomed and received by senior members of the Confederate Government, including General Randolph, the Secretary of State for War, who provided them with the necessary papers to travel to Winchester, where General Lee currently had his headquarters, after the recent inconclusive battle of Antietam (17 September 1862). In an accompanying letter to Lee Randolph wrote, 'I have not asked Colonel Wolseley to take the usual oath that he would not disclose nothing of what he sees here to our enemies, because I know I can rely upon the honour of an English officer'.[4] Before the pair left Richmond, they visited many of the recent nearby battlefields, including those close to Mechanicsville, such as the battles of Beaver Dam Creek and Gaine's Mill. Wolseley later wrote that he was surprised how difficult the wooded terrain was for the passage of large armies and expressed his admiration that the opposing forces were so effectively coordinated. On a more sombre note, he also described how hundreds of mass graves marked the spots where the fighting had been fiercest.

In the immediate aftermath of his visit Wolseley did largely keep his council as to what he had seen during his travels but both he and Lawley were to later write of the shortages of even the most basic foodstuffs and provisions in the South, as the Union economic blockade hit the Confederacy hard. Travelling from Richmond to Winchester, via a train to Staunton, proved a significant challenge not just because the two men were unable to purchase sufficient food for the journey, but they also struggled to find suitable transport for the 90 miles from Staunton. Finally, they were able to secure a ride with a group of ambulance wagons. These vehicles had been recently constructed and both the materials used and the build quality were very low, and Wolseley and Lawley endured a most uncomfortable few days in transit, during which the wagons underwent constant running repairs. Again, the state of the ambulance wagons reflected the economic turmoil the Confederacy was now facing. The delay would seriously hamper Wolseley who was very aware that his period of leave was running out and that he simply could not be late in returning to his Staff role. This meant that when he finally reached General Lee's command his stay was a brief one.

On arriving in the vicinity of Lee's camp Randolph's letters were duly examined and delivered and Wolseley was astonished how easy it was to gain almost immediate access to the General. Lee welcomed the two travellers personally and Wolseley sat with him for some time discussing the recent campaign which had culminated at Antietam. Even though Wolseley would have liked to have stayed longer at Lee's headquarters his writings are both militarily descriptive and evocative of a unique moment in his own life. Wolseley would later write, over 40 years after meeting Lee, that 'Every incident in that visit to him [Lee] is indelibly stamped on my memory. I have taken no special trouble to remember all he said to me then and during subsequent conversations, and yet it is still fresh in my recollection. But is natural it should be so, for he was the ablest general, and to me, seemed the greatest man I ever conversed with … General Lee was one of the few men who ever seriously impressed me and awed me with their natural, their inherent greatness.'[5]

General Lee provided one of his Colonels as a chaperone who took Wolseley to meet Lee's corps commanders, Generals Longstreet and Jackson. 'Stonewall' Jackson, who was to die just a few months later at the battle of Chancellorsville, impressed Wolseley with his affability but also his weariness to discuss military matters in any detail. Longstreet was more forthcoming and even arranged for Wolseley to inspect part of his force, including the Texan Brigade. Although most of the troops were dressed in little more than rags and poorly shod Wolseley noted that every man's Enfield rifle was spotless and clearly well maintained. Although these troops did not conform to European standards of drill or dress Wolseley recognized them as true soldiers and was duly impressed with their drive and determination.

Although he was unable to meet the Confederate cavalry commander, Jeb Stuart, for he was leading a reconnaissance raid at the time, Wolseley spoke to Lee and other commanders on the importance of cavalry forces in the war. From these debates he would conclude how essential such units were in warfare at this time. Wolseley developed his own thinking into the belief that mounted infantry, rather than specific cavalry forces, would offer a greater flexibility and more potency to commanders with him becoming a leading proponent of the use of such troops. The few days Wolseley spent with Lee's army was the only time he was to see and experience what amounted to a continental army in the field, for his own career would result in him commanding relatively small numbers of troops in colonial campaigns. These days clearly left a lasting impression upon Wolseley and would influence his thinking when he secured the position of Commander-in-Chief and was faced with the threat of a potential European war.

In the short-term Wolseley had to race back to Montreal to return to his Staff position, but not only was the 'expedition' enlightening, it saw the beginning of a fledgling writing career, which would continue, with varying degrees of success for the next 40 years. Wolseley wrote an article on his visit to the Confederacy which appeared in the January 1863 edition of *Blackwood's Magazine* and he was astonished to discovered the piece earnt him the sum of £40 (roughly equivalent to £6,000 today) and in later life Wolseley would gain some income from his writing. He also used his pen to further his cause for army reform, which on occasions resulted in some consternation at the War Office and especially with the Duke of Cambridge.

Apart from a short period back in England for surgery on his old leg wound acquired in the Crimea, which continued to give him pain, Wolseley was to remain on service in Canada for the next seven years. In the early years of this period he was frustrated, and even depressed, at the lack of opportunity for active service Canada provided. In the spring of 1863, Wolseley resumed his duties as Assistant Quartermaster-General, under Colonel Lysons. Wolseley quickly fell into a malaise for he needed to be busy and active, but instead he felt he was stagnating in a Canadian backwater. He wrote to his brother Dick in 1864 that his recent years of service 'have pushed away the ladder from under me and I am left hanging here [Canada] without any prospects. I am no use to anyone and all my visions of being able to advance have all vanished.'[6] Wolseley even began to consider a career away from the army, as an engineer, which had the bonus of better pay. This would, perhaps, allow him to consider marriage to Louisa for his love for her had not diminished. Yet, although tensions between Britain and America had lessened the memories of the Trent Affair still lingered and in Canada there was a growing awareness that the 18,000 British troops stationed there were insufficient to defend the country and that the Canadians would have to largely look to themselves for their own defence. The requirement for a 'home' defence force would provide Wolseley with the opportunity he needed.

In addition to the realization that America might present a danger to Canada, especially after the conclusion of the Civil War, another external threat was becoming apparent. In 1859 the Fenian Brotherhood was established in New York with the aim of establishing an independent republic in Ireland. At the end of the American Civil War many of the Irish troops who had fought in the conflict now reignited their republican ideals and began to meet in Philadelphia. Once established there the Brotherhood, with a president, a senate and a firm constitution, turned its attention on the formation of an Irish republic. With a return to Ireland out of the question, the logical place to find territory was across the border in Canada and from 1865 a series of potential Fenian invasion scares rocked both the Canadian and British authorities into action.

Considering the Fenian threat, General Sir Patrick MacDougall was sent out from Britain as Adjutant General to organize and develop a Canadian militia force and to establish a Camp of Instruction for cadets. Like Hope Grant before him, Wolseley was to form a great friendship with MacDougall who recognized Wolseley's drive and ability and within months had appointed him to establish the first ever militia camp in Canada. The place selected was at La Prairie, around nine miles from Montreal. Here Wolseley was in overall command with a General and Regimental staff under him. Whilst some of the three battalions formed had quartermasters and sergeant-majors who had previously seen military service in the British army, the majority of those serving came from cadet or volunteer forces with no or very limited military experience. To bring such men to a state of fighting readiness was the task that now faced Wolseley.

The camp was a huge logistical undertaking for over 1,100 cadets took part in the three weeks of instruction, yet Wolseley thrived under the challenge. Two divisional field days were arranged with the regular troops of the Montreal garrison, and on the second day Wolseley himself commanded one of the cadet battalions observed by MacDougall and Sir John Michel, the then commander of British troops in Canada, both of whom were full of praise for Wolseley. Indeed, MacDougall's report on the camp was glowing as to Wolseley's contribution, 'I desire to record as strongly as possible my sense of the ability and energy with which the immediate command of the Camp was exercised by Colonel Wolseley, and to which is attributable a large share in the success of the experiment. It was a charge requiring unusually delicate management; but in Colonel Wolseley's qualifications tact is combined with firmness, and both with an intimate knowledge of his profession in an unusual degree.'[7] Subsequently a considerable number of those trained at La Prairie joined Wolseley in his first independent command in 1870.

By March 1866, the threat of a Fenian invasion looked increasingly likely and whilst Horse Guards quickly despatched two regiments from Britain, the Canadian government called for 10,000 volunteers to join the recently established militia; 14,000 men answered. British troops were pushed westwards to face any likely invasion and Wolseley was tasked to inspect their state of military preparedness, spending weeks touring these units. Finally, after months of speculation, on 31 May 1866, the long-predicted invasion took place. Led by a former Union cavalry officer, Colonel O'Neill, 1,500 Fenian troops, many of them seasoned veterans of the recent American Civil War, crossed the Niagara River from Buffalo into Canada. On the following day O'Neill led the majority of his force into the deserted British fort, Fort Erie, which had seen action in numerous previous conflicts, including the Anglo-American War of 1812–15, in which it was besieged by American troops in the summer of 1814. Here, on the south-eastern tip of the Niagara Peninsula, O'Neill reinforced his position and awaited developments.

Despite an awareness that an invasion was likely, the Canadian government reacted poorly. It rushed ill-prepared cavalry and militia units into the Peninsula, who were insufficiently armed and supplied. In addition, these men were also weakly led by ineffective officers. Wolseley would later write in his autobiography in damning terms of the poor leadership qualities of these officers and by doing so gave his readers a clear indication of his own philosophy for commanding troops. He wrote:

> … the art of commanding men, for it is essentially an art, and so high, so peculiar an art, that many officers even in all regular armies never master it. Good, pleasant manners, closely allied to firmness, a genial disposition, a real sympathy for the private soldier, and an intimate knowledge of human nature, are essential qualifications for the man who would command soldiers effectively anywhere. The art is born in some and comes naturally to many. In peace or in war it is a quality more necessary for the officer than any knowledge he can acquire by a study of the drill-book, essential though that knowledge be.[8]

These qualities were sadly lacking in many of the Canadian officers. The local commander of the province of Ontario, General George Napier, rather than leading all his available forces against the invaders sent them in piecemeal. Led by inexperienced officers, such as Colonels Peacock and Booker, they failed to coordinate effectively and indeed Peacock's unit managed to get hopelessly lost on the line of march. O'Neil learnt of Booker's advance and sallied out from Fort Erie. The veterans intercepted and thoroughly routed the inexperienced militia, at what the Fenians would call the Battle of Limestone Ridge.

Details of the invasion reached General Sir John Michel in Montreal, soon followed by news of Napier's inept handling of the Canadian response. Michel did not hesitate and immediately sent Wolseley south with orders to 'coach' General Napier 'and prevent him from doing anything foolish'.[9] Once in Toronto Wolseley gave Napier firm instructions to do very little whilst he then boarded a train south with whatever military resources he could muster. His first task was to reconnoitre the situation around Fort Erie and this must have brought back memories of perilous days in India. He spotted a United States cutter anchored in the Niagara River crammed full of Fenian reinforcements and Wolseley must have then feared the worst. Fortunately, the Fenians were almost as badly organizing as the Canadians and after securing a further victory in a brief skirmish with the militia, O'Neill, desperately short of supplies, decided that it would be prudent to withdraw back across the border before his reinforcements had disembarked. The whole invasion had become a fiasco and it was to end in disaster for whilst trying to return to America O'Neill and his command were captured midstream by the USS *Michigan*. Wolseley quickly heard of the interception and received a firm promise from the American captain that the Fenians would be taken to Buffalo. The so-called invasion had been an embarrassment for both the Canadian and American governments and President Johnson acted quickly, outlawing the Brotherhood, and sending American troops north to secure the border from any further incursions onto Canadian soil. The majority of the Fenians were deprived of their weapons and were paroled on the condition that they relinquish any territorial ambitions upon Canada.

Although the 1866 invasion had become something of a farce it served to further establish Wolseley as the man to turn to in an emergency, who could be relied upon for direct and firm action. Clearly, his superiors, both Michel and MacDougall, recognized his ability but Wolseley was also developing a reputation amongst the Canadians, both civilians and military men alike. Soon after the O'Neill debacle Wolseley took command of a mixed brigade of regulars and militia at Stratford, on Lake Huron. He remained here a few weeks before returning to his normal duties in Montreal. Within days, with a clear panic in the Canadian government, Wolseley was sent to command a force at Thorold, close to the Welland Canal, which it was reported that some Fenians had threatened to attack. Wolseley was tasked in not only protecting the Canal, but also the Niagara region and he quickly turned his fledging force of militia into a tight, well-drilled unit, with the help of regulars from the Bedfordshire Regiment and a field battery of Royal Artillery. With the onset of winter, the Government finally decided that the Fenian threat had passed, the camp at Thorold was broken up and Wolseley returned to Montreal. In January 1867 rumours again spread of a further Fenian incursion and Wolseley was sent to Toronto to organize the brigade there. Once more the threat turned to nothing and with the arrival of spring Wolseley's term as assistant quartermaster-general came to an end. In the space of four years Wolseley's emotions had switched from the despair of never being able to leave a stagnating posting to one in which he was now reluctant to depart back to Britain for as he departed, he felt that more conflict was likely and with war came advancement.

The next months in Wolseley's life were to significantly alter his position for on his return to Ireland on leave his love for Louisa was reignited and he resolved to finally end his bachelor days. Despite the fact Louisa was not wealthy, he found his future wife to be his intellectual equal who in later life would correct and help Wolseley with his letters and speeches as well as be a confidant in both his public and private life. Louisa manged to introduce an element of tact and diplomacy into Garnet's future correspondence, something he badly lacked. The marriage had to be delayed a year when Wolseley was recalled to Canada to serve as Deputy Quartermaster-General in September 1867, upon the retirement of Colonel Lysons. Now aged 34, Garnet was the youngest officer ever to assume such a senior Staff role. He returned to Ireland in time for his 35th birthday and here he married Louisa during a two-month period of leave which at its end, he returned to Canada without her. They were reunited in the autumn of 1868, when Louisa joined her husband, and they began their married life together.

In the summer months of 1868, whilst awaiting the arrival of his new bride, Wolseley naturally kept himself busy. He returned to his earlier role of map-maker for which he had become renowned during his service in both India and China, and mapped the contested regions along the Canadian-American border that had not been properly surveyed for decades. He also turned his attention to writing, based on an idea given to him by Sir Richard Airey, then Quartermaster-General of the British army. Airey had proposed a practical handbook for the Staff to be written by officers in his department but the need for economy had meant the idea had been dropped. Wolseley, who was one of the officers Airey had wanted to employ in his pet project, decided to accept the challenge on his own initiative and, singlehanded, wrote the handbook in his own time. His mantra for the book was a reflection upon himself, and focused on guidance and information troops had needed, but not received throughout the four campaigns in which he had already fought. Thus, the book would be based on tangible requirements and needs rather than parade ground musings. The result was the *Soldier's Pocket Book for Field Service*, which was first published in 1869 and was to run to several editions.

The work was to become the defining authority on all things pertaining to army life and service and it successfully augmented the *Field Exercise* and *Queen's Regulations* which were the then standard works. Uniquely it was useful and relevant for all ranks from private to general. The book is divided into three parts and the level of detail Wolseley provided in all is truly outstanding and clearly reflects his amazing foresight and attention to detail at this time. Part One of the work examines the duties and equipment of every branch of the army and includes such details as the amount of supplies and equipment each wagon can carry to how much rations an elephant should receive daily! In addition, Wolseley prepared the private soldier with instructions on how to boil his coffee and make a stew from his rations. Part Two looks at the establishment of camps on the line of march, as well as the logistics of transporting troops to the seat of war by land and sea and even includes measurements for the size of horse stalls required on transport ships, and even describes how important it is for morale that troops sing on the line of march. The final part looks at the army in the field; from the deployment of troops, to building bridges, running railways and construction of telegraphs.

On publication it became an immediate success and the War Office itself later decided to buy the copyright from Wolseley and distributed the work as an official publication. Although Wolseley was clearly a brilliant soldier, he certainly was no diplomat and his candid and dogmatic statements in *The*

*Soldier's Pocket Book*, and the fact that he rarely disguised his own intellectual superiority, soon alienated many in the War Office and throughout the service. He made little attempt to hide his personal disdain of those officers who considered that their careers should focus on 'Queen's Regulations' and drill and learnt and understood nothing of the actual welfare and management or command of troops. Wolseley was primarily driven by the need for reform of the army away from what he would consider the inherent conservatism of the officer corps and in particular the senior officers in the War Office, yet by doing so he was viewed by many of these officers as an egotist and something of a pompous and presumptuous self-publicist. He was undoubtedly all these things but at the heart of his actions was a crusade for change and improvement. Naturally, anyone would have made enemies or rivals with such an approach, but at the same time Wolseley was preaching the correct sermon for many senior politicians and the stunning success of the *Soldier's Pocket Book* catapulted Wolseley from an ambitious colonel to someone whom the political world now took note of and this was to serve him well as his career progressed.

Although the threat of a direct Fenian invasion of Canada diminished with each passing month, the Dominion was now to be rocked by the possibility of insurrection from within and this latest danger was to allow Wolseley to shine once more. This challenge was centred upon lands in the Red River Valley acquired by the Canadian government from the Hudson Bay Company (HBC) in 1867. The HBC had held this land under Royal Charter from Charles II and continued to trade there with the indigenous Native Americans, though it was not this trade that interested the Canadian government but the land itself for the Red River Valley abutted an imaginary line drawn across the prairie which separated it from the United States. With tensions still high between the two countries the Canadians were anxious that the area become part of their own domain for if the USA pressed a claim to the Red River Valley, then this could threaten Canadian control of its north-west region. London assumed the role of negotiator for the Ottawa government but was placing enormous pressure on the HBC to agree a transfer of lands. Under this two-pronged assault the directors of the HBC conceded defeat and for the sum of £300,000 in compensation, the HBC were to hand over the lands of the Red River Valley, an area larger than Europe, to the Canadian government. By the time of the Red River Expedition these lands were still to be legally and formally bound to Canada and were still technically HBC territory. This was a technically that could and was conveniently ignored to suit the whim of politicians.

Of course, negotiations and pieces of paper do not always make for good policy, and the politicians on the ground and in London were insensitive in their dealings with the population of the Red River Valley. These were a mixture of British subjects and the Metis, people of French-Canadian descent who had also frequently intermarried with the Native American population. No explanation was forthcoming from the government of the inhabitant's status nor were guarantees provided for their rights or possessions. In addition, the Metis population were alarmed by the sudden appearance of English-speaking surveyors who quickly descended upon the newly-acquired domain. Integration of the new territory away from the HBC and to Canada was thus at best botched and was certainly thoughtless handed by the politicians.

While the English-speaking inhabitants were largely prepared to await developments, the Metis became more discontented and in this situation the eccentric, if not mentally unstable, Louis Riel became the self-appointed figurehead of Metis disquiet. Riel was a highly educated in philosophy, classics and law, a natural leader and firebrand orator who was expert at rousing a crowd and on 2 November 1869, he was at the forefront in establishing a provisional Metis government at Fort Garry, now modern-day Winnipeg. In December, with some inhabitants of the area growing uneasy about the legality of a provisional government and concern that it be considered as insurrection against the Crown, Riel called The Red River Convention of both French and English-speaking parishes along both the Red River and the Assiniboine River. The aim of the Convention, in Riel's mind at least, was to strengthen the resolve of the parish representatives and although some English-speaking members decided to withdraw their support, French-speaking parishes overwhelmingly supported Riel's position. A 'List of Rights' was agreed upon and Riel, feeling that he was now in a more secure position, issued a statement to the effect that the HBC had ceased to function as a government and the settlers of the Red River Valley did not recognize the authority of the newly appointed lieutenant-governor, William McDougall, whose tactless decrees from afar had inflamed the delicate situation. Riel concluded that the Metis were now effectively free to form their own government. With this declaration, and the raising of the Metis flag at Fort Garry, Riel's followers became more hostile. The English surveyors were rapidly evicted from the area and McDougall was refused entry at the border. The leader of the surveying team, Lieutenant-Colonel J Stoughton Dennis, called upon those 'Friends of Canada' in the area to resist Riel and a small group under the leadership of Dr John Christian Schultz did assemble to discuss forming a resistance. However, before any plans could be considered Riel led an armed group and arrested and imprisoned Schultz and his supporters; the Metis were prepared to fight their new overlords.

Whilst both the British and Canadian governments were concerned that Riel's actions could led to insurrection and bloodshed, the biggest fear was that any conflict, however small, could result in an escalation of the fight and even involve further difficulties with the United States, perhaps even military conflict. It was noted that Riel's secretary was an active Fenian supporter, and the flag of the new Metis provisional government displayed the French fleur-de-lis alongside an Irish shamrock on a white background. The flag had been sewn by nuns from a nearby Catholic convent and there was undoubtedly a religious element to the dispute, with many politicians and military men, Wolseley including, thinking that the Catholic church was actively encouraging the Metis revolt. Sir John Macdonald, head of the Ottawa government, was extremely concerned that Fenians in America might cause such agitation amongst the public, that the United States government might use this as an excuse for supporting the Metis territorial and political claims. Macdonald wrote that '... the United States Government are resolved to do all they can, short of war, to get possession of the western territory and we must take immediate and vigorous steps to counteract them'.[10]

During the first weeks of 1870 it looked, however, as if sense would prevail and that a peaceful negotiated settlement could be concluded. Donald A. Smith, a level-headed emissary of the Ottawa government had succeeded in building a working relationship with Riel and managed to convince the Metis leadership that they should agree to a meeting at Fort Garry. Here Smith hoped to explain the Canadian Government's position and from there begin negotiations to find a common path towards a political settlement. The subsequent two meetings of 19 and 20 January produced firm results, and Smith did manage to convince the Metis Provisional Government to send a delegation to Ottawa to ease a final agreement between the two opposing parties. As a gesture of goodwill Riel agreed to release Schultz and his small band of prisoners from the cells at Fort Garry.

Yet, any negotiations were taken firmly out of the hands of the politicians for Schultz and his followers managed to escape their imprisonment before they could be released and they sought refuge in the English-speaking areas further north, principally the settlement at Portage la Prairie. From here Schultz and a former British officer, Charles Boulton, as well as Thomas Scott who had been working on a road scheme for the Ottawa government when the revolt occurred, attempted to rally support for a military attack upon Riel. Thus far they found little appetite for a fight amongst the English-speaking Red River settlers and whilst Schultz decided to head for Ontario, Boulton led his dwindling force south. Unfortunately, this group passed close to Fort Garry and their mere presence was viewed as provocative by the Metis and Riel ordered them to be intercepted. Boulton, Scott and their comrades quickly surrendered to a small group of mounted Metis and found themselves back in the recently-vacated cells. Riel was in no mood for leniency and Boulton was charged with levying war against the new Metis provisional government. Fortunately for him, Donald Smith still possessed sufficient weight with Riel that he was able to personally intervene on Boulton's behalf who was granted a reprieve.

Thomas Scott, however, was not so fortunate. He could not hide his disdain for his captors and delivered a constant stream of abuse towards them, which finally resulted in a demand for Scott to be brought before a Metis court martial. On 3 March 1870, Scott was duly found guilty of sedition and sentenced to be shot. Even an intervention by Smith and a group of Protestant and Catholic clergy failed to secure a reprieve and the following day Scott was executed. Had Riel listened to Smith and others then perhaps a political settlement might had been concluded between the Metis and the Canadian government but neither the Canadians nor the British were going to stand by and accept, what they considered to be the murder of a British subject. Riel had badly miscalculated, and the writer Alexander Begg recorded that, 'A deep gloom has settled over the settlement on account of his deed'.[11] Many of Riel's supporters now knew that the situation had escalated to one in which military conflict was likely.

Wolseley had been watching events in the Red River with increasing professional interest. He was always on the lookout for an opportunity that would advance his own cause and he saw in the Red River dispute a chance to secure his first independent command. When he learnt of Donald Smith's political mission Wolseley tried to use his influence amongst both his political and military friends to persuade Macdonald, head of the Canadian Government, that he should accompany Smith. Macdonald, however, felt that to send a high-ranking serving officer on a peace mission would have been potentially provocative. MacDonald wrote:

> It would never have done for Colonel Wolseley to have gone with him [Smith]. Smith goes to carry the olive branch, and were it known at Red River that he was accompanied by an officer high in rank in military service, he would be looked upon as having the olive branch in one hand and a revolver in the other. We must not make any indication of sending a military force until peaceable means have been exhausted.[12]

Instead, Wolseley busied himself writing reports on the scale and route of any expedition, which he circulated amongst both politicians and military superiors, and he made no secret of his desire to lead such a force.

With the death of Scott, political and public opinion had shifted in both Canada and Britain towards military intervention. Negotiations did continue in Ottawa between Metis representatives and the Canadian Government, resulting in the passing of the Manitoba Act which recognized a Metis provisional government but with far less power and territory that Riel had wanted. Macdonald realized that anger amongst the Canadian populace towards Riel's decision to execute Scott could only be quelled by military intervention and for his own political survival Macdonald needed to be seen to be acting decisively and he thus sought the help of the Home Government. However, under William Gladstone, the British government had been following a policy of retrenchment across the Empire, and the garrison in Canada was in the process of being reduced. It was clear that Macdonald would need the support of senior British officers and administrators then serving in Canada if he was to secure British regulars for any military intervention against Riel. Macdonald first turned to the Governor-General, Sir John Young, who as early as February 1870 was writing to the British Colonial Secretary, Lord Granville, to lay out the case for intervention by British troops. Although initially reluctant, by March Granville had changed his mind and conceded that a small contingent of British troops should go to the Red River, '... to act in conjunction with a force of Canadian Militia with the view of restoring order in that Settlement'.[13] Despite securing British troops, both Young and Macdonald hoped and envisaged that the military expedition would be viewed not as a hostile force but as a friendly garrison.

The death in service of Sir Charles Windham, in February 1870, the Lieutenant-General Commanding in North America, resulted in something of a hiatus in military circles until Windham's replacement, Lieutenant-General James Lindsay, arrived from London. In the meantime, Macdonald was clear in who he wanted to lead any potential military expedition when he wrote, 'Should these miserable half-breeds [Riel and his followers] not disband, they must be put down, and then so far as I can influence matters, I shall be very glad to give Colonel Wolseley the chance of glory ...'[14] By April it was clear that Wolseley's canvassing was delivering results for in a letter to Sir Edward Lugard, Garnet's former commander, Sir John Michell, wrote of the Red River Expedition that, 'They [the British and Canadian governments] are going, I believe, to send in command the best officer for the purpose that I know of (Colonel Wolseley). Whatever can be done by every foresight, good sense and judgement, and for having the perfect confidence of his troops will be done by him.' Despite all his outward bravado Wolseley was to comment on this when he wrote to Louisa that, 'This almost makes me afraid when I hear what others expect of me'.[15]

Macdonald was delighted to hear that Lindsay was to be sent to Canada for he had previously worked alongside him when Lindsay was commander of the British troops in eastern Canada at the start of the American Civil War. Macdonald found Lindsay to be a man of great energy. Yet Lindsay had been given what appeared to be contradictory orders by the British government; for he was 'to supervise the rundown of the British army in central Canada and to cooperate with the Canadian government in providing a force to secure the transfer of the Red River colony to the dominion'.[16] The War Office made it very clear to Lindsay that his primary objective was to withdraw British troops from Canada by the close of 1870 and that the proposed Red River Expedition must not interfere with that timeline and certainly no troops could be stationed at Fort Garry beyond the winter of 1870–1. Thus, time was clearly of the essence and Lindsay, true to form, wasted none and on his arrival appointed Wolseley to command the Red River Expedition. Both the British and Canadians favoured a mixed expeditionary force of British regulars and local militiamen so as to demonstrate to the American government and people that Canada and Britain were working as one to retain the north-west of the Dominion under British sovereignty. It was also felt that the Metis would be less likely to resist militarily if they had to face British regular troops.

Wolseley knew that he would likely have to incorporate Canadian militia into his expedition and was indeed delighted to do so for he had worked so well with such troops during the various Fenian invasion scares and had respect for their abilities if well led. At first Wolseley's appointment was kept secret for negotiations were still underway with the Metis representatives over the Manitoba Act. This shows a degree of duplicity by Macdonald and Lindsay but once the Act was agreed the following month, news of Wolseley's command was released, and it was greeted with approval by the Canadian press and public alike. Wolseley's good reputation as a man of action would, as it was felt by many, including those members of the 'Canada First' organization, guarantee the success of the expedition.

Wolseley had already made Lindsay's choice for commander of the expedition a very easy one for as soon as the new Lieutenant-General had arrived in the Dominion Wolseley presented him with the *Memorandum Regarding the Despatch of an Armed Force to the Red River Territory* which he had been compiling for several months. In truth Lindsay had probably made his decision to appoint Wolseley to lead the expedition whilst he was in transit from Britain, but this memorandum reaffirmed his decision. Indeed, Lindsay wrote to the War Office that Wolseley 'has the full approval of his Excellency the Governor-General and his Government, and I consider it very fortunate that an officer who knows Canada and its Volunteers so well and who has so much ability and experience, should have been available for this service'.[17]

The breath and scope, as well as level of minute detail, in Wolseley's *Memorandum* was truly staggering and demonstrates that the author was a master of his trade. Undoubtedly the early writing of the *Soldier's Pocket Book* had framed his thoughts and although Wolseley had been working for months to ensure that he would be granted his first independent command he must have been slightly daunted by the enormous challenge he now faced. Yet, he had the intelligence and foresight to realize that the success of the expedition would rest on careful planning and organization, both areas in which he excelled. In the *Memorandum* Wolseley outlined the number of troops that would be required (around 1,000), and the amount of ammunition per man: 210 rounds, 60 rounds to be carried in pouches, with the remainder stored in ammunition barrels. Wolseley also specified that wooden boxes would have to be constructed, with exact measurements, to transport ten rifles in each as well as the clothing required and camp equipment. He also outlined the type of boats that would be needed to not only cope with the large distances that would have to covered across lakes and along rivers but be sturdy enough for portage over land to transverse rapids and waterfalls. The level of detail in the *Memorandum* was such that the contents and weight of each boat was specified from the number of men to their equipment and supplies; from the size of the axes to be taken to fell trees, to the number of nails required for boat repairs, to additional blankets and cooking utensils for it was envisaged that each boat would be a self-sufficient unit with all the equipment stored within. Wolseley overlooked nothing. He even tried out each piece of equipment and discovered, for example, that the regulation-issue axe was useless at cutting back brushwood and adopted the double-edged axes as used by the American army. This design was later utilized by the British Army as their standard model. Wolseley was to later write in his memoirs that the Red River Expedition was, '... my first independent command, so I was on my mettle, and felt that if I possessed any genius for such practical work, the time had at last arrived for me to show it'.[18]

Lindsay initially focused on ensuring that the Canadian Government provided sufficient troops, who were of the right calibre, for the expedition, as well as seeking a financial commitment largely covering its costs. He insisted that the expedition have an additional 40 boats built, to add to the 100 that the Canadians already had constructed and paid for. Both Lindsay and Wolseley realized that the design and durability of the boats would be crucial for the success of the expedition and thus both men spent much time in ensuring that their testing requirements were met. The boats were between 25 to 30ft long, equipped with masts, sails and oars and were designed to accommodate fifteen men, twelve troops and two or three voyageurs, or boatmen, as well as four tons of supplies, which Wolseley calculated would last 60 days per boat.

Both the British and Canadian governments were involved in deciding upon the strength of the force, which largely followed Wolseley's advice. The British regulars came from the 1st Battalion of the 60th Rifles, 373 officers and men, a battery of Royal Field Artillery, comprising four 6-pounder mountain guns, which could be rapidly assembled when and if required, a detachment of Royal Engineers and finally members of the Army Service and Hospital Corps. Wolseley was fortunate in the choice of the Rifles for not only were the troops of a high quality but the battalion also possessed some impressive officers, including Captain Huyshe, who would serve under Wolseley in the Asante Expedition, and Captain Redvers Buller. The latter would become a member of Wolseley's famous or infamous Asante Ring and his career would be intertwined with that of Wolseley's for many years. The two men would become colleagues, friends and then ultimately rivals as they actively fought Victoria's foes over the next 15 years in West Africa, Egypt and the Sudan. The remainder of the 1,200-strong force came from militia volunteers who Lindsay ensured reached Wolseley at the earliest possible moment, so he and his British regulars had time to assess and train them in the requirements of the expedition. In the end, the men came largely from two militia battalions: the 1st Ontario Rifles and the 2nd Quebec Rifles. Lindsay also reaffirmed the stance from the War Office, that no imperial troops would remain at Fort Garry once it had been secured and that the Canadians would have to provide and supply the new garrison there. Lindsay's whirlwind approach was not always appreciated in Canadian government circles but both he and Wolseley worked well together. Indeed, Garnet was to write fondly of Lindsay, who would die just four years later at the age of only 58, stating he was as 'an able, energetic soldier, whose heart was in his work …'.[19]

At the start of the expedition, Wolseley was confident that his troops would prevail in any hostile encounter with the Metis rebel forces but he was under no illusion as to the scale of the physical challenge his men would face. There was no easy route from the then political and geographical heart of Canada to the far-off HBC lands. The troops mustered in Toronto had a distance of 1,228 miles to cover before they would reach Fort Garry. Much of the terrain was over lakes and fast-flowing rivers, with dangerous rapids and when waterborne travel was impossible the boats would have to be unloaded and supplies and vessels carried to the next body of water. Such 'portage' as it was known would be time consuming and laborious work and require the troops to assail difficult slopes, travel along mountain passes, through swampy valleys and dense forests in which mosquitos would prey upon them. Alongside this was the fact that the expedition would be travelling through lands which was still home to significant numbers of Native American tribes and no one, Wolseley included, knew how the presence of a large military force marching through tribal lands would be perceived by them.

There was an easy route, south of the Great Lakes, via American territory, where a railway was already in operation that could transport the force to St Paul in Minnesota, only 100 miles from Fort Garry and where boats could be taken along the Red River to the fort itself. However, this route was very much closed to Wolseley and his men. Not only did many Americans sympathise with the Metis, but there was no doubt that in 1870 the American administration still had designs upon the vast north-west region. The American press were vocal in their demands that the north-west was part of the country's geographical destiny and Senator Chandler of Chicago, a Fenian supporter, even tried to push through a resolution in Congress for the United States to annex the Red River region. As early as November 1869 the American Secretary of State had informed the British Ambassador in Washington that if the British government sought permission to move troops along this route, then the answer would be a firm no. Knowing the political situation, it is unlikely that Wolseley ever seriously considered this American option.

Instead, Wolseley turned to the practicalities of the only two other possible routes, neither of which were ideal. The first was the northern route traditionally used by the staff of the HBC. This option covered 723 miles and ran up the Hayes River to Lake Winnipeg and then along the Red River to Fort Garry. The problem with this route was that Hudson Bay was only ice free for a limited time in the summer months which would mean that any expedition would be forced to 'winter' at Fort Garry, and this was politically and financially unacceptable to the British government. The second option, or the so-called southern route, although considerably longer, did allow for a passage by steamers on the Great Lakes which permitted a faster transit across Lake Superior. Again, like the 'northern' route, ice restricted the months in which steamers could operate but there was just enough time for the expedition to leave in early May and return before ice once more closed off the region. Though both Wolseley and Lindsay favoured this route, they would need some reassurance before completely committing to it fully for it relied on a number of factors being in place. First the men would be carried by rail from Toronto to Collingwood on the Georgian Bay, a distance of 94 miles. From here steamers would take the troops 524 miles across Lakes Huron and Superior to Thunder Bay. The force would then march 48 miles along

Dawson's Road to Lake Shebandowan and from here the final stretch of 550 miles to Fort Garry would be in the specially-constructed boats.

This final part of the journey was to take the expedition across Lake Shebandowan into the Hudson Bay watershed, then into Lac des Mille Lacs to Fort Francis and from here the force would sail down the Rainy River to Lake of the Woods. This followed the border with the United States, and into the Winnipeg River and the southern end of Lake Winnipeg, which flows into the Red River and onto Fort Garry. Although little was known about this stretch, Wolseley was aware that the force would have to cope with nearly fifty portages, ranging in length from as little as 100 yards to over a mile during which the boats would have to be unloaded, manhandled and then reloaded, which would of course be both time consuming and laborious. Another concern was whether Dawson's Road would allow for an easy transfer of troops and supplies and here Lindsay and Wolseley were very dependent on the advice and intelligence of the surveyor Simon J. Dawson of the Canadian Public Works Department who had been employed to construct the road from Thunder Bay to Lake Shebandowan.

During the autumn of 1869 Dawson and his team of surveyors had been working on the construction of a road from the Lake of Woods to Fort Garry, and it was this work that had so infuriated the Metis rebels and saw the surveyors physically expelled from the area. Work then continued on Dawson's Road from Thunder Bay to Lake Shebandowan and Dawson was able to reassure Wolseley and Lindsay that before work had ceased with the onset of winter, the engineers had completed 25 miles of the 48-mile route to a such a sufficient degree that it practicable for use by wagons. Furthermore, Dawson had left firm instructions with his engineers that once the snows had melted, they were to recommence their work and that there were now eighty men working to complete this last section. He also stated that he would arrange for two steamers, the *Chicora* and the *Algoma*, to be hired for the whole of the summer to regularly run supplies between Collingwood and Thunder Bay. With Dawson's optimism ringing in their ears, Wolseley and Lindsay finally committed to this 'southern' route and the work of the expedition now began in earnest.

Wolseley went ahead of the mustering troops and journeyed to Collingwood to begin to assemble some of the supplies for the expedition. Dawson's plan to hire and use steamers to ferry materials was put to an early test for any vessel leaving Collingwood had to travel along the St. Mary River, which divides Canada from the USA. Three miles of this river were unnavigable because of rapids at Sault St Marie and these could only be by-passed by using a canal on the American side. Wolseley tested American resolve by sending first one and then the other steamer through the canal. The first travelled undetected but the second was stopped by the American authorities, who then ceased all Canadian traffic, although this was later relented to only banning steamers carrying supplies for the Red River Expedition. Whilst the Canadian and American governments argued over access to the canal, Wolseley used his initiative and bribed the captain of an American steamer to carry supplies and a potential bottleneck was avoided.

The troops left Toronto on 12 May and were able to board steamers for the journey across Lake Superior. Yet before they sailed each man was issued with a copy of Wolseley's Standing Orders for the Red River Expeditionary Force. In thirty-five separate points Wolseley outlined all the basic information that the troops would need to make the expedition as successful and as smooth running as it could possibly be. The information included what time reveille would be each day (3am) and that each man would have hot tea before starting on the line of march. Breakfast would be at 8am with an hour's rest, whilst lunch was served at 1pm. The march would always halt at least one hour before dark so that the night's camp could be prepared. It also explained how the force would be structured as it advanced and Wolseley stated that movement would be by detachments consisting of one or more companies and to each company a brigade of five boats would be attached. Wolseley was to use similar Standing Orders in the Asante expedition and both documents left none of the participants with any doubt as to what was expected of them and what they could expect. The final point, number 35, reflected Wolseley's concern as to what his force might encounter from the Native Americans. It stated:

> All Officers belonging to this Force will be most careful in impressing upon those under their command the great necessity there is for cultivating the good will of the Indians and others employed as voyageurs. Colonel Wolseley will punish with the utmost severity anyone who ill treats them. The same rule applies to all Indians who may be met on the line of route. It must be remembered that the Government has made a treaty with them securing the right of way through their country; all are therefore bound to protect them from injury, and it is of special importance that our intercourse with them should be of the most friendly nature.[20]

With these instructions impressed upon officers and men, the steamers set out on their 524-mile journey across Lake Superior to Thunder Bay.

Wolseley maintained his working relationship with *Blackwood's Magazine* and after the completion of the expedition, and on his return to Britain, he wrote two articles both of which were published in 1871. In terms of the planning for the trip Wolseley wrote, 'Every probable, indeed almost every possible, contingency had to be thought of and provided for; and it may be confidently asserted that no expedition has ever started more thoroughly complete or better prepared for its work'.[21] This was a bold claim, but in terms of the British Army, it was probably an accurate one.

Wolseley and his men arrived at Prince Arthur's Landing at Thunder Bay on 21 May and were greeted with a depressing sight for a recent forest fire had swept through the area and had caused devastation. He was to write that, 'I have never looked upon a drearier or less inviting prospect in any of my many wanderings'.[22] Yet Wolseley knew how vital it would be to maintain the expedition's morale throughout the long and difficult journey to Fort Garry, and so although he had many moments of frustration and even despair over the next weeks, to his men he was always cheerful and resolute. No problems were too insurmountable, and this was demonstrated on the first night when a panicky chief control officer approached Wolseley with the news that due to an oversight the tent poles had been left at the quayside in Collingwood. Wolseley's response was not one of anger but of laughter and he enquired whether the axes had been left behind too? On receiving the news that the axes were with the expedition Wolseley pointed to the half-burnt trees in the vicinity and said, 'Then you can help yourself to as many tent poles as you require'.[23] Similarly on the first night a young officer, Lieutenant Riddell, was struggling to cook a meal of salt pork. Wolseley took the time to show him how best to prepare his meal and in Riddell's words 'He [Wolseley] showed me, in the scientific manner of an old campaigner, how to dig a trench in the ground, and with stones and sticks to construct a fender over it, on which to place my cooking utensils ... '[24] Wolseley's hands-on, cheerful approach to any difficulty gave his men confidence and inspired them to give all to their commanding officer.

Prince Arthur's Landing, which Wolseley named in honour of the Queen's third son, was soon transformed into the main supply depot as his men busied themselves unloading stores and constructing a stockade around the perimeter. Over the next days this was made into a more defensible position for Wolseley intended to leave a detachment of militia here with two of the expedition's artillery pieces to protect his rear and lines of communication from possible Fenian intervention. Wolseley ventured forward to inspect Dawson's Road from Thunder Bay to Lake Shebandowan Lake and was horrified to discover that despite Dawson's assurances the road was far from finished. The construction was to have been based on a corduroy road; that is to say that as the virgin forest was cut down and the ground levelled and boulders removed, the timber from the fallen trees was used to form a surface over which men and supplies could travel. Yet Wolseley found that work on the last 18 miles of the 48 had not begun and that the quality of the first 30 miles was poor, with boulders and tree stumps disrupting passage.

This was a major setback to an already tight timetable and Wolseley's cheerfulness rapidly turned to anger. He found the men of the Land Transport Service a useless workshy bunch who he suspected of trying to deliberately sabotage the expedition, for he believed many of them held a loyalty or allegiance to the Fenian cause. Wolseley was even convinced that the Minister of Public Works, a man named Langevin, was a firm supporter of Riel. Although Dawson was a hard-working dedicated public servant, his men were clearly taken from the dregs of society. Wolseley was left with no alternative but to utilize his own men, both troops and the voyageurs, to form fatigue parties to push forward the construction of the road. Even officers were expected to carry and use picks and shovels like their men. The work was laborious, and the men were not helped by the weather. Thunder Bay was well named for between the end of May to mid-July it rained incessantly for 23 days, often with severe thunderstorms. Not only did the rainfall slow the construction of the road, turning everything to mud and frequently washing away what had already been built, but storms on 11 and 15 July damaged boats moored on the shore and soaked supplies. Also, the men were hampered by swarms of mosquitos and other flies which made already difficult conditions sometimes almost unbearable. Remarkably, morale was maintained. Wolseley ensured the men were rotated from time spent on road construction and on their 'rest days' he encouraged canoe races not only to improve their nautical skills for what lay ahead but to induce a competitiveness amongst the troops. The men were also creative in devising songs to sing as they laboured on the road, one of which went –

> Twas only as a volunteer that I left my abode;
> I never thought of coming here to work upon the road.
> But never mind, we'll struggle on, not heeding wind or weather, For we're sure to get along, if only we pull together.
> If the girls of Manitoba are as kind as they are charming
> The half of us will stop behind and settle down to farming.[25]

Although publicly Wolseley displayed his usual cheerfulness and optimism in front of the men, privately he was increasingly concerned that the delays imposed on the expedition by the incomplete road would threaten its success. He confided in a letter to his brother Dick that 'I have always made it a rule through life, no matter whether it was in the danger of battle or any other position or circumstance when men of ordinary characters are likely to be *glum* to appear jolly – and the consequence I that everyone thinks I am of that happy sort of disposition'. But he concluded that at times he was in such low spirits he could '… sit down and cry like a schoolgirl'.[26] Now was such a time, for the schedule to get the canoes on to Lake Shebandowan was slipping dangerously. The press, both the Canadian and British, were writing that the road would never be built in time and the expedition would be recalled even before it had really started, and the American press were jubilant and confidently predicted that Wolseley's force would have to turn back. Wolseley realized that he had to consider an alternative to the endless road construction which was sapping both hope and patience. Although some progress was being made his horse-drawn wagons could only move a single boat at a time along the slowly increasing roadway and he had 150 boats to move.

Wolseley decided to enquire amongst the staff of the HBC to establish whether an alternative route existed and discovered from them that Lake Shebandowan was connected to Lake Superior by the Kamasnistiqua and Mataway Rivers. Dawson was adamant that these waterways were not navigable, and the men of the HBC also declared that it was impossible to move his boats along these wild-rushing waterways, whose rocky bottoms would surely wreck the vessels. Yet Wolseley felt it was worth the risk and detailed Captain John Young of the 60th to make a reconnaissance and attempt to see if these rivers could be utilized. After 10 days of effort, which included portage over a waterfall 120ft in height, Young and his party forced their way up the 50 miles of rushing water. Wolseley was delighted to receive Young's positive news, for he knew that he could now divert the boats and most of the haulage of supplies along these river routes, thus saving his force between four to six weeks of toil along the Dawson Road route, bringing the timescale for the completion of the expedition back on track.

After two months of hard labour, countless delays and frustration, the expedition had succeeded in hauling and paddling over 150 boats and two months of supplies to McNeill's Bay on the shores of Lake Shebandowan where a depot was established. Wolseley arrived on 14 July and despite suffering from dysentery he rallied his men to begin the last, and most difficult stage of their journey to Fort Garry, which was to begin in two days. A violent storm on 15 July threatened to delay their departure, but the following morning was clear and bright, although a brisk onshore wind meant that the flotilla of boats, with Wolseley at its head, did not set their paddles into the lake until the late afternoon. Someone from the 60th Rifles in the first boat shouted, 'For Fort Garry!'[27] This was quickly followed by resounding cheers from both the troops in the flotilla and those left on shore. Wolseley had determined that to ease congestion over the numerous portages the men of the expedition would face, the force would be divided into brigades of fifty men in six to eight boats, with the 60th Rifles and the Royal Engineers in the first tranche. It would not be until 1 August that the last troops left McNeill's Bay and by then Wolseley and the men of the first brigade had reached Bare Portage, 150 miles along the route.

It was not only the numerous portages the men had to face that delayed progress but passage across the many lakes was also slow for they were strewn with dozens of small islands and to thread the right course between them proved problematic. It was very easy to paddle for miles into a cul-de-sac of bays and waste many hours retracing the route until the right passage was located. In a letter to his sister Henrietta, Captain Redvers Buller described the difficult in paddling through these lakes and even mentioned that Wolseley himself became lost on route. Buller wrote:

> I loaded 6 boats and having some difficulty succeeded in getting them equipped with a portion of the allotted stores; for things at Shebandowan were in a sadly backward state; I started up the lake at 4 pm, on Sunday evening the 17 July 1870. We were to be accompanied by 12 voyageurs two for each boat but there was no kit ready for them and so we went on leaving them to follow. We rowed about 3 miles up the lake and camped waiting for Dundas who with his company joined us about 8. The next morning our troubles began. No guide had been forthcoming; & Wolseley had said 'Oh! You have your map, keep the righthand shore all the way & you cannot miss the portage. Shebandowan is over 20 miles long, full of islands and all bays and inlets; & most unfortunately although my map was the W.O. one yet the Hydrographer General had omitted (sic) to its existence. We rowed till about 11 when I happened to notice that the water in front about 4 miles was then visible right ahead was dead calm, while through an opening we were passing I could see rippled water. I at once judged that it must be the longest part, & turned sharp to the right; & by this lucky accident we were the only detachment (without a guide) that came direct to the portage and escaped rowing about 5 miles up a bay and back again. In another half a day we reached heights of land portage about 1 ½ long & a very rough one; this took us a day and a half; we then had 2 days down a large & very lovely lake; Lac des Milles Lacs; I think it rather ought to be called lake of a thousand islands we had some difficulty in finding our way as we were still without a guide but we were lucky for we did not lose more than an hour altogether and Col. Wolseley himself with a guide was lost for a whole day in it ...[28]

Writing in *Blackwood's Magazine* Wolseley left an equally descriptive passage on the difficulties surrounding portage that the expedition had to endure;

> The brigades of boats were to move singly or in groups of two or three, according to circumstances; but three was the largest number that could work together on a portage, two being the best ... the men began to carry over the stores without delay, piling them in heaps, one for each boat ... The ordinary method in vogue with Indians and the regular North American voyageurs for carrying loads, is by means of a long strap about three inches wide in the centre, where it is passed across the forehead, but tapering off to an inch in width at the ends, which are fastened round the barrel or parcel to be portaged. Men accustomed to this work will thus carry weights of 400lb., and some 500lb., across the longest portage, the loads resting on the upper part of the back and kept there by the strap going round the forehead. The great strain is thus upon the neck, which has to be kept very rigid, whilst the body is bent forward. As it could not be expected that soldiers untrained in such labour would be able to carry loads in that manner, short pieces of rope with a loop at each end were supplied to the boats, by means of which two short poles – cut in the woods at the portages as required – were easily converted into a very efficient hand-barrow, of just the dimensions required for the conveyance of the small barrels in which our pork and flour were packed. After, however, a little practice, a large proportion of the men soon learned to use the common portage-strap, their officers setting them the example by themselves carrying heavy loads with it. As soon as all the stores had been conveyed across the portage, the boats were hauled ashore, and dragged over their keels resting on small trees felled across the path to act as rollers. The labour involved by hauling a heavy boat up a very steep incline, to a height of about a hundred feet, is no child's play. In each boat there was a strong painter [a strong line used for towing a boat] and a towing-line, by means of which and the leather portage-straps a sort of man-harness was formed when required, so that forty or fifty men could haul together. Say the portage was a mile long (some were more), and that each man had to make ten trips across it before all the stores of his brigade were got over, he would have walked nineteen miles during the operation, being heavily laden for ten of them. At some portages considerable engineering ingenuity was required – small streams had to bridged and marshy spots to be corduroyed over. By the tie our men returned many of them were expert axemen, and all were more or less skilled in the craft of the voyageur and American woodsman.[29]

Many of the men on the expedition left their own accounts and they often differ from Wolseley's rather stoic description of the work surrounding the portages and illustrate just how exhausting such work could be. Describing the first serious portage at Kashabowie Buller wrote, 'The portage was about three-quarters of a mile long. Over it we had to carry on our backs all our loads, consisting of about twenty-eight barrels a boat, and then to drag the boats over. This took us just a day, and we camped the other end … I carried five loads over. I thought them heavy then; they averaged about 100lb. a piece …'[30] Later in the expedition Buller recorded that he could carry around 180lb. at a time, reflecting how the men became accustomed to the hard work. John Kerr wrote of portaging as 'horrible work' and stated that as difficult as pork barrels were to carry, the boxes of rifles were the worst for their sharp edges cut into the flesh of arms. Although each portage offered its own degree of difficulty, the Height of Land Portage was viewed by many of the men as one of the worst for it covered 2½ miles of steep ground and the sheer effort meant that it took some brigades two or three days to get across. The men were rewarded in their efforts though for once across the expedition was travelling with the current rather than against it and this remained the case until the Red River itself was entered. For many, it was the first time they were able to look up and take a moment to marvel at the scenery around them of a largely untravelled wilderness.

Again, Buller was to write of the early progress the expedition made, the quality, in his opinion, of many of the voyageurs, and the need for constant boat repairs and the ingenious solutions he and the men employed:

> About the end of the first week, Col. Wolseley overtook us he was pleased with the way we had made & promised to blaze tree [score the bark with an axe] to guide us for the future and after that we never had any difficulty in finding our way. Down the River Maligne there were some heavy rapids to descend & here my special labours commenced; the voyageurs who had been sent with us to manage our boats, instead of being skilled boatmen were simply Canadian adventurers who wanted a free passage to the Red River to see what it was like. I can fearlessly state that not one of them was as competent to manage a boat as I am myself. The boats hit rocks got damaged & had to be mended right and left; my own which I steered myself escaped unhurt, but I had to do all the tinkering to the others we mended holes by putting a lot of canvas with white lead and covering with tin.[31]

Whilst Wolseley might have thought of everything the expedition required in terms of supplies and materials, one area in which his choices were not popular amongst the men concerned food. Wolseley had hoped the men would have been able to supplement their diet by catching fish, but the speed of the 'march' allowed little time for fishing and the noise created during portage ensured game was rarely seen. So, the men were largely reliant on the salted provisions they carried, principally pork. Captain McCalmont named the daily ration 'choke dog', which was a mixture of pork and flour and which he claimed '... one would not have found either appetizing or digestible under any other circumstances'.[32] The monotony of the diet was recorded by Captain Wallace who wrote how, towards the end of the day the men would joked about what they would have for dinner; 'what a delicious change ... hot boiled pork instead of cold boiled pork'.[33] It seems quite incredible that the men could achieve such acts of physical toil day after day on such a diet and although Wolseley's troops did all that he asked of them, the Colonel learnt from his error and in subsequent campaigns Wolseley ensured that the diet of his troops was more varied and nutritious.

By the 19th day out from McNeill's Bay the lead elements of the expedition, Wolseley included, reached Fort Frances, an unimpressive collection of HBC shacks, which were however significant for the force had covered roughly half the distance to Fort Garry. Here Wolseley was greeted by Captain William Francis Butler, who Wolseley had earlier appointed as an intelligence officer. At a time when campaigning frequently covered unknown or unmapped terrain in which commanders rarely had much of an appreciation of what was over the next hill yet alone where the enemy might be, Wolseley fully understood the importance of obtaining as much intelligence as possible. His employment of young, energetic officers in the role of intelligence gatherers although not unique in British colonial campaigns certainly placed Wolseley at the forefront of information-gathering and the adoption of an intelligence department which reported directly to him was a key feature of all of Wolseley's subsequent commands.

The careers of Butler and Wolseley were to become intertwined from the moment Butler introduced himself to the young Colonel when he volunteered for the position of intelligence officer for the campaign. The men would campaign in West and Southern Africa, Egypt and the Sudan as Butler became one of Wolseley's so-called 'Asante Ring' of trusted and loyal subordinates. Butler's role in the Red River Expedition was that of a spy and his mission was personally highly dangerous for the task Wolseley set him saw Butler travel incognito through America and into Canada to reach Fort Garry and if his identity had been discovered Butler could have faced imprisonment or even death. Both Wolseley and Lindsay wanted Butler to cross into the United States to gauge the strength of American support for Riel's rebellion before trying to rendezvous with Wolseley and his men somewhere on route. In his orders, Lindsay gave Butler almost a free hand as to how he was to accomplish his mission, writing, 'We must leave matters to yourself, I think ... you will be the best judge of how to get on when you know and see the ground. I will not ask you to visit Fort Garry, but if you find it feasible, it would be well if you could drop down the Red River and join Wolseley before he gets to the place. You know what I want, but how to do it, I will leave altogether to yourself.'[34]

Wolseley was keen to ascertain the attitude of the people in the American states bordering Canada and he was especially anxious to discover if the Fenians were likely to support Riel with any military intervention. Dressed as a frontiersman Butler had entered Michigan from Toronto on 10 June and travelled widely by train across the border states. His constant enquiries on Fenian activities soon identified him as a British intelligence officer so after just three weeks he felt it was prudent to cross back into Canada having a most arduous journey north via train, stagecoach, paddle steamer and on foot. Butler not only succeeded in reaching Fort Garry but even managed to secure an interview with Riel himself. On learning of the expedition's approach Butler hurried to Fort Francis and was able to greet Wolseley with some vital intelligence.

Butler's meeting with Riel had, however, yielded little intelligence, for it was Riel who attempted to gain information from Butler as to the size of Wolseley's force and its intentions. Naturally, Butler circumnavigated his way around Riel's questions, and he learnt from Riel that he had no intention of offering armed resistance against Wolseley's expedition and Riel stated, '... I only wish to retain power until I can resign it to a proper Government'. Riel, therefore, made it clear, that with tensions running high between the local French and English-speaking settlers, he would not resign to anyone but a government representative; 'I will keep what is mine until the proper Government arrives'.[35] Riel also firmly stated that he required an amnesty for the execution of Scott or else his loyal band of supporters would likely resist Wolseley's advance. With these contradictory words Butler left Riel and sought out the Protestant bishop, Macrae, and other prominent Government loyalists. To a man all gave Butler the firm impression that the settlement was close to anarchy, with the rival camps threatening violence, and over this was the risk that the local Native Americans might use the chaos as an opportunity to rise up. Armed with letters from the bishop and others, who urged Wolseley to hurry to their aid, Butler journeyed for his rendezvous at Fort Francis.

Despite the urgency impressed upon him Wolseley lingered at Fort Francis for a few days for his men to rest and repair their battered boats and threadbare clothing before the advance continued in earnest. He left a company of the Ontario Rifles at the fort and pressed the remainder of his troops up Rainy River and into the Lake of the Woods. Rainy River formed the boundary between America and Canada and if the expedition was to encounter any American intervention it would have likely to have been here. Despite Butler's reassurances that such American or Fenian action was highly unlikely, Wolseley was keen to hurry his men on and here his impatience got the better of him. Deciding that he would not wait for a guide he soon got hopelessly lost amongst the many small islands and inlets of the lake. Unlike his early navigational mistake this time Wolseley lost many hours as his flotilla had to repeatedly retrace their steps. When his party finally arrived at Rat Portage, at the mouth of the Winnipeg River, they were close to collapse. Here, Wolseley found that the officials of the HBC had sent additional boats to ease the passage along the Winnipeg River and he was greeted with further desperate appeals for haste from the English-speaking settlers.

The next stage of the expedition was arguably the most dangerous and exhilarating, for the Winnipeg River has numerous dangerous rapids and fast-flowing sections, as well as steep waterfalls. Indeed, Wolseley's canoe nearly foundered when his voyageurs chose the wrong passage down a steep rapid, but fortunately only two boats were wrecked during this dangerous crossing and no men were lost. Success, and fortunately no loss of life, was partly due to luck, but the skill of the local voyageurs sent by the HBC undoubtedly made the transit possible. On reaching Fort Alexander, Wolseley learnt that at his approach Riel had decided to backtrack on his earlier reassurances to Butler and had called his followers, who amounted to 600 men, to arms. After three days' rest Wolseley pushed on and entered the Red River. Once more the expedition was battling against the flow of the river and progress was difficult and was made more so by the extremely hot weather. Also, the boats kept grounding in shallows. Yet when the flotilla reached the Lower Fort on 23 August, just 20 miles south of Fort Garry, the troops were greeted by an amazed group of loyal settlers and Native American chiefs, for they could not believe that the expedition had made such a fast passage. Here supplies were unloaded, and horses and carts commandeered so that a small, mounted unit could be formed to reconnoitre forward. Whilst most of the militia were left behind to guard the stores, Wolseley and the men of the 60th Rifles returned to their boats for the last leg of their epic journey. Wolseley later described this as something of a triumphal procession for they were greeted by cheering crowds of loyal settlers and the bells of the Protestant churches on route rang out. Riel was in no doubt that the British were coming.

However, the grand entrance was delayed by the fast-flowing river current which impeded the advance and forced Wolseley and his men to camp out one more night, just six miles from Fort Garry. Wolseley had planned to advance on the fort, but overnight the weather broke, and a torrential downpour greeted the troops when they awoke. Wolseley thus resolved to return to the boats and the men once more paddled and by 8am they were within two miles of the fort. Here, at Point Douglas, Wolseley received the news that Riel was prepared to make a stand and that he had placed his artillery on the walls of the fort. Through the constant rain Wolseley drove his men forward. With both feet and the two brass cannons that had been manhandled numerous times on and off various boats sticking in the mud, the troops struggled on. They swept around the fort with the intention to cut off any potential escape by Riel. The expedition had reached its finale.

Buller in his letter to his sister describes the assault and its frustrating ending:

> Reveille sounded at 3 but it was raining so hard that we did not get off till about 7 & then we had no breakfast as the rain beat us in all our attempts to make fires. We rowed to within 1½ miles of the fort and then all landed & in pitiless rain marched to the attack; B.Company skirmishing in front of H. behind, the remainder Guns Staff & foot in the middle up to our knees in thick, sticky, slippery black mud we splashed our way; cutting through the corner of the town of Winnipeg a scattering collection of indifferent wooden houses on a muddy road where we were enthusiastically greeted by a half-naked Indian very drunk. We marched across half a mile of prairie & reached the back door of Fort Garry just as Riel & O'Donoghue his secretary walked out the front door. Finding the back door shut we marched round to the front which we found open we formed line fired 21 guns presented arms gave three cheers for the Queen and stood at ease in the rain and so ended the attack & capture of Fort Garry; Just at this moment a supposed loyal citizen showed me two men standing on the opposite side of the river whom he informed me were Riel and O'Donoghue they were looking at us & in about 10 minutes mounted their horses and rode off leisurely; (From what I have since heard I have no doubt that it was really them). Well we took the fort & marched in the band playing the Regimental quick step & the men were given quarters in some of the H.B. store house which Riel's gang had left pretty empty and the officers went into Riel's house which we incontinently proceeded to loot. He evidently was rather hurried in his

> departure as we found his breakfast served on the table still warm & only half eaten, we finished it having had none ourselves turned the house upside down and found nothing worth taking unless perhaps I should mention this elegant paper of sheets on which I am writing. Having cleaned out the House we went into the good town of Winnipeg where we got a very good dinner including as much beer as we could drink for 2/6. I fancy we rather frightened the man with our capacity for beer. Fort Garry itself is an enclosure of about 4 acres the front and half each side wall being stone the back and the other half of the side walls wood, there are 10 stone bastions – 4 corner ones two to each gate & one in the centre of each side. It is a strong structure and as Riel had plenty of guns, rifles, and ammunition he might have made a very considerable fight within it; I wish he had. It does so disgust one to have come all this way for the band to play God save the Queen.[36]

As Buller stated, 'it was a long way to travel for a band to play' but the expedition, the men taking part, and its commander, had achieved all that could be possibly asked of it and them. Sitting down to breakfast, Riel had heard approaching bugles and, deciding upon prudence over valour, had fled. Wolseley made no attempt to pursue Riel, for although he had the power to defend and overcome if his force had been fired upon, he had not been given any civil powers by the Canadian government and he felt it best to reframe from entering the world of politics. As hinted at by Buller, the troops, after weeks of hardship and a journey which had been alcohol-free, had a wild night to which Wolseley looked the other way. Discipline, however, was quickly, if not painfully, restored the following morning!

Despite attempts by the local settlers to encourage Wolseley to assume civil powers he wisely resisted, although Fort Garry was placed under martial law. With the arrival of both militia forces to garrison the fort and the new Lieutenant-Governor, Mr Archibald, to the region Wolseley's work was done and by early September he was free to depart and return to England. The expedition had been a triumph on many levels. Not only was it bloodless, indeed no shots had been fired in anger, but it had resulted in the return of Her Majesty's authority to the region and the end of a potentially serious rebellion, which had the real possibility of extending beyond the Canadian border. In addition, the whole campaign had been a remarkably inexpensive enterprise at only £100,000, of which the Canadian Government paid three-quarters, and this can be attributed to two factors. First, Wolseley had clearly demonstrated his incredible ability of organization, planning as well as foresight, which both undoubtedly helped in keeping waste and thus costs down. Yet the second factor, and one which Wolseley himself highlighted, was that he and Lindsay had been able to plan the whole expedition away from the normal War Office meddling and Wolseley was indeed fortunate that this had been the case for he was clearly able to demonstrate his inherent organizational skill and in subsequent campaigns he was given a great deal of latitude by the War Office.

All the British regulars had departed for their return journey to Toronto by 3 September and Wolseley left Fort Garry a week later. With the British government keen to reduce its military garrison and thus expenditure in Canada, both Wolseley and Lindsay were recalled to Britain and both men sailed on 1 October. Just before Wolseley left the people of Montreal hosted a banquet in his honour. Praise was justly directed towards Wolseley and the closing speech by William Workman, the Mayor of Montreal, was indeed fulsome, 'The citizens of Montreal, who watched the progress of the Expedition with the most anxious concern, will ever remember your admirable management of it with feelings of the warmest gratitude. We regret your departure from Canada, where your conduct as a soldier, and your character as a citizen, have won for you so many warm friends ...'[37] Wolseley was also given the honour of having Fort Wolseley, at the north-west corner of the Lake of the Woods, named after him, whilst his wife also shared the honour of having Fort Louisa, at the mouth of the Winnipeg River, named after her.

During the transit home, Wolseley must surely have reflected upon his first command with huge personal satisfaction and having received such praise and notoriety in Canada, he was perhaps expecting the same in Britain. Yet he was to be disappointed. The Franco-Prussian War of the summer, and with it the crushing defeat of France, had completely dominated the news and indeed Wolseley's Red River Expedition had hardly featured in the British press. However, although he was not yet generally known amongst the British public, Wolseley's exploits and clear ability had been noticed in both the War Office and more importantly in Whitehall where he was soon to become a firm favourite, advisor and confidante of the new Secretary of State for War, Edward Cardwell. Wolseley's already impressive career was to now enter a new phase in which he would achieve worldwide fame and glory.

# Chapter 3
# The White Man's Grave

Wolseley's return to Britain was met with a combination of indifference and suspicion. The author of the *Soldier's Pocket Book* and the commander of the Red River Expedition had already acquired for himself a reputation as a reformer within Army circles and he was thus not well received by those of a more conservative nature. Led by the Duke of Cambridge, Commander-in-Chief and cousin to the Queen, this group longed for the status quo surrounding officer promotion and the training and tactics of the Army to continue and in Wolseley they saw a man of radical ideas who was a threat to their inertia. Yet, for all these reasons the Secretary of State for War, Edward Cardwell, saw in Wolseley the drive he needed to help him push through his own ideas for reform. Over the next few years Cardwell and Wolseley worked closely together and in many ways Wolseley's career was given a new direction by Cardwell that would take him for the first time to Africa, a continent in which Wolseley was to secure his greatest military successes but also his one and only command failure.

Back in London, Wolseley was formally recognized when he received a knighthood from his monarch for his services in Canada. Yet at Horse Guards the author of the *Soldier's Pocket Book* found himself with no firm position, and Wolseley was placed upon half-pay, which after his service was clearly a ludicrous situation to find himself in. He wrote, 'I soon found that according to the views then entertained by our old general officers, I had committed a serious crime in presuming to express my views on military matters as freely as I had done in *The Soldier's Pocket Book* ...'[1] With his financial position reduced Wolseley returned to writing to supplement his income. He wrote several anonymous articles on the Red River Expedition, although no one could doubt the authorship for Wolseley was candid in his criticism of many of the Canadian politicians he had had contact with. There were implications that contracts granted to supply many aspects of the Expedition were given to gain political favour. His less-than-diplomatic musings antagonised some in the War Office and many in the Dominion, but as he confided to his brother Dick, the articles kept his name before both the public and those in Whitehall. Eventually, after a nearly six-month delay and with the insistence of Cardwell, Wolseley was appointed to the position of assistant adjutant-general, discipline branch. Wolseley was under no illusions that his forthright views on reform had made him many enemies at the War Office and that without Cardwell's support this opposition, 'would have contrived to have him honourably deported to some command at the Antipodes where his tiresome brain would have ceased to worry the War Office'.[2]

The relative ease of the Prussian victory against what was initially considered the mighty French Army in the latter half of 1870 had sent shockwaves across the world, and in Britain it startled the Liberal premiership of William Gladstone. It was apparent to many that the country was unprepared to wage a European war in its current state and that much of the underlying problems with the readiness and professionalism of the British Army could be explained by the existence of the purchase system, by which officers' commissions, and indeed subsequent promotions, could be purchased. Such a system not only excluded many talented young men who were unable to afford the high costs of purchase, but it also served to perpetuate an elite who appeared more interested in their social standing than the art and science of soldiering. Cardwell had already targeted the abolition of the purchase system as his number one priority, much to the disquiet of the Duke of Cambridge and other senior War Office incumbents, where his efforts had encountering significant opposition. In the summer of 1870, as war was raging in France, Cardwell had concluded that the only way to ensure that purchase was abolished was to offer compensation to those officers who had already paid significant sums into the system. So, with the approval of Gladstone and his Cabinet, Cardwell was able to bring the Abolition of Purchase Bill to the House of Commons on 13 July 1871. With support from the Conservatives the Bill duly passed but it was rejected in the House of Lords. Eventually Cardwell had to resort to a Royal Warrant which the Queen signed in November 1871 and by this means the purchase, sale and exchange of commissions were finally ended.

Wolseley had joined the purchase debate towards the end but had soon made his own views clear, which were fully supportive of Cardwell's stance for Wolseley was evangelical in his desire to end purchase. During the latter half of 1871 the two men were constant companions in both the War Office and in and around Parliament as they sought to educate, oppose, and cajole those members of both Houses who were against the reform. As Wolseley's biographer, Joseph Lehmann, wrote, '... the politician and the soldier developed an intimate friendship and worked efficiently as a team – Cardwell with the blueprints and Wolseley giving them practical shape'.[3] Wolseley wrote with real affection of his relationship with Cardwell, 'There is no Statesman for whose memory I entertain a greater regard than I do for that of Mr Cardwell

… Personally I became much attached to him, as I think all were who knew him well.'[4]

Cardwell was particularly astute at choosing talent, for as well as Wolseley he surrounded himself with like-minded young officers who were keen on reform; men such as Sir Patrick MacDougall, George Colley, Henry Brackenbury and Frederick Maurice, the last three of whom would serve under Wolseley in his next campaign. In addition, Cardwell employed Lord Northbrook as his very able under-secretary, and Northbrook and Wolseley developed a strong working relationship around Parliament. Apart from the abolition of purchase Wolseley worked alongside Cardwell in the construction of the 1872 Localisation Act, which had at its heart the linked two-battalion system that envisaged one battalion serving at home and one on foreign service at any one time. The home battalion was regionally based, in a town or city, with a local depot centre for training and recruitment, which it was envisaged would encourage both regimental cohesion and enlistment. It was considered that such a local approach would also attract men to Militia battalions to serve as volunteers. This radical reorganization was an extremely complex undertaking and Wolseley was to serve under Patrick MacDougall, who he knew well from his time in Canada, on the Committee to decide upon the division of the military districts and the location of the depots across the country. Although the linked battalion system was well intentioned it was largely taken over by events for as the Empire expanded rapidly in the 1880s and 1890s, and with it the demands placed upon the Army, so the home battalions were frequently depleted of men.

During his period at the War Office, Wolseley was not slow in putting forward his own thoughts and ideas about reform and the future tactics of the Army. In August 1871 Wolseley entered an essay competition run by *The Times* newspaper which offered a prize of £100 for the best essay on 'The System of Field Manoeuvres Best Adapted for Enabling our Troops to Meet a Continental Army'. Although Wolseley did not win, his work and five of the other best essays were later published in book form. Unsurprisingly Wolseley's essay demonstrated his contempt for the current training of British troops in the offensive. It took great notice of how massed firepower and innovations in rifles, such as the breech-loader then being introduced across Continental armies, would force troops to advance in small formations in skirmish order and that frontal attacks would become obsolete or too costly. He advocated flanking movements, with cavalry used for scouting and intelligence-gathering rather than for grandiose massed charges, which would suicidal up against modern armaments. These views were not only contrary to the thoughts and practices of many in the War Office but would also be very prophetic.

Wolseley did on occasions venture out behind his War Office desk and was involved in the large-scale army manoeuvres held for 16 days at the end of August 1871 near Aldershot. Woloseley was appointed to the role of Chief of Staff to the 2nd Division under Major-General Sir Charles Staveley. The following year Wolseley was again involved, this time on the Staff of General Sir John Michel. Wolseley reported to Louisa that in his role as umpire he had made numerous enemies. The Duke of Cambridge reported to Cardwell on the success of both manoeuvres and, although critical of some aspects of the infantry, was largely happy with how staff work had improved over the two years. Wolseley was less fulsome in his assessment. Writing in *Blackwood's* Wolseley stated, 'Judging from our selections made for our operations of both years, a stranger would be led to think that England was not rich in talented generals. With a few brilliant exceptions, it will be generally admitted that the great majority of generals and brigadiers employed this year were not men to whose care the lives of soldiers could be entrusted in war.'[5] Such language did not endear Wolseley to many of his contemporaries nor those in the War Office. He himself was fully aware of how unpopular he was becoming in some Army circles;

> I realized … that I was hated in certain quarters because of my opinions upon all points of military organization, and because I alone of those in office at the Horse Guards would not follow the dictates of my military superiors, and presumed to express openly my views to Mr. Cardwell at War Office meetings … Because I held strong views upon the great military value of our Auxiliary Forces, and of the Volunteers especially, I was looked upon as a sort of traitor to the old traditions of the Army.[6]

Fortunately for Wolseley he was not to be reliant on the Army hierarchy for his future advancement but instead it was to Cardwell that he looked for his next field command.

Wolseley was in exactly the right place to benefit from the latest colonial conflict when tensions began to rise between Britain and King Kofi Korikari, leader of the Asante nation of West Africa. For centuries European powers, such as the Dutch, Portuguese, British and even the Danes, had been actively trading along the Gold Coast, primarily in slaves, gold, and ivory. The warlike Asantes had built a substantial empire based on conquest with many of the subjugated peoples of other tribes traded by the Asantes as slaves with the European nations. Britain had led the way to end the slave trade with the Abolition of the Slave Trade Act of 1807, and although some nations such as the Dutch continued this hideous trade as the century wore on British intervention saw a decline in activity. This naturally put Britain on a collision course with the Asante nation and conflicts occurred in the 1820s and again in 1863–4. By the end of the 1860s, with the slave trade much reduced the Dutch Empire decided to focus its economic attention on the Dutch East Indies and sold and then ceded its loss-making Gold Coast territories to the British. Whilst the Dutch had maintained a presence on the Gold Coast the slave trade was secretly tolerated but with Britain now having territorial control of the whole coastline, King Kofi knew that if the Asante were going to maintain this lucrative trade, then he would need to push the British away from the coast, and in particularly back from the coastal defences at Elmina. The King skilfully manipulated the inept British Governor, John Pope Hennessy, into believing that his intentions were peaceful, whilst at the same time preparing his army for conflict. With the 'war party' at the Royal court in the Asante capital of Kumasi calling for the King to act decisively, Kofi had no alternative, if he was to maintain his authority and standing, but to invade British-held territory which he duly did in January 1873.

Both British officials in the Gold Coast and London were taken completely by surprise by the Asante invasion. On the ground, the British could only put a force of Hausa Police and troops from the West Indies Regiment into the field to oppose the enemy and these men, fighting under a small group of colonial officials and Fante allies, initially slowed the Asante advance. Yet at the Battle of Yancommassie in March 1874 and then again at the Battle of Dunkwa, the Fante allies retreated on masse and armed resistance against the Asante effectively ceased. The British were aided by the Asantes' pedestrian advance and by the fact that many of the warriors were struck down by sickness and disease, but the situation was critical, for the castle and settlement at Elmina was now under real threat. Initially, Lord Kimberley, the Colonial Secretary waited on events, largely to see if the British officials could galvanize the Fante into an effective fighting force, but with the debacle at Dunkwa Kimberley called a meeting at the War Office in May 1874. Here the despatch of 100 Royal Marines, under Colonel Festing, to Elmina was sanctioned, as well as an additional four companies of West Indies troops from Barbados.

Whilst Kimberley might have been slow to act against the Asante threat Cardwell had already instructed Wolseley to devise a plan for an expedition to the Gold Coast. Wolseley later wrote, 'Mr Cardwell had in confidence already informed me that he would like me to go there should it be determined to undertake active operations against the invading Ashanti ... I submitted privately to Mr Cardwell a rough outline of a military scheme ...'[7] The plan assumed that Wolseley would be appointed to the governorship of the Gold Coast and that he then be allowed to relinquish the position and return to

England at the end of operations. He also requested that he should be able to pick a small group of special service officers with which to train and raise a force from the local tribes to drive the Asante army back across the Prah River, the border between British territory and the Asante empire. Wolseley stated that he envisaged the need for two battalions of British regulars to march upon Kumasi, although it would be many weeks before Cardwell and Wolseley could convince Prime Minister Gladstone of the need to despatch British troops to the Gold Coast. Wolseley was to write in later life that he had felt a lasting peace with a warrior nation such as the Asantes could only be achieved once they had been utterly defeated in battle and any other solution 'was merely the wild dream of timid men'.[8]

Festing and the contingent of Royal Marines arrived off the Gold Coast on 7 June 1873 and headed at once to Elmina Castle. This was now being effectively besieged by the Asante army, who with the support of the local inhabitants had infiltrated the town to within a few hundred metres of the castle. On 12 June Festing issued a proclamation demanding that those in the town surrender all arms and retire. This, however, provoked two sharp clashes in which the British, armed with the Snider rifle, the first breech-loading rifle to enter service with the Army, took a heavy toll upon the Asante warriors and the army withdrew. Although the immediate danger to Elmina had gone, the large Asante army was nearby and still presented a real threat. Cardwell, Kimberley and Wolseley knew that for the British Protectorate to be secure once more the Asante forces would have to be at least driven back across the Prah and all three men realized that the total defeat of the Asante and the occupation of Kumasi would be the only way to truly secure peace in the colony.

Wolseley, as in the Red River Expedition, had thrown himself into the planning and logistics of marching British troops from the coast to Kumasi, through dense dark jungle in which the enemy was at a huge strategic advantage, and one in which Wolseley and his men would have to deal with the most unforgiving tropical climate. The Gold Coast was also known as the 'White Man's Grave' for away from the coast the humid climate turned minor scratches into festering wounds and caused dysentery which was often fatal. In addition, heat exhaustion, dehydration, malaria and typhoid fever were real threats. Indeed, Wolseley's in-depth planning and research convinced him that the climate of the Gold Coast would be the biggest threat to British troops, and he knew that any campaign must be completed during the healthiest months of the year, between December and March, when a hot dry wind blew down from the Sahara Desert and rainfall was at its lowest. Wolseley envisaged that the troops would begin to march north from the coast on the day they disembarked, to minimize their time in the region. He planned for a route to be laid out as far forward as the Prah River, the boundary into the Asante nation. Staging posts, with enough raised beds and canteen facilities would have to be constructed, for they could not risk slow baggage convoys hindering the march. This work was to be undertaken by local tribes, under the guidance of the special service officers to avoid any unnecessary delay or fatigue for the British troops, whose role would be to spearhead any advance upon Kumasi. A dose of quinine was to be administered to each man before the start of the day's march in either his tea or hot chocolate, to deter malaria and when British battalions were eventually disembarked upon the Gold Coast strict health guidelines were issued. This included the need to keep heads always covered from the sun, to avoid direct contact with damp earth and that sleeping just a few inches off the ground was essential to preserve health.

Wolseley provided exact designs for kit and dress for the troops; he personally designed a simple grey uniform of strong serge for both officers and men which would allow for freer circulation of air than the traditional uniforms, thus reducing the risk of heat exhaustion. The officers were to be provided with Norfolk jackets, pantaloons, gaiters and shooting boots, cork helmets and puggarees, with which to shield exposed necks from the worst of the sun. Sword bayonets and revolvers alone were to be employed for it was felt that in the dense jungle swords would be a hinderance. Men were issued with helmets, smock-frocks, trousers, and long sailors' boots and armed with the short Snider rifle and a sword bayonet. Wolseley even designed a special harness so that the artillery pieces could be efficiently and comfortably pulled through the bush by native allies. Wolseley also realized that both horses and mules would not survive the climate for long and that all stores would have to be carried by native porters. The need for large numbers of such, both men and women, was to become the greatest logistical problem of the entire expedition.

Wolseley was given the local rank of major general and was officially appointed as administrator and commander-in-chief on the Gold Coast on 13 August. Now at last he had been given the green light to press on with his own plans for the first stage of the operation, which until he received the go-ahead from the Cabinet for the use of British troops, would be to create a fighting force from local tribes. He realized that if the British had any hope of transforming these men into an effective force he would require special service officers of the highest calibre in terms of physical strength, intelligence, commitment, and ability to display initiative. As soon as his appointment was announced he was besieged with applications from officers who were desperate to join the expedition. Yet, it is clear from the final twenty-seven who were chosen, many had already been selected in Wolseley's mind at least, probably

A miniature of Ensign Wolseley before he departed for Burma.

British troops lift the Siege of Lucknow. This painting illustrates the brutal nature of the fighting in which Wolseley was engaged.

Lieutenant-Colonel Wolseley serving in China in 1860.

A picture of Lady Wolseley, circa 1870.

Colonel Wolseley at the time of the Red River Expedition of 1870.

Wolseley and his Staff at the Prah River Camp before the invasion of Asante territory.

A *Vanity Fair* print of Wolseley after his success in the Asante Expedition of 1873–4.

'The Double Perambulator and the Nurse for all our South African Babies'. Wolseley takes care of Generals Chelmsford and Crealock, *Fun Magazine*, 11 June 1879.

Wolseley accepts the surrender of Zulu chiefs at Ulundi on 1 September 1879 and imposes his own settlement upon the Zulu nation.

Wolseley presents the Victoria Cross to Major Chard at the end of the Zulu War.

Wolseley cheers on the Swazi warriors as they assault Sekhukune's stronghold on the morning of 28 November 1879.

Wolseley in 1879 in South Africa.

A portrait of Wolseley by the artist Paul Albert Besnard, 1880, upon Wolseley's return from South Africa.

Brigadier Sir Baker C. Russell, who served under Wolseley in the Asante Campaign of 1873–4, the assault upon King Sekhukhune's stronghold in November 1879 and in the Egyptian War of 1882.

General Sir Evelyn Wood VC, who served under Wolseley in the Asante Campaign, in the Egyptian War and during the Gordon Relief Expedition. He would later work alongside Wolseley to introduce reforms in training whilst serving at Aldershot and as Adjutant-General. This photograph was taken in 1880 on Wood's return from South Africa.

General Sir Redvers Buller VC, who served under Wolseley in Canada, on the Asante Expedition and in Egypt and Sudan.

Lieutenant-General Sir Gerald Graham, VC, long-term friend of Wolseley. Both men fought together in the Crimean War, in the China Campaign of 1860, in the Egyptian War of 1882 and Graham led forces in the Suakin Campaign of 1884.

Major General Charles Gordon. Long-term friend of Wolseley from both the Crimean War and the Campaign in China of 1860. Wolseley's inability to save Gordon from Khartoum was his only campaign failure.

The Black Watch lead the assault upon the Egyptian position at Tel-el-Kebir, 13 September 1882.

Wolseley and his Staff viewing the British assault at the Battle of Tel-el-Kebir, 13 September 1882.

'After the Battle': arrival of Lord Wolseley and Staff at the bridge of Tel-el-Kebir at the close of the action – a painting by Lady Butler – oil on canvas, 1885.

A contemporary cartoon of the Gordon Relief Expedition showing Wolseley bearing the full burden of Prime Minister Gladstone's indecision.

Wolseley whilst on the Khartoum Relief Expedition of 1884–5.

Lieutenant-Colonel Fred Burnaby lies mortally wounded at the height of the Battle of Abu Klea, 17 January 1885.

Evacuating Herbert Stewart to the Jakdul Wells after he had received a mortal wound at the Battle of Abu Kru.

Wolseley as Commander-in-Chief of the British Army.

Wolseley's statue in Horse Guards Parade, London.

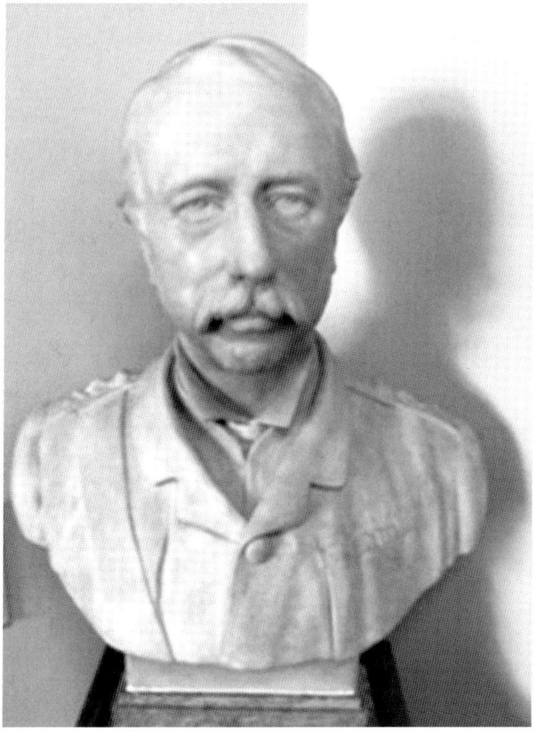

A bust of Wolseley held in the National Army Museum.

Wolseley's coat of arms.

The plaque in St Paul's Cathedral to mark the grave of Wolseley.

HERE RESTS IN GOD
GARNET JOSEPH,
VISCOUNT WOLSELEY,
FIELD MARSHAL IN
HIS MAJESTY'S ARMY,
COMMANDER IN CHIEF
1895–1900
BORN JUNE 4, 1833
DIED MARCH 25, 1913
HIS WIFE HAS PLACED THIS
TABLET TO HIS MEMORY.
SHE NOW RESTS HERE WITH HIM
BORN JAN. 27, 1843
DIED APRIL 10, 1920

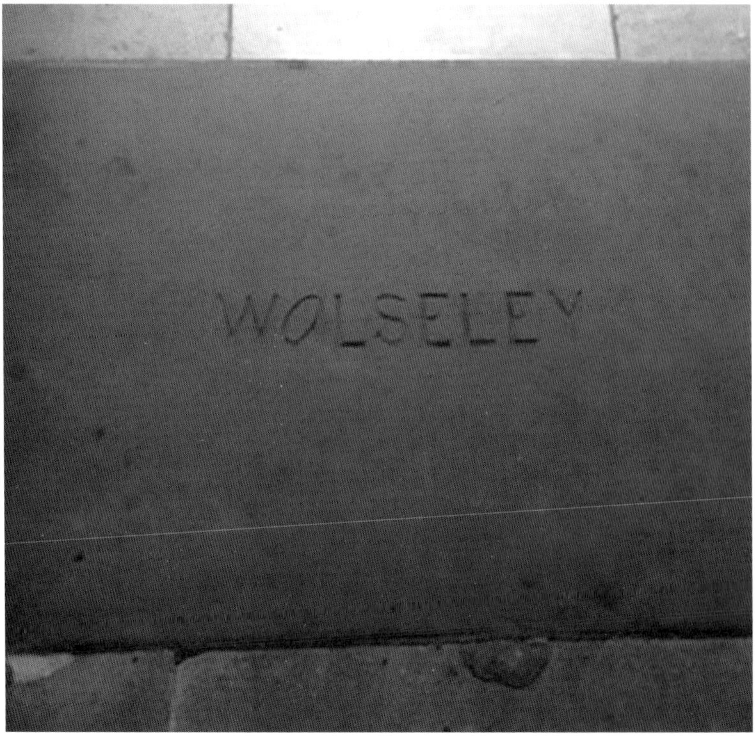

as early as May 1873. Although given free rein to pick from the officer corps, several had already served alongside Wolseley in the Red River Expedition. These included Captains Redvers Buller, George Huyshe and Colonel John McNeil VC, who would be Wolseley's chief of staff in Asante. In addition to these men, some, such as Evelyn Wood VC, had already come to Wolseley's attention and almost all were to distinguish themselves in future years. The careers of these men often followed Wolseley's patronage, so much so that they became known in later years as 'The Asante Ring' and Wolseley undoubtedly saw them as his 'trusted men', which would sometimes blind him to their failings, particularly in the expedition down the Nile to Khartoum.

In late August Colonel Harley, Acting-Governor of the Gold Coast, wrote to Kimberley to state that if the British were to reassert their authority and prestige upon the Gold Coast then they must go on the offensive and that Kumasi would have to be taken. Harley's letter at least reaffirmed the thinking of Kimberley, Cardwell and Wolseley that to assert British sovereignty, a march upon Kumasi would probably be essential and raised the need for British troops to be involved in the undertaking and this must also have pleased the three men.

Whilst rumblings continued between Cabinet colleagues as to the cost and goals of the expedition, Wolseley and his special service officers received instruction that they were to depart for the Gold Coast on the *Ambriz*, which sailed from Liverpool on 12 September. As September progressed both Cardwell and Kimberley sensed that the prime minister and his Cabinet colleagues were either cooling or actively against the thought of British intervention. At a meeting at the War Office on 22 September Cardwell and Kimberley agreed and conceded that the decision-making on all aspects of the Wolseley plan would have to enlarge to include the whole Cabinet. The matter was finally discussed in detail in a five-hour-long Cabinet meeting held on the afternoon of 4 October 1873, but by then Royal Naval personnel had been attacked by Asante warriors on the coast at the mouth of the Prah River. This act swung public opinion firmly towards the direct use of British troops in the Gold Coast and despite misgivings the Cabinet finally approved the despatch of three battalions. Wolseley did not get everything his own way for he had proposed to Cardwell that he should select the twelve best battalions then currently stationed in Britain and from these take only volunteers with no man under two years' service to be accepted. Every man would be medically inspected and only the strongest would be taken to face the rigours of the climate. Wolseley suggested that the engineers and artillerymen be selected in a similar manner. He also requested that these men should be ready for service upon the Gold Coast from 1 December 1873. Cardwell would not accept either the date or the composition of the battalions for he argued there was no precedent for such a course, that the traditions of the British service were contrary to it and that such a scheme would undermine the very nature of the British regimental system. Wolseley was advised that the next two battalions on the roster for foreign service would be informed of the possible requirement for active service in West Africa and that they would be brought up to full strength and readiness for service. These were the 23rd Royal Welch Fusiliers and the second battalion of the Rifle Brigade. In addition, Gladstone was insistent that a third battalion, the 42nd Highlanders, also be sent, and it was envisaged that all three would be arriving on the Gold Coast at the beginning of January 1874.

After a most uncomfortable voyage, for the *Ambriz* was barely seaworthy, Wolseley and his special service officers arrived off the coast at Cape Castle on 2 October 1873. Wolseley's fears regarding the dangers of 'The White Man's Grave' were discovered to be well-founded. Of the 130 English officers and men in the country only 22 were fit for duty. British troops in the protectorate amounted to just 30 officers and 770 other ranks, comprising the 2nd West Indies Regiment and the Royal Marines contingent. Of the Marines, one-fifth were sick. Clearly if Wolseley was to force the Asante back across the Prah, before the arrival of British battalions, much would depend not only on raising sufficient men from amongst the local tribes but also how well and how quickly these natives could be turned into a fighting force by the special service officers. However, it seems clear that Wolseley had already made up his own mind that the local natives would be unequal to the task, and he fully expected that British troops would be required to march on Kumasi. In a letter to his wife during the voyage Wolseley wrote, 'the negroes are like so many monkeys: they are a good-for-nothing race'.[9] At a time when the vast majority of British officers, and their men, would have held some level of racist views, Wolseley seems to have been exceptionally racist and for these opinions, which he would hold throughout his life, he should be condemned, not just by the standards of the twenty-first century, but also by the standards of his own times.

The first, and most important, military task facing Wolseley was to go on the offensive with the limited means he then had at his disposal. Crucially he required the support of the local chiefs but Wolseley's initial meeting with them was not a great success. There were many promises but little enthusiasm to fight again amongst the Fante tribes. Wolseley was able to promise £10 per month to each chief for every thousand men he could put into the field and each of these men would be paid 1*s.* ½*d.* per day and be supplied with arms, ammunition, and some rations. Wolseley spoke for several minutes and was clear in his aims when he said,

> I can assure you that if you place all your available resources at my disposal, and are loyally determined to fight your hereditary enemies [the Asante] now, I will guarantee to you that I, with God's assistance, shall drive them out of your territory, and that I will inflict such a terrible punishment upon them, that for all time to come you can have nothing to dread from them. My intention is to chase them out of your country, and, if necessary, to pursue them into Ashanti territory.[10]

Despite this statement Wolseley could clearly see that the locals were reluctant to fight and although he received a promise from them that they would respond to his request as a matter of urgency Wolseley was not surprised or deflated when he heard the news that the local natives were ready to work as porters but not as fighters. He wrote, 'Seeing that we left them entirely to themselves at the beginning it is scarcely to be expected that the whole of a much dispersed and dispirited people will suddenly come to believe in our serious intentions vigorously to aid them. To get the people to act with that rapidity which is essential we must act energetically ourselves.'[11] Wolseley was correct in his assessment for there did exist a belief amongst the locals that the British would be no match for the Asante in battle, particularly in the jungle. Thus, he resolved to strike at the enemy as soon as practical to win back some confidence amongst the natives and to restore British morale and prestige throughout the protectorate. The chiefs of the coastal settlements around Elmina, who had been supplying the Asante army with food, offered an obvious target for his first punitive act. On 10 October a company of Hausa troops arrived from Lagos and with the addition of these men Wolseley was able to cobble together a force comprising 180 white troops, Royal Marines, several of the special service officers and around 50 sailors commanded by Captain Fremantle, and 330 black troops which were composed of men from the 2nd West Indies Regiment, the Hausa company and around 30 Fante labourers. At around 4am on 14 October the contingent slipped silently through the gates of Elmina. Such was the secrecy surrounding the preparations only Wolseley and Wood knew the target of the raid.

After three hours of marching through the bush, the force, led by Colonel Wood with Wolseley observing, neared the village of Essaman, hoping to surprise the enemy. Yet before the troops could deploy, one of the Hausas was killed outright by Asante fire at point-blank range, and the surrounding jungle then erupted in volleys of 'Long Dane' fire. These weapons were crudely-made muskets, which the Asante had utilized in battle for several decades. Based on imported Danish weapons, the 'Long Danes' were widely inaccurate and had a limited effective range. Their main attribute was to produce large amounts of noise and smoke which had been used in the past to shock and overwhelm rival tribes in battle. In addition, the Asante had limited access to ammunition and often used pebbles or pieces of metal, such as nails, as projectiles, and produced their own gunpowder which was variable in quality and frequently ineffective. For Wolseley the technological advantage his troops possessed with their Snider rifles and 7-pounder artillery pieces would be decisive. Wolseley would later acknowledge that with a high level of British wounded in the set-piece battles with the Asante, he and his men were fortunate that the 'Long Dane' fire was ineffective or else the British could have been forced from the battlefield with high numbers of fatalities.

As the Asante fire poured in, Wood ordered Lieutenant Eyre to lead the West Indian troops onto a hillock to draw fire away from the main force and sent Buller forward with the Fante labourers to clear the undergrowth leading to the village. However, Wolseley could not now control his instinct for command and without consulting Wood he ordered Brackenbury and Lieutenant Charteris to charge forward at the head of a detachment of Royal Marines. At the same time, the chief of staff, Colonel McNeil, led a party on a left-flanking advance and Captain Fremantle was able to fire both a 7-pounder and rockets into the village. Both these men were wounded in the assault and McNeil was so badly injured in his wrist that he had to return to England. Wolseley would greatly miss the support of his old colleague from the Red River Expedition. Although the Asantes tried their usual tactic of using the cover of the surrounding jungle to try and outflank Wood's command, they were beaten back and when the British made a dash into the centre of the Essaman they found it deserted. Wood ordered that the village be burnt, and the resulting explosions demonstrated that the Asantes had been using the village to store vast quantities of gunpowder.

After an hour's rest the column marched five miles on to the town of Amquana. The sounds of battle and exploding powder had forewarned the inhabitants for the town was found to be deserted. Again, Wood ordered its destruction. It was now noon, and the effects of the powerful sun began to take a toll and Wood was forced to let many of the British rest. Yet with 30 white and 250 native troops he moved onto the villages of Akimfoo and Ampeene which were also burnt to the ground. The force returned to Elmina in the early evening having covered 22 miles across mixed terrain, much of which involved the troops pushing their way along jungle paths. Wolseley could take many lessons from this punitive action; the Hausas had proved themselves brave, but excitable and difficult to control. The West Indian troops had behaved well under fire whilst the Fantes had fled at the first signs of battle, dropping their loads. However, the biggest lesson was how difficult it was for British troops to operate across such terrain and in the humid climate of the Gold Coast. Although the men had carried as much water as possible, and despite receiving additional supplies from the Royal Navy cutters that landed between Akimfoo and Ampeene, this had proved inadequate, and they were left with none for much of the afternoon. At one point the British had only advanced four miles in three hours and Eyre collapsed with exhaustion. Brackenbury wrote of the day, 'The march was intensely fatiguing. The thick bush shut out every breath of air, and there were no forest trees to give shade. The path was rugged, and the way seemed never-ending. Then for the first time we learnt the terrible strain of performing staff duties on foot in such a climate.'[12]

Although Wolseley knew that much would have to be done to prepare for the arrival of British troops at the end of the year, he was still keen to take the fight to those Asante warriors still south of the Prah and thus occupying territory within the Protectorate. To this end he desperately needed more manpower and Wood and Major Baker Russell set about training their respective regiments of native troops. Not only had the local Fantes failed to volunteer in significant numbers but the attempts to entice volunteers from Sierra Leone and other West African countries had largely been unsuccessful. As the campaign progressed the British would be forced more and more to 'press-gang' the local tribes into service, particularly as porters. Wood found the task of establishing his own regiment of native troops extremely frustrating. His four companies comprised men from Fante tribes as well as Bonny and Kossos men. The best Wood could say about the Bonny tribesmen was that they had an aptitude for basket work but not for war. Yet these men had been thrown together often with little thought for tribal rivalries and with their British officers having little regard for them or an ability to converse effectively, so it is perhaps not surprising that these troops would prove reluctant in battle.

Wolseley was keen to see for himself how effective these native forces might be and on 27 October, he ordered Colonel Festing to lead a company of the 2nd West Indies Regiment and about 600 local natives in an attack upon a small enemy camp at Escbio. The Asantes were totally surprised whilst cooking and initially they fled into the bush, but from there they returned a hot fire. Whilst the West Indies troops again performed well, Festing lost control of the native troops and withdrew, having destroyed the camp. The following day, Wolseley himself led a reconnaissance force of 500 troops from Abakrampa to Assanchi and ordered Festing to move his force so that the two converged. However, Festing was unable to induce the native troops to advance at all and when Wolseley arrived at Assanchi he discovered that the enemy had fled into the bush.

November was a particularly difficult month for the British for the climate began to take a toll upon the newly arrived officers and within six weeks 70 per cent had fallen sick, many seriously. Lieutenant Charteris passed away on the hospital ship back to England after being evacuated suffering from fever and dysentery, and Wolseley himself became dangerously ill. He was moved to the hospital ship *Simoon* and when Wood visited there he was shocked at his commander's condition, although he found him coherent. What Wood didn't realize was that on the day of his visit Wolseley was in relatively good form for in the previous days the doctors had considered that the commander's life was in danger. Wood thought it unlikely that Wolseley would be fit enough to accompany a march on Kumasi, but, like many before him, he underestimated Wolseley who eventually was able to return to duty. In Wolseley's absence Colonel Festing took the fight to the Asante with another reconnaissance in force, this time to Dunkwa. Here the Asantes were prepared and waiting for the attack, and the British march was stalled by 'Long Dane' fire. A stalemate ensued for over two hours as troops of the 2nd West Indies Regiment returned the Asante fire. Lieutenant Eardley Wilmot of the Royal Artillery was wounded in the shoulder by the first Asante salvo and was later killed as he led an advance. Festing himself was hit in the back as he recovered Wilmot's body and a further four officers were wounded. Wilmot was the first of the special service officers to die and, with Wolseley himself sick, morale was low amongst the British.

The Asante now decided to go on the offensive and on 5 November, they attacked the village of Abakrampa. This was the furthermost western settlement which had been garrisoned by the British, and in a surprise attack the defenders were only able to hold on due to the effectiveness of their breech-loading Snider rifles. The battle raged all day and the Asante fire only ceased at midnight. Major Baker Russell had been able to utilize a recently-laid telegraph cable to inform Wolseley, then at Cape Coast Castle, of the Asante assault. The news was received by Wolseley and his staff with almost disbelief but once the full implication of the attack was appreciated Wolseley reacted swiftly to reinforce Abakrampa. All the available sailors and marines onboard the five Royal Navy ships off the coast were commandeered and Wolseley was able to cobble together a further 300 men and 22 officers, as well as a detachment of rockets. With these men Wolseley set off towards Abakrampa. Yet in the extreme heat over a tenth of the force fell out suffering from heat stroke and exhaustion. After only 10 miles the whole column had to rest for some hours, and it was not until nearly dark that Wolseley led his force into the column. Although they were met by enemy small-arms fire, they were able to enter the defences and collapse for the night.

Wolseley also ordered Wood to support Baker Russell and, with 1,000 new recruits from the coastal tribes, the colonel led his regiment on an equally gruelling march through the bush. They arrived on the morning of 7 November and despite the efforts of Wood and his officers the new recruits could not be persuaded to attack. Fortunately, the Asante felt it prudent to withdraw back into the jungle, but the engagement had been something of an embarrassment for Wolseley and again showed that any thought of crossing the Prah into Asante territory would have to wait for the arrival of British troops and this view was reinforced by further smaller actions.

The British continued to harass the Asante army as it inched, roughly five miles a day, north towards the Prah. There were frequent clashes between the Asante rearguard and various detachments of natives. On 8 November Captain Charles Bromhead, commanding a combined force of Hausas, Kossos and Cape Coast men, engaged the rear of the Asante army at the village of Ainsa. Here they met determined resistance from the Asante and were driven back. Bromhead thought it prudent to withdraw, but the Fante panicked and fired wildly, killing twenty of their own and then, fleeing across a stream, they rushed over the Hausas and drowned one, trampling him under the water. They continued to run until they reached the safety of their own homes on the coast where they dispersed. Wolseley was absolutely furious at their cowardly behaviour.

The British officers now lost sight of the Asante army for nearly three weeks, although Wolseley was kept informed of the enemy's movements by his intelligence officer Redvers Buller who was able to ascertain that Amankwa Tia, the Asante commander, was cutting fresh jungle paths parallel to those main tracks being used by the British. The armies clashed again on 27 November at the village of Faysowah. The skirmish was later to be magnified into something of a defeat for the irregular forces. Wood learnt that Amankwa Tia and several important chiefs were resting at Faysowah with a large body of troops. All were celebrating an *Adai*, or holy day, and Wood thought it a great opportunity to attack the enemy whilst they were so engrossed. Initially the engagement went well. The Hausa and Kossos advanced in skirmish order and pushed back the Asante pickets. However, once they came up against the main Asante camp the advance stalled and the enemy quickly reacted by adopting their usual battlefield flanking movements. Unfortunately, the men from the coastal tribes once again panicked and ran off without offering any resistance, and this panic spread to both the Hausas and Kossos and the orderly withdrawal became a rout as weapons and ammunition and baggage were lost in the confusion. Only a spirited rearguard action by

Wood, Eyre, Gordon and the other special service officers, firing their Snider rifles to keep the enemy at bay, prevented what could have become a disaster.

Although once again humiliated by the poor performance of the local tribesmen, Wolseley were fortunate in that the action convinced Amankwa Tia to take the last of his army, ravaged by sickness, disease and malnutrition, back across the Prah. In less than two months Wolseley could congratulate himself and his officers that the invaders had been forced back to their homeland. Although how much credit can be attributed to the harassing stance taken by the British is difficult to determine, but the fact remained that the invading army had left the Protectorate. It was at this point that Wolseley might have pursued a policy of peace and appeasement. Yet, Wolseley now knew he had public opinion firmly on his side; a lesson had to be taught to these African barbarians for passions were running high at home and these increased with every story of Asante savagery and tales of human sacrifice. The government could not ignore public opinion and more importantly Wolseley knew how to use it to his advantage. Queen Victoria was also firmly on his side and Wolseley was not going to let peace interfere with the prospect of a successful and brilliant campaign which would further enhance his own standing and reputation. Thus tentative peace moves from the Kumasi court were ignored and Wolseley set about planning the next stage of the campaign; the march on Kumasi.

In truth, Wolseley had been planning the attack upon Kumasi for several months and whilst the harassing of the Asante army in October and November had been largely left to his special service officers, particularly Wood, Wolseley had used the time to put his plans into action on the ground. His main concern was to ensure the fast transit of British troops from the coast to Kumasi and back, for Wolseley was determined to expose his men to the debilitating climate for the least possible time. Linked to this was the requirement to recruit thousands of local porters and labourers to assist the British and remove many of the harsh physical demands from the newly arrived troops.

The task of ensuring that the British battalions could arrive at the base of Prahsu, on the southern banks of the Prah, in relative comfort and with the least amount of effort, rested with the energy and planning of Wolseley and the efficiency and dedication of Major Robert Home of the Royal Engineers. Even though Wolseley had chosen the dry season for his expedition he knew that with the troops needing to march the 70 miles from the coast to the staging post of Prahsu high losses from heat exhaustion could jeopardize not only lives but the success of the campaign. Working in extremely difficult conditions, Home built seven stations at roughly 10-mile intervals. Each had accommodation for 400 men, as well as a hospital, storage sheds and water purifiers. Two of these stations had bakeries and four abattoirs. Although Lieutenant Gordon had managed to extend the path up to Yancommassie Fanti before Wolseley's arrival, there remained around 50 miles of paths to widen and improve before the British troops arrived. In addition, 237 footbridges had to be constructed along this route, including a 200m bridge across the Prah River from which the British would launch their assault into the Asante nation. Such works required both a herculean effort and an incredibly detailed level of planning, something which Wolseley revelled in.

Of the seven staging posts it was the forward base at Prahsu that was particularly elaborate; accommodation for 4,000 troops was built, along with a hospital for a hundred patients, a battery and magazine, canteen, post office and headquarters for Wolseley and his staff. Both Baker Russell's and Wood's regiments of native troops were employed in the widening of the path and on 16 December, they began to clear the area for the Prahsu base. Work continued for a month and the surroundings were denuded of palm leaves, which were to be used for thatching both walls and roofs. Thousands of poles were cut for uprights and supports, and all were transformed into the buildings of the camp. Raised beds with bamboo frames were also made to ensure the troops did not have to sleep on damp ground. Wolseley and his staff arrived at Prahsu on 2 January 1874 and were clearly impressed by the work of Home, Wood, and Baker Russell. Writing in his private journal upon his arrival at the Prah camp Wolseley wrote,

> ... it was so refreshing to see a clear open space and a fine river flowing through it ... A vast amount of work has been done here, large open spaces with huts all round them, the ground levelled, roads made etc, etc. My own hut stands overlooking the river being on the bank – it has actually two rooms, one to sleep in and the other to write and receive visitors.[13]

Yet, for all the incredible efforts and feats there remained one huge logistical problem that threatened the success of the expedition and to solve this problem Wolseley would have to resort to extreme measures.

The further the British moved from the coast, the greater the issue of recruiting and keeping local tribesmen to help with construction became, and the same applied for the need of porters. With the Asante army now back across the Prah, the Fante viewed the war as a European war and not their affair. In despair Wolseley was driven to characterize his Fante allies as 'too cowardly to fight their own battles and too lazy, even when well paid, to help those who are risking their lives in their cause'.[14] Yet, all the blame in securing sufficient manpower did not rest with the Fante chiefs alone for the army commissariat, with civilian administrators, lacked an understanding of how to best utilize the available local manpower. Men from different tribes, often with long-standing historical grievances, were forced to work alongside each other and in the chaos, some were paid twice for the same job whilst others received nothing. Many were overworked to the point of exhaustion and often it was only the threat of physical violence that got the men to work. Hundreds deserted because they were not fed, for the British relied on food subsistence payments for the men to buy their own provisions. Whilst this worked on the coast, they could hardly use this money in the jungle where there was nothing to purchase. The British, and indeed Wolseley himself, seem to have been guilty of thinking that the local populace would be grateful to work for them and that this alone would suffice. The British could not understand why the locals did not relish the opportunity of carrying 50lb loads on their heads for over 70 miles and for once Wolseley can be considered to have been somewhat complacent in his logistical thinking and this was perhaps clouded by his inherent racism.

Finally, realizing that the portage issue could seriously jeopardize the campaign, Wolseley acted and called for a former colleague from the taking of the Taku Forts and the War Office, Colonel George Pomeroy Colley. Wolseley was able to entice Colley away from his position of Professor of Military Administration at the Staff College, and as soon as he arrived on the Gold Coast in December Wolseley appointed him as commander of transport. On assuming his role, Colley calculated once the British battalions had arrived and had begun their march towards Kumasi that at least 8,500 porters would be required. Of this figure, 2,500 would be required for daily provisions, 3,500 for the transport of regimental supplies and equipment and the remaining would be needed just to maintain supplies at Prahsu. To illustrate the immense challenge, the porters had to move over a million rounds of Snider ammunition and 400 tons of food rations which was the equivalent of 30 days' rations for 6,500 men. Colley systematically set about improving the porterage system, based on the basic premise of providing the carriers with reasonable working conditions. He divided the line of communication into sections, with specific porters allocated to their own area and they would not be expected to work in another section. Allocation would be by tribes, with their own headmen reporting to a British officer who would individually pay each porter after the work had been completed. When possible, each porter would be given a day's rest after every four days' work. It was hoped that this humane approach would lessen desertions and although it proved successful to some degree, the loss of porters remained a problem and Wolseley resorted to taking direct punitive action to secure more locals. He harangued local chiefs, threatening that the British soldiers would withdraw from the Gold Coast and thus leave the local tribes at the mercy of Asante retribution. Colley was ordered to lead a reconnaissance to the villages around Dunkwa and Agoonal from where earlier porters had deserted en masse. As an example, Colley and his men burnt the settlements to the ground. Within a few days this tough stance had worked, and the number of porters was edging back to what was required. The most direct action owed more to the eighteenth-century practice of the 'press gang'. One of Wolseley's biographers wrote:

> Desperate for carriers, Wolseley cast [aside] all forms of legality. Kidnapping began on a large scale ... The commandant of Accra, with a man-of-war at his disposal, went up and down the coast collecting carriers. If the chiefs were unco-operative, a party of sailors would land at night, surround his village and carry off the entire adult population, leaving only a few old women to care for the infants.[15]

Women porters were also recruited, particularly from Anomabu, and they were found to complain less and smile more than the men. Although the porterage system did not collapse, it would always remain a constant cause of concern for Wolseley and his staff.

With Wolseley and his special service officers working frantically to overcome the logistical problems, the government had finally acknowledged that British troops could be used to march on Kumasi. Much to Wolseley's surprise the first troops from the 2nd Battalion of the Rifles arrived off the coast onboard the *Himalaya* on the evening of 9 December. Two days later the *Senegal* brought the Royal Welch Fusiliers and, on 17 December, the *Sarmatian* appeared with the last battalion, the 42nd Highlanders. With the neither the passage to Prahsu or the camp itself yet complete, Wolseley had no choice but to order the crew of the troopships to sail along the West African coast for three weeks, rather than risk the men to the climate. The troops finally begin to disembark from 1 January 1874 and straight away they commence the march to Prahsu.

With his usual attention to detail, Wolseley had pamphlets printed and issued to the troops with guidelines on how best to maintain health, such as not exposing the head to the sun and never to drink water until it had been filtered. He also provided a detailed description of what troops could expect when fighting in the alien jungle environment. Wolseley was clearly trying to convey to the men what they could expect both in the jungle and from the likely fighting with the Asante. The pamphlet stressed independence of action for small units of men in skirmish order and stated that self-confidence and reliance on comrades would be required in the dark, dense jungle. Wolseley wrote of how difficult it would be to maintain contact through the bush and along narrow jungle paths and that bugle calls would be essential to maintain cohesion. The pamphlet was, in essence, the first detailed description of jungle warfare.

Wolseley concluded the pamphlet with what can only be described as a rousing Victorian call to arms, or in modern language something of a pep talk. He wrote:

> It must never be forgotten by our soldiers that Providence has implemented in the heart of every native of Africa a superstitious awe and dread of the white man that prevent the negro from daring to meet us face to face in combat. A steady advance or charge, no matter how partial, if made with determination, always means the retreat of the enemy. Although when at a distance, and even when under heavy fire, the Ashantis seem brave enough, from their practice of yelling and singing, and beating drums, in order to frighten the enemies of their own colour, with whom they are accustomed to make war, they will not stand against the advance of the white man. English soldiers and sailors are accustomed to fight against immense odds in all parts of the world; it is scarcely necessary to remind them that when in our battles beyond the Pra they find themselves surrounded on all sides by hordes of howling enemies, they must rely on their own British courage and discipline, and upon the courage of their comrades. Soldiers and sailors, remember that the black man holds you in superstitious awe; be cool; fire low; fire slow and charge home; the more numerous your enemy the greater will be the loss inflicted upon him, and the greater your honour in defeating him.[16]

Whether Wolseley's troops remembered these clearly racist words at the height of their battles with the Asante is unknown. What is clear is that by the end of the war, all, even Wolseley, would view their enemy with respect for his bravery and tenacity.

With the reputation of the region for sickness, and with Cardwell impressing upon Wolseley the need to minimize the risk and to deal quickly and efficiently with any cases of illness or battlefield wounds, Wolseley turned his mind for detail and order on this area. Each of the stations along the line of march had designated buildings for the sick and a separate hut for infectious cases. At the Prahsu and Mansu sites, as well as at Cape Coast, there were hospitals for up to 500 patients. The system in place for moving the sick was a 'conveyor belt' of hammocks with native bearers working in relays between each of the way stations until the patients were delivered, in relative comfort, to the coast. A total of 150 hammocks and 85 cots were sent out with the troops and it was envisaged that around 200 men could be moved speedily at any one time. Once at the coast the sick and wounded became the responsibility of the government. HMS *Victor Emmanuel* was sent from England as a hospital ship for 240 patients. In addition, the *Himalaya* and *Tamar* were moored offshore with an additional 100 beds each. A steamer service was established from Cape Coast back to St Vincent, where the *Simoom* was stationed as a floating nursing home for patients awaiting transfer back to England on the regular Cape Town to Southampton mail boats. Every ship that the government chartered for the Asante Expedition, whether as a troop or supply ship, was also fitted with additional sick cots. Despite these measures the system would be severely tested during the first months of 1874 as both the climate and the fierce fighting took a heavy toll upon the British troops.

Brigadier General Sir Archibald Alison arrived with Colley in December and was given command of the British brigade in the expedition. Although senior to Wolseley, he would defer to him, though Alison would lead the battalions in the subsequent battles of Amoaful and Ordashu. Wolseley was clearly not pleased with Alison's appointment for he wrote in his journal on 10 December, 'Heard from Horse Gds that Sir A. Alison is coming here as Brigadier General & second in command. I am very sorry for this as I don't care much for him & don't think he is the man I want.'[17] Despite Wolseley's misgivings the two generals would work together and their cooperation in battle was crucial to British success. Wolseley initially gave Alison responsibility for the disembarkation of the British battalions. The first men to arrive on shore were sailors from the so-called Naval Brigade. All 251 men were carefully selected volunteers from all the ships anchored off the coast, and Wolseley described them as splendid physical specimens in his journal. The detachment left the coast on 27 December, and they covered the 70 miles to Prahsu without mishap by 3 January.

Next to disembark were the Rifles followed by the 42nd Highlanders, the Black Watch and then the 23rd Royal Welch Fusiliers. At first the march went well, but the appearance of the British troops led to a realization that a fight might be imminent, and this resulted in a significant increase in the desertion rate amongst the porters. Alison recognized that there was a real risk that not enough food and supplies could be carried forward for all three battalions so, acting on his own initiative, he stopped the disembarkation of the remaining half of the 23rd as well as the gunners from the Royal Artillery. When Wolseley assessed the supply and porter situation he agreed with Alison's assessment and ordered the leading half of the 23rd, which had already marched 13 miles to the Accroful station to return to the coast and re-embark. Naturally, the officers and men of the regiment were bitterly disappointed at being denied their part in the campaign and after protestations from the commanding officer, Colonel Savage Mostyn, Wolseley relented slightly. Although there could be no question of the supply situation allowing more than two battalions to go forward, Wolseley did agree that 100 of the least fit officers and men of the 42nd would be replaced by troops from the 23rd. The gunners did not receive any such concession and they saw no active service. Wolseley had been impressed by how one of his special service officers, Captain Rait, had trained his sixty Hausa gunners and Wolseley realized that any additional Royal Artillery personnel would be superfluous. Furthermore, Wolseley conceded that the Hausas' ability to dismantle and carry their guns through the jungle meant that they offered a great advantage over British gunners. As a solution to the immediate porterage problem, men from Wood's and Baker Russell's commands, as well as troops from the 1st and 2nd West Indies Regiment were added to the porterage detachment. Wolseley's ingrained racism towards the men of the local regiments meant that he had no hesitation in transferring these men from a fighting unit to more menial duties and despite the men of the West Indies regiments showing a reliability in battle they too would be used as porters and later as guards for baggage and supplies.

Asante spies reported to King Kofi Karikari of the growing British strength and on the movement north of troops. This intelligence seems to have spurred the King to seek some sort of terms with Wolseley. Asante envoys arrived in the Prahsu camp from 2 January, staying for four days whilst limited negotiations took place and letters were sent from the camp back and forth to Kumasi. Wolseley was in no hurry to respond to the King but when he did his demands were firm; Wolseley stated that the British government refused to acknowledge the Asante claims to the Assin and Denkyira peoples and demanded that European hostages taken by the Asante king be released immediately. Furthermore, the general stated as the Asante had waged an unjust war by invading the protectorate the British sought 50,000oz of gold in compensation and that royal hostages would have to be provided to guarantee future good behaviour. If Wolseley's terms were not met, then the British would advance upon Kumasi. The Asante envoys stayed at Prahsu until 6 January and were then marched across the newly completed bridge and escorted by Buller for a few miles before being sent on their way to deliver Wolseley's terms to the king. Wolseley did not slow the plans for invasion as they waited for Kofi Karikari's response. It seems most likely that by demanding a large amount of gold in compensation, as well as royal personages as guarantors, Wolseley knew the terms would be too costly for the king to accept. In addition, the king had a record of duplicity in dealing with the British and Wolseley had no reason, or desire to believe that he could be trusted now. Wolseley was in command of a powerful force, and he was not willing to simply turn it around in the face of Asante promises.

Wolseley's invasion of Asante territory began on 5 January as scouts from Buller's intelligence team crossed the Prah and headed towards Kumasi. Led by Lieutenant Lord Gifford these men would, over the next weeks, place themselves far in advance of the main body of British troops and would encounter many dangerous moments as they clashed with Asante pickets. Most of Gifford's scouts were from the local Assins tribe. These men were natural forest dwellers and hunters and could speak the dialect of the Asante without an accent. Even the hard-to-please Wolseley was impressed with these men. The rest of the scouts were composed of other special service officers and Hausas, Kossos, and a few West Indies troops. Covered by the scouts, Baker Russell's regiment crossed the Prah on 5 January, followed by Wood's regiment ten days later. Each of these native regiments also carried eight to ten days' supplies forward.

The next round of diplomacy began on 12 January when Gifford's party met a senior envoy along the path from Kumasi who was accompanied by one of the missionaries, Mr Kuhne, whom the king had decided to release as a gesture of goodwill. Kuhne stated that the king was unable to pay the high indemnity Wolseley demanded but had asked for the British to halt their advance. This Wolseley refused to do and the British marched on. Wolseley received Kofi Karikari's response on 21 January, which was delivered by another senior court official who was accompanied by the last of the missionary hostages. The king's latest negotiation stance was again dismissed by Wolseley for although Kofi Karikari indicated that Amankwa Tia would be required to pay an indemnity for the invasion, the released hostages confirmed that the king was not able to pay the 50,000oz of gold. With the release of the hostages and with the withdrawal of the invading army most of the original needs for the campaign had been settled and a moment probably existed for the peaceful entry into Kumasi of perhaps a token force. However, Wolseley was not going to let the opportunity to enhance his own military reputation be missed. Indeed, at the time there was a strong argument that British public opinion expected a decisive defeat of the 'savages' and even stronger one that the Asante had to be taught a firm lesson to ensure that the Protectorate would not be threatened by a further invasion. Thus, Wolseley in replying to the king's pleas to halt, demanded that all Fante prisoners were also released, for half of the gold to be paid immediately and for six hostages, to guarantee Asante behaviour, be handed over to the British at Cape Coast Castle. These were to include the

*Asantehemaa*, the queen mother, as well as the king's brother and designated heir. The king simply could not hand over such royal personages and maintain his own throne, and Wolseley would have known this and by demanding such hostages he effectively put an end to the peace negotiations.

As Gifford continued to probe further north the British battalions were now finally over the Prah River. Gone were the comfortable way stations and now the British troops sought shelter in tents and on groundsheets as they marched further into Asante territory. As January grew to a close so the number of sharp encounters between Gifford's men and the Asante grew, and sniping became an increasing problem. At the village of Borborasi Captain James Nicoll was killed by an enemy sniper and the British responded forcefully and cleared the village with several volleys and captured in the process the state umbrella of the veteran Asante general, Asamoa Nkwanta. The presence of such an important figure suggested that a major battle was close and indeed Asamoa Nkwanta and the king of Adanse were trying to lure Wolseley on to the main Asante army. Buller's spies confirmed that the enemy were holding a reversed arrowhead-shaped defensive zone on raised ground around the village of Amoaful. With Amankwa Tia out of favour, command was given to the *Mamponhene*, or the king of Mampon, a man named Kwabena Dwumo, who usually led the army's right wing. Wolseley accepted the challenge laid down by Kwabena Dwumo for, hoping to avoid more than one engagement, he saw the coming battle as an opportunity to destroy the enemy, although he had hoped that the battle would be nearer Kumasi.

With the clear intelligence that the following morning would see British troops facing the Asante army in battle, Wolseley called together his battalion and regimental officers for a full briefing on what they could expect. He reiterated how the jungle would mean that close control of the men would be essential and reaffirmed the expected Asante plan of attack. Wolseley stated that to counter the Asante flanking movements he resolved to advance in a large open square formation, or parallelogram, with each side having its own selected commander. The position to be occupied by each battalion and regiment was explained in detail to each of the commanders. The front fighting line was to be 600–700m wide, with its centre marked by Captain Rait's two 7-pounders, which would move forward on the Kumasi Road. Rait would be surrounded by the Highlanders of the 42nd, commanded by Major Duncan Macpherson, with Alison in overall command of the front face. The rockets were deployed on the front two angles of the square.

The left and right faces, commanded by Colonels McLeod and Wood respectively, would initially cut at 90 degrees to the front of the square, at a maximum distance of 300m from the road and then turn and cut a path parallel to the main path. Wolseley, his staff, the newspaper correspondents, the medical orderlies, and the reserve of a detachment of the 23rd Royal Welch Fusiliers were placed in the centre of the square. The baggage was held at Ahkankuassie under the guard of a sick Baker Russell and one company of his regiment, whilst the West Indies troops guarded the field hospital and reserve ammunition held at Insarfu. Wolseley knew that his force of 1,508 Europeans and 708 native troops was too small to prevent the enemy, estimated at between 15,000 and 20,000 warriors, from surrounding it and that the Asante would be much more mobile moving through the jungle than the British could ever hope to be. Wolseley impressed upon the officers that the Asante were a formidable enemy who would use drums, horns and screams to try and intimidate the troops and that to prevail the British needed to be brave, confident and highly disciplined. He stressed that all faces of the square were equally important and that each would be very reliant on the other. Yet for all his outward signs of confidence Wolseley's real state of mind was reflected in a letter he wrote on the eve of battle to his wife; 'Fighting against great odds is all very well on the plains of India or China, where one can see what you are about, but in the forest, where one can never see a hundred yards, it is nervous work, especially with a mere handful of troops and so far from their base'.[18]

At 8am on the morning of 31 January 1874 Wolseley ordered Gifford's scouts to move in advance of the British square as it pushed forward. They passed through the village of Quarman without seeing the enemy but three-quarters of a mile further on, as they approached Egginassie, they came under musket fire. However, Gifford urged his men on and took possession of it without further resistance. Gifford's scouts then discovered a large body of Asante across and around the road leading out of Egginassie. It was now time for the British infantry to be deployed and Alison ordered forward two companies of Highlanders and they pushed on through the scouts to engage the main Asante army.

Almost immediately after moving forward, the two leading companies of the 42nd had to be reinforced by a third as all became hotly engaged with the enemy. It soon became clear that the Asantes were endeavouring to turn the left flank of the Highlanders and in order to meet this movement two more companies were sent up a narrow bush path branching off to the left, but with firm orders not to lose contact with the three leading companies. The Highlanders were now hit by close-range fire from Asantes lying flat on the ground. These warriors were virtually invisible until they fired their 'Long Danes' and this point-blank fire hit several troops, including the commanding officer, Major Macpherson, and Major Baird, who was severely wounded. By 10am Alison reported back to Wolseley that the enemy were holding their ground determinedly and that he was suffering many wounded, and this was evident in a steady stream of Highlanders returning to seek medical attention. Wolseley sent forward more surgeons and Alison called for reinforcements of half a battalion of the Rifle Brigade. Wolseley could not spare such numbers but sent the 83-strong detachment of the Welch Fusiliers and later one company of the Rifles.

This was a battle of noise and confusion, like none the British troops, including Wolseley, had ever experienced. An invisible enemy, hidden by the jungle foliage produced nerve-testing noise; drums, tom-toms and horns and war cries, whilst the 'Long Danes' emitted an enormous explosion as they discharged. For the Asante too this was a battle like no other. At such close quarters the Sniders and Rait's 7-pounders left heaps of Asante dead and wounded. The Asante soon realized that they were seriously outgunned, and their only hope of success was to infiltrate the British square. Asante skirmishers slipped between two British units and fired upon both. Frequently the British did not know where the firing was coming from and simply fired back in the general direction from whence it had come and at least one wounded officer had a Snider bullet extracted from him. Officers from the Naval Brigade complained that they were fired upon by men of the Welch Fusiliers who had been sent to reinforce the Highlanders, as well as by the Highlanders themselves, whilst both these regiments claimed that the Naval Brigade had fired upon them. In this pandemonium Wolseley's calmness, as he smoked one cigar after another, was evident. He smiled confidently as troops were directed to check each threat from the enemy.

The British flanks were now attacked but Wolseley was prepared for this and had warned his troops to expect it. He ensured that the Welch Fusiliers he sent forward maintained contact with the Highlanders, whilst the Rifle Brigade had the responsibility of linking with the rear of the Welshmen. Even this deployment did not stop the British centre coming under close-range attack from all sides. The enemy fire was so intense that Asante black powder smoke hung in the air making the already poor jungle visibility significantly worse. As the Highlanders edged forward so the British flanks tried to join this general movement. This was the responsibility of Wood's and Baker Russell's irregulars, supported by the 180-strong Naval Brigade, split evenly between each regiment. Baker Russell's men advanced with some Highlanders under the command of Colonel McLeod to the right of the centre, but this was stalled by fierce Asante fire. It was in this attempted advance that Captain Richard Buckle of the Royal Engineers received a mortal wound whilst leading labourers from Sierra Leone who had been tasked with cutting a path. Wood's advance on the left also stalled. The men found themselves unable to move under intense fire and Wood ordered them to cut a clearing in which they laid down and returned fire and here they remained for over an hour, under constant Asante fire. Captain Luxmoore was part of Wood's wing, and he later described the confusion of the battle, 'My men lying down to escape the enemy's storm of bullets and slugs, and there we had to remain over four hours without being able to advance ... We ourselves fired into the 23rd Regiment once I afterward found out, but the bush was so dense that one could scarcely see one's own men ... The whole day I only saw one living Ashantee about 50 yards from me ...'[19]

At around noon, the Asante fire began to slacken, and Rait and his Hausa gunners used the opportunity to carry forward the 7-pounder to support the Highlanders. This weapon, firing over open sights at a mere 50m range, inflicted serious casualties upon the enemy and after each shot the Highlanders were able to advance a few extra metres under cover of the confusion and destruction. After fifteen rounds of this pulverizing fire the Highlanders were able to stand up and charge forward. They poured into a now-vacated Asante camp but as they continued onwards, they were met by renewed resistance from the ridge behind it. Rait's gun was again brought forward, and this combined with Snider fire lessened the Asante threat. A fresh charge was made, and the last serious stand of the enemy was broken. A little after 12.30pm Sir Archibald Alison was able to report to Wolseley that he village of Amoaful was now in British hands

The capture of Amoaful was certainly not the end of the day's fighting. As the Welch Fusiliers advanced to join the Highlanders, they met resistance from Asante who had infiltrated behind the Scotsmen. Having lost the centre, the enemy broke off their attacks on the flanks, allowing the centre and irregulars to move forward, the latter with war cries. The Asante now focused their attention upon the line of communication and the stores at Quarman. This was held by a detachment of the 2nd West Indies who held back the Asante attack until companies from the Rifle Brigade could be rushed from the rear to support them. Even with these additional troops Quarman was hard pressed for two hours. As Colley approached the harassed base with fresh supplies in a convoy of porters nearly five miles long, he too was attacked from the bush and many of his carriers fled. A company of the Rifles sallied forth from Quarman and rescued Colley from immediate danger before returning to the base. Colley salvaged what supplies and porters he could and fell back to Insarfu. The maintenance of the line of supply, Egginassie to Quarman to Insarfu, was now critical. The Asante would continue to harass this over the next few days, which would severely threaten Wolseley's subsequent advance.

A relieved Wolseley moved forward and established his command in Amoaful. After several hours of severe fighting the exhausted troops secured a perimeter defence and tried to gain some rest. Wolseley wrote in his private journal that the battle was, 'A hard fight that lasted all day: the enemy fought like men … '.[20] Considering the intensity of the fight, the casualty toll was remarkably light: 21 officers, 144 troops and 29 irregulars had been wounded, whilst one officer and two men of the 42nd were dead and in addition one irregular had been killed. Yet these figures do not tell the whole story for one in four of every Highlander had become a casualty and Wolseley realized that although fatalities had been thankfully few, he would still probably have to fight another pitched battle before reaching Kumasi with a much-weakened force. It is not known how many Asante warriors were committed to the battle or how many were killed, for the Asantes' practice of carrying off their dead from the battlefield meant that numbers were impossible to establish, although it is likely to have been in excess of 1,500. The bravery of the Asante warriors had been conclusively proven at Amoaful, as had the inferiority of their weapons.

The critical moment in the campaign had now been reached and it says much for Wolseley's clarity of thought and confidence in his own abilities, and that of his troops, that he was able to make what was a bold and courageous decision. Although the Asante army had been comprehensively beaten, it was still offering resistance and threatening the British supply line which was a real concern. The British were still 16 miles from Kumasi, with a much-reduced force which could expect another pitched battle before the city could be entered and furthermore the rains were due at any time. In Kumasi the fearful number of dead and the sight of the wounded returning from the battlefield had brought the peace party to the fore in the king's council. Again, attempts were made to negotiate with Wolseley, but the commander held his ground and his insistence that royal hostages must be provided was just too great a demand for the royal court to accept. The council was forced to take the unpopular measure of remobilising an already-beaten army. The role of commander was accepted by Asamoa Nkwanta, a key member of the peace party, and it says much for the respect in which the veteran commander was held that he was able to bring the army together once more to oppose Wolseley.

Wolseley concluded that the real threat to reaching Kumasi was delay. Colley was doing his upmost to ensure supplies were brought forward but repeated enemy attacks on the lines of supply, even as far south as the supply depot at Fomena, had so frightened most of the porters that they simply refused to work. In these circumstances, Colley informed the general that it would be several days before he would be able guarantee enough supplies could be brought up. Wolseley knew his force only had four days' rations for a march on Kumasi. Wolseley thus instructed the captains of the companies to ask their men if they would accept limited rations for the work ahead. All agreed, whether out of duty or loyalty it is not known, but what is certain is that the troops, like Wolseley, were keen to press on and return to the coast before the arrival of the rains. On his return to England Colonel Wood had a meeting with the Duke of Cambridge. Wood informed him that if Wolseley had not been appointed to lead the Asante Expedition, Kumasi would never have been taken for nobody else would have ventured to enter the Asante capital with only one day's food in hand and it was indeed a risky move by a brave and determined commander.

On the morning of 2 February Wolseley continued the advance and once again Gifford and his scouts led the way. Although no serious opposition was encountered the British faced constant sniping from an invisible enemy, which made the tired and exhausted men trigger happy. In addition, nerves were not eased by the sight of numerous human sacrifices for at each settlement the British passed through either the body of a young man or woman was laid out, feet in the direction of Kumasi and their severed heads directed towards the troops. As the day progressed so the Asante resistance increased. Rait's guns were used to soften up any significant Asante opposition and at times Gifford and his scouts were dangerously exposed. Yet by the end of the day the British had reached the River Oda and here they rested for the night. Wolseley counted the cost of the day; of the eleven Hausas serving Rait's guns, seven had been wounded by Asante skirmishers and there were a further thirty-three casualties amongst Baker Russell's irregulars and the Rifles. Wolseley knew he could not sustain such casualties, and this made him more determined to press on to Kumasi. A further deputation from the Asante king arrived which stated that all Fante prisoners would be freed if the British would only halt their advance, yet Wolseley' insistence that royal hostages be provided again put an end to negotiations.

The British experienced a horrendous night as the first rains of the new season arrived and all, Wolseley included, suffered from want of shelter. Throughout the night the Engineers had toiled away and by 6.30am when the British renewed their advance the Oda had been bridged. Buller's intelligence scouts reported that 10,000 Asante warriors were in place to oppose Wolseley at the village of Ordashu and it seemed that Wolseley would have another hard fight to face. The British marched in a single column with Wood's irregulars leading the advance followed by three companies of Rifles and the remaining native regiments all under the command of Colonel McLeod. The rest of the Rifles, Rait's artillery and the dwindling band of Welch Fusiliers and

Highlanders formed the main body, again commanded by Archibald Alison. Wolseley followed with his staff whilst the Naval Brigade was tasked with the safe crossing of the baggage across the Oda and to then form a protective rear to the column.

Within minutes Wood's men were under accurate fire from Asante pickets and to his dismay the natives flung themselves to the ground and fired widely into the air, without even looking up. Wolseley relinquished the vanguard from Wood's petrified troops and the three companies of Rifles, with the support of one 7-pounder, pushed forward. The opposition from the Asante force stiffened and McLeod was forced to deploy more and more troops forward. At 9.30am, after nearly two hours of hard fighting, the Rifles gave a cheer and McLeod led them forward in a sudden rush which carried Ordashu. By 11am Wolseley had established his headquarters in the village but at this moment the position was attacked on all sides in an inferno of musketry for the Asante were determined to retake the village. The Naval Brigade in the rear was also attacked in some force and they and the baggage had to rush forward to seek the relative sanctuary of the village.

The sound of war drums, the screams of the warriors and crash of incessant musketry from an invisible foe, began to take a toll on the British troops who had now endured three weeks of privations in the jungle with their nerves on edge. The Asante moved closer to the British and the right and rear was initially under much strain and soon the left was also pressed. Some men of the Rifles began firing indiscriminately and had to be rebuked, whilst the warriors encroached nearer and nearer. Suddenly Wolseley himself was down, bowled over by an Asante slug that hit him on his helmet. His staff jumped to his aid and Colonel Greaves emptied his revolver in the direction of where the shot had come from. Fortunately, the folds of the puggaree on Wolseley's helmet had taken most of the impact. The general was helped to his feet, and he was able to joke that perhaps he and his Staff should move to a less exposed position. Although he suffered from a bad headache for the rest of the day, he was otherwise unharmed. On examination the 'slug' proved to be a lump of tin, roughly in the shape of a dice, which seemed to have been sliced off a longer bar. Wolseley's luck was still with him. Writing in his journal Wolseley was philosophical about the incident; 'Whilst sitting on a stool a heavy leaden slug gave me a crack on the side of the head ... my helmet and puggaree saved my old nut.'[21]

Wolseley quickly regained his composure and realized that the advance had stalled badly. It was only the steady volleys of the Sniders that were keeping the determined Asante from overrunning the British position and Wolseley knew he had to move forward or risk defeat and annihilation as the enemy pressed nearer. At this point Wolseley was critical of the performance of the Rifles, whose Colonel he described as always looking '... as if he was going to his own funeral' and that the Brigade '... did not do as well as they ought to have done', and even described them as 'useless'.[22] So, Wolseley ordered Rait's guns to fire up the road for a few minutes and then he called upon McLeod and the remaining 340 men of the 42nd to charge in rushes towards Kumasi. With pipers playing and a hearty cheer, the Highlanders made a dash for the capital. Firing volleys by companies the Highlanders took turns to run forward and reload, without stopping. The Asante were bewildered by this rapid advance. Each ambuscade was simply brushed past in the pursuit of the target of Kumasi. As they marched in double time or even ran along the path, the Highlanders ignored each flank attack. The Asante had never seen an enemy behave in such a manner and their surprise shifted to fear and many broke and fled. Within little over an hour the now-exhausted Highlanders reached the village of Karsi, the last remaining settlement before the capital. Here they rested and Alison sent word to Wolseley that his men would be in Kumasi before nightfall.

Wolseley at once ensured that this good news was communicated to all his troops, both European and native, and all raised ringing cheers at the news. This sound made the Asante cease firing. They seemed instinctively to know what it meant, and this was reinforced when Asante speakers in the native regiments confirmed their fears with taunts. The warriors withdrew in silence and the battle was over. Realizing that he now had a great opportunity, Wolseley ordered a rapid advance of his whole force upon Kumasi. Leaving a small garrison at Ordashu, the general himself soon passed through the leading troops of the Rifles and overtaking them he smiled and said, 'Come on, my lads, you will have a house to sleep in tonight, perhaps a palace'.[23] The march was largely unhindered by Asante opposition. As Wolseley neared the capital a note was received from Dawson warning him that if the British pressed on to Kumasi that he and the remaining Fante prisoners were likely to be executed. The general's only comment to his troops was for them to quicken their pace.

At about 5.30pm McLeod led his weary troops down the wide streets of Kumasi, without facing any opposition from large numbers of Asante warriors. The Highlanders positioned themselves in the main market square where, an hour later, just before dusk, they were joined by Wolseley and the rest of the contingent. Wolseley ordered his men to give three hearty cheers for Her Majesty, and although Wolseley must have been hugely satisfied that he had reached the capital, he knew his position was a delicate one. His men were hungry, wounded or sick and all were utterly exhausted; he needed to find shelter for them quickly and there were still thousands of sullen-faced warriors in and around the city. Wolseley was also keen to negotiate a peace treaty with Kofi Karikari who seemingly had fled the capital and was now in a country residence a few miles north. Wolseley realized that he and his men could not stay long in Kumasi for the rains were threatening, the arrival of which could seriously jeopardize the return march to the coast. The casualties of the Battle of Ordashu were not as severe as at Amoaful; one officer, Eyre, and one native soldier had been killed but six officers and sixty men had been wounded and Wolseley knew that he could not risk another battle with so many troops sick or wounded. Wolseley wrote poignantly in his journal of Eyre, 'We buried poor young Eyre in the village – He knew he was dying and was conscious to the last – an only child and heir to a good fortune – but above all things as gallant a young soul as ever wore Her Majesty's uniform. We covered over his grave to prevent it being desecrated.'[24]

Frustratingly, the correspondence he received from the king promised his imminent arrival which never came and although he waited another night, Wolseley knew the king would never appear. In the early morning of 6 February, the British headed south and back to the coast. The British forces had looted the royal palace the day before. The captured booty was carried by thirty porters to Cape Coast Castle and some of this subsequently found a home in the British Museum. Major Home and his engineers blew up the royal palace and set fires across the capital. The Naval Brigade led the march south and McLeod and the Highlanders were the last to leave the smoking ruins of Kumasi as they took the rear of the column. Wolseley's decision to make a dash for Kumasi after the Battle of Amoaful proved to be not only a brave but also a correct one for the threatened rainy season arrived on the night of 6 February and the early days of the return march were severely hampered. The road which had been dry and firm only a few days before was now a swamp with mud that was so deep the men frequently disappeared up to their waists and it was with great difficulty in these early days that the troops wearily marched on. On 8 February the Rifle Brigade reached the battlefield of Amoaful on their march back to the coast and here a proclamation from Wolseley was read out to all the returning troops which praised them for their efforts and reaffirmed that their mission had been to tame a 'savage' people:

> After five days' very hard fighting, under very trying circumstances, your courage and devotion have been rewarded with complete success … You have repeatedly defeated a very numerous and most courageous enemy, fighting on its own ground, in well selected positions. British pluck, and the discipline common to Her Majesty's land and sea forces, have enabled you thus to overcome all difficulties … and you have proved to

> this barbarous people that England is able to punish her enemies, no matter what their strength in numbers be, or the position they hold.[25]

The return to the coast was a more sombre affair for the casualty rate amongst the officers was disproportionately heavy and there were too many 'empty' spaces. Captain Brackenbury was the only surviving member of the thirty-five special services officers who had journeyed with Wolseley from England to accompany the general back to the coast. The remainder were either dead, like Charteris, Eyre and Huyshe, wounded, like Wood, or sick with fever. Of about 2,500 white troops who had set out for Kumasi, 71 had died, 394 were wounded, and a total of 1,018 were invalided home. Thus 59 per cent of the combined strength was either killed, wounded or succumbed to sickness and in the two months of the main campaign sickness affected 71 per cent of the total force. This was despite Wolseley's attempts to minimize the effects of the climate.

Wolseley could claim a stunning success; the Asante had been decisively defeated, Kumasi taken and the king humiliated, and all these were required to enhance Britain's reputation on the Gold Coast and ensure that the threat of a future invasion of the protectorate was nullified. Yet, Wolseley had not achieved all his aims for, as Gladstone predicted and Kimberley had feared, the king had fled Kumasi, and no one was there to sign a peace treaty. The king's envoys did not reach Wolseley until 13 February when the draft of the Treaty of Fomena was handed to him, and he had already left for home when the treaty was signed and ratified by the administrator at Cape Coast on 14 March 1874. In it the king agreed to renounce his claim on Elmina and he also agreed to pay the 50,000oz of gold Wolseley had demanded. However, this was never fully paid and would be used as an excuse for future conflict. At the start of the 1874 general election campaign, Gladstone stated in his Greenwich manifesto that it was never the British government's policy to destroy the Asante nation, but it was to secure a treaty which would result in long-term peaceful relations. The Treaty of Fomena did nothing to secure good relations between the Asante and the British, only resentment, and it was to undermine political stability in Kumasi. This resulted in years of turmoil and would lead to further British intervention within 25 years. Wolseley, as he would do in the 1879 settlement between Britain and the Zulu nation, was able to claim success and raise his own personal standing whilst leaving others to deal with the medium to long-term consequences of a failed political settlement.

The Anglo-Asante War of 1873–4, or the 'Segrenti War', as the Asantes called it (this being a corruption of 'Sir Garnet'), was a decisive British victory. Although Wolseley's logistical and operational planning was inspired, and his decision to make the 'dash' to Kumasi was a brave one, made by a confident commander, luck, as in all wars, played a part in the final result. Undoubtedly the vast technological superiority the British possessed was an important factor, but equally, poor Asante ammunition and gunpowder meant that despite high numbers of wounded, battlefield fatalities amongst the British were mercifully low. Wolseley could have been dealing with large numbers of dead troops if the Asante had been well resourced in munitions and this alone could have swung the war in their favour. However, the comparatively low casualty rates hid many personal tragedies of aspiring young lives cut short. Back in Government House in Cape Coast a grand reception was held to make the end of the campaign and when a melancholy Wolseley was asked about those lost in the fight or to sickness, Wolseley said with sadness, 'Don't talk of it'.[26] This is undoubtedly why Wolseley was later to write in his autobiography that the Anglo-Asante War of 1873–4 was 'the most horrible war I ever took part in'.[27] As he sailed away from Cape Coast Castle on 4 March he wrote, '… never did I leave any spot on earth with such pleasure'.[28]

## Chapter 4

# Our Only General

After the success of the Asante Expedition, Wolseley had become a household name and Britain's most celebrated general. Such was his fame that, at his own request, the place and time of his arrival back to England was kept a secret from the press. When he arrived in Portsmouth on 21 March 1874, he dressed as a civilian and took the first available train to London to avoid detection. The following day the Queen summoned Wolseley to Windsor where Her Majesty found him 'thin and grey, but well' and '... a very smart, active, wiry-looking man, full of energy, and calm and decided-looking'.[1] The Queen and Wolseley would have a rather turbulent relationship going forward, but as Wolseley regaled his Queen with tales from the expedition the two enjoyed the moment.

On 30 March, in Windsor Great Park the Queen inspected Wolseley's returned forces and Her Majesty presented him with an honorary knighthood, but for someone who rarely displayed modesty, he declined a baronetcy. Later Wolseley did accept a sword of honour from the Lord Mayor of London at a lavish banquet at the Guildhall. In addition, he received honorary degrees from both Oxford and Cambridge universities. Finally, the House of Commons awarded Wolseley a vote of thanks and a personal grant of £25,000. According to the War Office, the cost of the campaign had been £660,978, under the budgeted £800,000, and when compared to the figure of £23,412,223 for the Second Afghan War of 1878–80, it can clearly be seen why it was considered an inexpensive conflict.[2] The performance of the British troops reflected well upon Edward Cardwell and his contentious reforms to the battalion system. This and the fact that the campaign was low in cost and casualties was also viewed as a personal triumph for him. Clearly, he and Kimberley had chosen the right man in Wolseley, and they showed their political bravery in backing him to assume military, operational and administrative responsibility once on the Gold Coast.

Wolseley drew huge praise for his logistical and operational skills which in turn had kept the feared high levels of loss amongst the troops relatively low. The phrase 'All Sir Garnet', became synonymous for many years with something that was well planned or organized or going well. His fame was such that in 1879 he was caricatured as the very model of a modern major general by W.S. Gilbert in the comic opera *The Pirates of Penzance*. With Wolseley's Asante success would come continued fame and fortune, and many of those who had served alongside him would also rise to higher command.

Wolseley was always tantalized by the prospect of an Indian command and although he expected that he would now be despatched there as adjutant-general to Lord Napier, it was to Africa that Wolseley was soon to be drawn. Yet before this posting he was attached to the War Office as Inspector-General of the Auxiliary Forces. Here his main task was to extend the Cardwell Reforms to the localisation of Militia, Yeomanry and Volunteer units in military districts which covered the country. Ever since Prussia's crushing victory against the French in the war of 1870, many of Britain's military and political leaders, as well as the press, had become obsessed with the need to improve home defences against a potential invasion threat and the reform of Britain's part-time infantry units was considered a priority. Although Wolseley attacked his new role with his usual vigour, what progress he made was cut short after only eight months for he was appointed to his first civil post as Lieutenant-Governor of Natal.

With hindsight Wolseley's decision to accept the Natal position was a surprising one. His role, as outlined by Lord Carnarvon, Secretary of State at the Colonial Office, was multi-faceted and extremely complex and as such was open to potential failure. Whilst Wolseley was prepared to accept a military appointment anywhere in the world and face the most difficult of challenges and overcome them, as he had demonstrated so effectively in both Canada and Asante, he had a loathing for both politicians and politics. As Lieutenant-Governor of Natal he would be faced with huge challenges from the political complexities of the region. Wolseley was still very much the 'hero of the hour' and surely could have waited for the next great military challenge that the growing empire would send his way, but he had a great sense of service to his country and when he was approached to accept this new and difficult role, he felt that he should accept.

Although Carnarvon clearly wanted Wolseley in Natal, he felt it unlikely that he would accept the position, but there clearly were other factors involved. Garnet's reforming zeal and determination to pursue the Cardwell reforms to their successful conclusion had antagonized many at Horse Guards, as had his blunt and abrupt manner. In particularly the Duke of Cambridge was keen to remove Wolseley from Whitehall, even if that meant a political appointment in South Africa. The Duke pressed Carnarvon for Wolseley's appointment and in return Carnarvon played upon Garnet's sense of duty and 'asked in a way that made it impossible for a public servant to refuse'.[3] Yet crucially Wolseley was able to dictate some terms for his acceptance and these included that the role was to be of only six months' duration and that he would be able to take his own staff with him. Once agreed, in February 1875, Wolseley was seconded to the Colonial Office and left soon after for South Africa.

Carnarvon's priority was to extend his policy of the confederation of white-controlled states across South Africa, as had been earlier achieved in Canada. There was a precedent in the region for the Cape Colony had gained responsible government two years before and Carnarvon was keen to extend this to include the independent republics of the Orange Free State and the Transvaal. Natal, largely populated by English-speakers, was geographically sandwiched between these two Boer states and Carnarvon felt that it was essential for Wolseley to convince the colonists of Natal to renounce much of their constitution, including the control of their own finances which had only been granted by royal charter in 1856. To complicate Wolseley's already difficult task the Natal legislature had, only a few months before Wolseley's departure, carried a resolution requesting that London provide a new constitution which would give them responsible government free from 'the interference of political parties in England'.[4]

If this was not enough of a challenge for Wolseley, he was also given the task of devising a policy directed towards the indigenous peoples of the region. The interests of the colonists had frequently clashed with local tribes and in 1873 the Hlubi clan, an offshoot of the Zulu nation, had rebelled under their chief Langalibalele. Although the rebellion was crushed, the performance of the colonial troops had been variable and with the potential of an external threat from the neighbouring Zulus, Wolseley hoped that the colonists could be persuaded that the presence of British regiments in Natal would be a price worth paying for the downgrading of their constitutional privileges. Once in Natal Wolseley became convinced that war with King Cetshwayo of the Zulus was inevitable and although his foresight was indeed correct, war would come because of British, not Zulu, aggression.

Wolseley journeyed south with his staff; four comrades from the Asante campaign, whose presence and hard work would become central to the success of the mission. These were Colonel George Colley, Major Henry Brackenbury and Major William Butler, while Captain Lord Gifford served in the role of Wolseley's private secretary. Wolseley realized that his six-month tenure would involve a great deal of travelling around Natal to not only assess the military and economic situation, but also to canvas local support for Carnarvon's proposed constitutional amendments. Wolseley also knew that he would have to initiate a 'charm offensive' to win over the populace and this centred around the holding of numerous parties and balls, the like of which Natal had never seen before. The new Governor even insisted that a ballroom be created in the Governor's residence in Pietermaritzburg. Indeed, one of Wolseley's biographers, Joseph Lehmann, described this period as one of 'champagne and sherry diplomacy'. Not a natural to such congeniality, Wolseley forced himself to a degree of social civility he had not before displayed but he also relied heavily on his staff to charm the Natal political and economic hierarchy. On occasion their approach exceeded the remit for both Brackenbury and Butler had affairs, the former with numerous married ladies, whilst Wolseley himself had to persuade Gifford away from an unsuitable marriage. Despite these potential embarrassing liaisons, Wolseley's charm offensive began to have results.

Fortune was with Wolseley and his team in that the two biggest and most vocal local critics of Carnarvon's plans, Barter and Foss, both of whom were members of the voting Legislative Council, were out of the country. Clearly neither of them thought Wolseley could possibly rush through major constitutional amendments in such a short period of time. However, Wolseley's drive and energy seemed to be able to move the most impenetrable problem and within three months of his arrival, on 5 May 1875, he was able to address the Legislative Council with the Natal Bill to modify the constitution. The proposed measures included the appointment of fifteen members to the Council, of whom eight would be directly chosen by the Governor, as well as modifications to how taxes could be raised. Wolseley argued this would enhance the economy by providing the confidence and stability that investment required while at the same time strengthening military readiness and defence of the Colony. The Bill required three readings before it could become law and Wolseley realized that the longer the debate went on the more likely that opposition would grow. So, after proposing the legislation Wolseley left the chamber and instructed Colley to lead the support for the Bill and push it through without delay. Although some members, particularly in the northern regions of Natal near the Transvaal border, would never be swayed by Wolseley's proposal, his focus upon those from Durban and Pietermaritzburg saw the Bill pass its final reading by ten votes to seven. Wolseley and his team had achieved what many in South Africa and London thought to have been impossible and with promises of defence and investment from Britain, particularly in railways and other infrastructure, many colonists appeared happy to display their loyalty to the Crown. Wolseley's success would be repeated the following year when Carnarvon was able to persuade the politicians of the then bankrupt Transvaal state to accept confederation into the empire and the Colonial Secretary's policy seemed assured.

However, Wolseley was more sanguine about his success for the longer he stayed in Natal the more he considered the colonists unsuited to run their affairs for he found them lazy and uninspiring, and his concerns centred on the military strength of the Zulu nation. He even petitioned Carnarvon that a small force of British regulars could and should cross the Natal border into Zululand and annex it by force and that to delay would allow the citizens of Natal to become complacent as to the threat. Carnarvon, a somewhat cautious politician when it came to direct action, would not be persuaded and Wolseley handed over his Governorship to the new incumbent, Sir Henry Bulwer, with regret and concern that his achievements would soon be overshadowed by conflict with the Zulu nation.

Wolseley returned to London in the autumn of 1875, to his old position at the War Office of Inspector-General of the Auxiliary Forces. With the apparent success of the Natal mission Wolseley's star had risen ever higher, particularly with Prime Minister Disraeli and his government. Yet Wolseley was viewed with growing suspicion by many of his War Office colleagues and although he returned to make proposals for the division of the military units in Britain into eight separate corps, he could not achieve the same level of success from behind a Whitehall desk. His plan envisaged that First Corps would comprise only regular army regiments whilst the remaining seven would be a combination of regulars, Volunteers and Militia battalions. But this somewhat grandiose plan was hamstrung by a lack of available troops to meet its demands and although Wolseley campaigned for greater government investment, especially in artillery and engineers, his plan had barely moved forward before once again he was called on for fresh service.

Wolseley initially accepted a move from the War Office to a seat on the India Council for the then Secretary of State for India, Lord Salisbury, wished Wolseley to advise on the implementation of the Cardwell reforms upon the Indian Army. This move had the benefit of a 20 per cent pay rise and Wolseley clearly saw an opportunity for higher command in India. Once again, Cambridge was happy to accept the request for a secondment. However, Wolseley was soon diverted by events in the Balkans in which Russia and Turkey had become involved, once again, in conflict, in the so-called Eastern Question. Disraeli saw that Britain's interests lay in Turkish battlefield success and Russian humiliation and he ordered the British fleet to proceed to Istanbul and extra funds for both naval and military expenditure were granted by Parliament. There was even talk of Britain sending an expeditionary force in support of the Turks. Wolseley was rapidly involved in planning for the many military scenarios that might possibly occur, and he identified that Britain's plans were seriously hampered by the lack of naval facilities in the Eastern Mediterranean. However, some of his thoughts and ideas displayed a huge degree of political naivety, including his proposal for a grand alliance of Muslim countries, with British and Canadian troops at its head. Despite these eccentric moments, in February 1878 Wolseley was appointed as Chief of Staff to Lord Napier who would command any expeditionary force. It was clear that the two men loathed each other, with Napier seeing Wolseley as something of an upstart and Wolseley considering Napier too old and frail to command.

Tensions in the Balkans continued to rise, and Wolseley was involved in the call-up of the Army Reserve which occurred in April 1878. Fortunately, however, the stoic defence of Turkish forces at Plevna halted Russian designs and Disraeli was able to claim huge political credit by bringing all parties together at the Congress of Berlin in July 1878 at which a settlement was agreed. Britain was rewarded in her support of Turkey when the Turks agreed to ceded Cyprus to the British, who thus gained a strategic naval base in the volatile region. Much to his amazement, for he was expecting a move to India and the Bombay command, Disraeli appointed Wolseley to the position of the first British High Commissioner to Cyprus.

Again, Wolseley turned to many of his tried and tested comrades from Asante and South Africa to join him on his Staff and the likes of Brackenbury and Lord Gifford, along with Colonel Greaves and Lieutenant-Colonel Baker Russell, journeyed to Cyprus in the summer of 1878. The island was now considered a vital British strategic asset and three British battalions, along with three Indian ones, were transferred from Malta to be under Wolseley's command. It was the brief of Wolseley and his team to improve the infrastructure of the island and to ensure that barracks and the new naval port rapidly became operational. Additionally, in his role as High Commissioner Wolseley travelled extensively around Cyprus, assessing both its economic needs as well as devising a system of tax collection to finance the administration and future developments, both military and economic.

Wolseley, like many, viewed Cyprus as a poor choice for a British naval base and it was clear that the hot temperatures and poor water supply adversely affected the troops. Indeed, the Indian contingent had to be removed after just a few months as so many troops had succumbed to sickness. Although Wolseley and his small team of officers achieved much in reducing corruption and increasing tax revenues, the island's finances had to be subsidised to a sum in excess of £90,000 per annum to balance the budget, a figure that raised objections both in Parliament and in the British press. Furthermore, Wolseley's attempts to attract investment to the island seemed to entice many less-than-scrupulous investors. Although he maintained an outwardly positive show, it is clear from letters to his wife and army confidantes that he found his time as High Commissioner in Cyprus a frustrating one, mainly because he felt trapped in a backwater when military command opportunities were passing him by. This was particularly true of the renewed conflict in Afghanistan, for Wolseley knew that he would have been ideally placed to command an expedition to Kabul and he even contacted George Colley, now serving in India, to ask him to inform the Viceroy, Lord Lytton, that he was ready to leave Cyprus and serve in Afghanistan. Despite this plea, and several to London, Wolseley was unsuccessful and as the Afghan war widened and became more intense Wolseley regretfully wrote from Cyprus that 'I feel like an eagle that has had his wings clipped'.[5]

Yet a new conflict, and one which he had predicted, offered Wolseley his chance to escape what he was beginning to view as his island prison. With politicians, principally the new Colonial Secretary, Sir Michael Hicks Beach, preoccupied with events in Afghanistan, the High Commissioner in the Cape, Sir Bartle Frere, convinced that the military threat from the Zulu nation was imminent, decided upon a pre-emptive strike. With the collusion of the British commander in South Africa, Lord Chelmsford, and using the three-week delay in telegraph traffic between Natal and London, Frere presented an ultimatum to the Zulus, which Cetshwayo was unable to accept. Frere used this non-compliance as justification for an invasion of Zululand on 11 January 1879 with the intention that a British victory would be secured quickly and before London could object to the invasion. However, both Frere's and Chelmsford's scheme was wrecked when the Zulu army inflicted a crushing defeat on part of the British invading force at the Battle of Isandlwana on 22 January 1879. Despite the heroic defence of Rorke's Drift by just 100 men of the 24th Regiment, questions were quickly being asked about Chelmsford's competence and whether he should be replaced.

It was not until 18 February that the news of the disaster of Isandlwana reached Wolseley in Cyprus and he quickly saw a personal opportunity. He sent a telegram to Cambridge stating, 'If required I could at any time reach Natal from Cyprus sooner than anyone could get there from England, and as I know the people and the country well, I think I might be of use'.[6] However, this shows a degree of political naivety, if not desperation, on Wolseley's part for Cambridge would never voluntarily agree to Wolseley's appointment over a commander, Chelmsford, whom he had himself appointed to the South African command. Wolseley also turned to politicians, such as the Foreign Secretary Lord Salisbury, offering his expertise on the country following his early stint as Natal's Governor, in the hope that this approach might secure a position. When Wolseley heard that a new commander was indeed to be appointed, he pointedly messaged Salisbury, 'Will you send me?'[7] However, weeks went by, and Wolseley's frustration rose. Finally, on 27 April he received a cipher telegram ordering him to report immediately to the War Office where in London he was to discover that it was not Salisbury, but the Prime Minister himself, Disraeli, now Lord Beaconsfield, who wanted him for the South African command. Wolseley left Cyprus without regret and a hope that he would never return to the island. Although he had achieved much to put the island on a stronger military and financial footing it seems clear that his heart lay elsewhere, and he was now desperate to move away from political appointments.

On arriving in London in late May, Wolseley met with Colonel F.A. Stanley, the Secretary of State for War, who told him in strictest confidence that it had been settled and that Wolseley was to go to Natal with full civil and military powers. Stanley asked him how quickly he could start for South Africa? Wolseley responded by saying, 'By the 4 o'clock train this afternoon if you wish it'.[8] Wolseley was then summoned to Downing Street for a private audience with the Prime Minister who was keen to discuss the military situation in South Africa. Beaconsfield told Wolseley that he was not satisfied in the way things had been conducted in South Africa and referred in strong terms to the mismanagement of military operations. After a series of Cabinet meetings, numerous letters to pacify the Queen, and to the disquiet of Cambridge, whose distrust of the progressive Wolseley would never abate, the Prime Minister was finally able to confirm Wolseley's appointment. He left London on 29 May for South Africa, with the overwhelming support of the Press and even the Liberal opposition. Victoria was both protective of her cousin, Cambridge, and Chelmsford, and was also herself unsure of Wolseley's character. Beaconsfield, in response to the Queen's concerns, wrote to her that, 'With regards to Sir G. Wolseley, Lord Beaconsfield will write to Your Majesty with that complete and unlimited confidence which has always, he trusts, distinguished the remarks he has had the honour of submitting to his Sovereign. It is quite true that Wolseley is an egoist and a braggart. So was Nelson.'[9] With these words the Queen's opposition was nullified. For Wolseley, his main concern was that he would reach Natal too late and that the war would be over.

As Wolseley journeyed south on board the *Edinburgh Castle* the lack of news from South Africa made him increasingly worried and frustrated. On arriving for a brief stop in Madeira he was met with the news that Chelmsford had begun a second invasion of Zululand on 21 May, but with no further details he became somewhat sanguine in his thoughts and musings. Writing to Louisa he shared that his believed that the heavy fighting would be over before he arrived and that his task would then be little more than, 'embarking the troops for England and endeavouring to settle matters with the Boers in the Transvaal'.[10] Finally, Wolseley arrived in Cape Town on 23 June and received the news that the war was still ongoing, and progress was slow. He was still hopeful that he might be in time to influence its conclusion. After spending one night at Government House in discussion with the now-censured Sir Bartle Frere, whose authority was now reduced to the Cape Colony only, Wolseley boarded the SS *Dunkeld* for Natal. From what information he was able to glean from Frere and other sources, Wolseley was appalled at Chelmsford's disposition of columns for the fresh invasion. Chelmsford and Major-General Crealock were advancing along different routes towards the Zulu capital of Ulundi, acting independently of each other and with no communication between them. Wolseley feared that the Zulu army might attack and overwhelm one of these columns, as they had so successfully done at Isandlwana. Wolseley had also received reports that Crealock's force was snail-like in its advance (the press named this force 'Crealock's Crawlers') whilst Chelmsford had been badly rocked by the death of the Prince Imperial on active service whilst under his command. All this reinforced Wolseley's opinion that Chelmsford was a hapless commander who was completely out of his depth.

News that Wolseley was to supersede him had reached Chelmsford only a week before and this seemed to snap him out of the lethargy he was clearly suffering, for he was now determined to end the war before Wolseley could reach the front, to avenge the defeat of Isandlwana and to restore some of his battered reputation. Wolseley was now clearly in a race. He arrived in Durban on 28 June and from here travelled by train to Pietermaritzburg where he was quickly sworn in by Sir Henry Bulwer as the chief authority, both civil and military in Natal. Bulwer had succeeded Wolseley in 1875 and he spoke candidly to Wolseley sharing his concerns as to Chelmsford's lack of competence and urging Wolseley to rein Chelmsford back from any further advance. Wolseley duly sent a message forward demanding an operational report and although Chelmsford did confirm that his column had reached within striking distance of Ulundi, he resolved to ignore Wolseley's orders to concentrate his forces and to undertake no further operations. Indeed, Chelmsford had no further communication with Wolseley, which astounded the latter who admitted to the Secretary of State for War that he was in absolute ignorance of Chelmsford's plans. A now-desperate Wolseley endeavoured to find a way to Chelmsford as fast as possible, yet once again he was frustrated. His aim of sailing from Durban and along the coast to Port Durnford collapsed when rough seas made it impossible to land and it was not until 5 July that Wolseley reached Fort Pearson to receive several telegrams, one of which reported that Chelmsford had secured a crushing victory the previous day and that Ulundi was in flames. Wolseley's premonition that he would be too late to influence the war had proved correct.

Chelmsford now followed Wolseley's instruction to lead the 2nd Division towards the coast to unite with Wolseley who was now with Crealock's column. Wolseley had acted in his usual direct manner and had ended the advance of the 1st Division leaving most of the troops to garrison the line of forts that had been built on route. He then pushed on to rendezvous with Chelmsford at the mission station at St Paul's. In his diary of 12 July Wolseley wrote,

> Chelmsford wants to go home to relieve himself from the 'false position' in which he finds himself, and to leave at once pending reply to an application he had addressed direct to Secty. Of State for War. I replied through Chief of Staff that I had no objection whatever to his retiring and wished to know whether he would resign or go home on leave. I can understand his being very much put out by my arrival, but his contumacious disobedience of my orders to correspond only through my Chief of the Staff does not recommend him to me as a soldier.[11]

Chelmsford and Wolseley finally met on 15 July and again Wolseley recorded his feeling in his diary of that day,

> I cannot say that my meeting with Chelmsford was a pleasant one. He has persistently ignored my military authority over him, although I have told him I have a Commission giving me command of the Troops in South Africa. However, I try to make every allowance for him for his feelings must be unpleasant finding a superior officer sent to supersede him.[12]

By 20 July Wolseley wanted rid of Chelmsford as he clearly illustrated in his diary entry, as well as showing his almost legendary disdain for those at Horse Guards:

> My line is to get Chelmsford out of the country as soon as possible: he has now no power, and although I have the poorest opinion of his ability as a general or a public servant, I have a feeling for the position in which he finds himself at present and don't want to rake up old complaints against him. Why kick a dead horse? In war he can never be again employed although I have no doubt Horse Gds. will cover him with Honours and give him Aldershot or some equally good place.[13]

Wolseley quickly set about formulating his plans for the political settlement of Zululand as well as breaking up Chelmsford's large army. He wrote, 'I shall thus get rid of useless Generals and reduce expenditure'.[14] Whilst he maintained some correspondence with Cetshwayo, who had fled Ulundi to avoid capture, Wolseley also began to entice various Zulu chiefs to agree a political settlement. He was adamant that Cetshwayo needed to be removed from the region or he would remain a rallying point for further dissatisfaction. Thus, when the king was finally captured by a British patrol on 28 August, he was dispatched to Cape Town prison where he was to remain for the next three years.

In discussion with Bulwer, Wolseley resolved to divide Zululand into thirteen independent chiefdoms. Wolseley confirmed his thinking by stating, 'Such breaking up of the cohesion of the country will, I firmly believe, preclude for the future all, or almost all, possibility of any reunion of its inhabitants under one rule'.[15] The Zulu people were informed of Wolseley's decision on 1 September when he summoned chiefs and dignitaries to Ulundi. Militarily defeated by the British, Wolseley now ensured the demise of the Zulu political system. All thirteen newly-appointed chiefs had either fought alongside the British in the recent war or had deserted Cetshwayo and it seems clear that their appointments were deliberately chosen to create political rivalry and disunity. Wolseley's imposed settlement also ensured that there would be no restoration of the Zulu military system and it allowed for Zulus to leave their territory to seek employment in the mines of the Transvaal and Orange Free State, which further undermined the cohesion of Zulu society. The writer and contemporary Rider Haggard was forthright in his criticism of Wolseley's Zulu settlement when he wrote,

> Of the chiefs appointed some were so carelessly chosen that they had no authority whatsoever over the districts to which they were appointed, their nominal subjects preferring to remain under the leadership of the hereditary chief. Several of Sir Garnet's [Wolseley] little kings cannot turn out a hundred men, while the hereditary chief who has no official authority, can bring up to three or four thousand.[16]

Anarchy was the almost immediate result of Wolseley's judgement, for within just a few weeks Zulu fought Zulu as the new kingdoms frequently cut across old tribal lands. It is thought that more Zulus died in the years following the Anglo-Zulu War in a period of chaotic civil unrest than did in the war itself. In addition, Wolseley appointed a Boundary Commission which confirmed that the northern limit of Zululand would be moved southwards, with the Pongola River as the new natural boundary and the Boers of the Transvaal gained former Zulu lands in the west. Although Wolseley's settlement had served to satisfy the immediate needs of the British government to remove their military and political responsibility for Zululand, the resulting chaos caused thousands of deaths and the collapse of the economic and political system. For this Wolseley must be considered to have been at fault and his actions and decisions seem to have been driven by haste as much as political expediency.

Before he was to leave Natal, Wolseley was faced with an immediate military issue which needed to be resolved. The previous year a small British expedition, commanded by Colonel Hugh Rowlands V.C., had advanced upon the Pedi people of Eastern Transvaal who, under the leadership of Chief Sekhukune, had resisted Boer encroachment onto their lands and had indeed repulsed numerous Boer commando attacks and even raided isolated Boer settlements. With Transvaal now officially part of a Confederation with Britain, Rowlands was tasked with bringing an end to the Pedi threat and although successful in a small skirmish at Tolyana Stadt on 27 October 1878, he was forced to withdraw before launching an attack upon Sekhukune's main stronghold, due to sickness amongst his horses and lack of water for his men. The British government and Wolseley saw the Pedi as the last organized indigenous opposition in southern Africa. Wolseley did try to avert war by offering Sekhukune the option of accepting a military post on his lands as an outward sign that the chief had accepted British supremacy, but this offer was scorned and in September 1879 Wolseley mounted a two-column assault against Sekhukune.

Wolseley was determined that unlike Rowland's efforts of the year before his expedition against the Pedi would not fail, for he believed that a quick, successful campaign was essential not only to subjugate Sekhukune, but also to restore the prestige of British arms after the less than glorious Anglo-Zulu War. This was particularly important as the Boers of the Transvaal, aggrieved that confederation had been imposed upon their bankrupt state, were muttering about restoring their independence, by force if necessary. Wolseley, once again, realized that the success or failure of the campaign would depend upon logistics for the distances over which the force had to travel were immense and far from established towns, whilst the terrain was demanding. Yet at no point did the troops or horses suffer from lack of supplies and this was very much down to the meticulous planning of both Wolseley and his Chief of Staff, Captain Henry Brackenbury. As the columns set out Wolseley boasted that he would be sipping afternoon tea in Sekhukune's hut by 28 November 1879.

The Transvaal Field Force was to consist of 1,400 British infantry, largely taken from the 2nd Battalion of the 21st Regiment, as well as companies from the 94th and 80th Regiments. The infantry was supported by a mounted colonial force which was in excess of 400 men and a native force in the region of 10,000 warriors. These local men came from various Transvaal tribes, all of which were natural enemies of the Pedi, but the majority, around 8,000, were

Swazis who as part of their enlistment would be allowed to keep any cattle that might be taken in the raid upon Sekhukune's stronghold. Although a few warriors had rifles, the majority were armed with short stabbing spears known as assegais. Wolseley deliberately decided to keep the use of British troops to a minimum to keep costs low and to avoid the ravages of the ever-present horse-sickness that racked the countryside and which particularly affected horses brought from Britain. In addition, with the Transvaal Boers looking increasingly threatening small British garrisons had to be maintained at strategic points, including in Pretoria.

Wolseley moved his headquarters to Middleburg in the middle of October and here he was delayed by both pain from his old Burmese leg wound and by a lack of wagon drivers, many of whom had returned home after the conclusion of the Anglo-Zulu conflict. Yet despite these setbacks Wolseley maintained an outward show of cheerfulness and resolution which gave confidence to those around him. By 28 October Wolseley and his Staff had moved forward to Fort Weeber where he discovered that transport delays had led to a shortage of supplies coming forward. With his energy restored he soon rectified the deficiencies and within days his leg pain had eased sufficiently for him to begin a series of reconnaissance rides of the area. He then rode the 86 miles to Lydenburg to meet Major Bushman who was to command the second column, composed mainly of the Swazis. Throughout this period Wolseley formulated his plan of operation and gathered every piece of intelligence he could muster on the enemy he was now to face.

Wolseley gave command of the main column to Colonel Baker Creed Russell, who had served so bravely and diligently throughout the earlier Asante expedition. Wolseley and his Staff accompanied this main column and the 'Transvaal Field Force' concentrated at Fort Albert Edward, which had been rapidly constructed on the route. Wolseley reached the Fort on 23 November and concluded that sufficient supplies and ammunition had been collected to allow the assaulting columns to advance. On the night of 24/25 November Fort Albert Edward was denuded of troops as all marched to Seven Mile Post, seven miles up the valley towards Sekhukune's kopje fortress, where Baker Russell had constructed a staging point. The following days were spent in reconnaissance with the occasional minor clash of arms with the Pedi, the heaviest of which was led by Commandant Ferreira of the Colonial Horse against the kraal of Chief Umkwane, one of Sekhukune closest allies. Ferreira's men caught Umkwane by surprise and inflicted a significant morale-boosting victory. The Lydenburg Column under Bushman arrived with the Swazi levies and with the two columns now combined Wolseley could begin his attack on Sekhukune's stronghold.

Although Sekhukune's kopje looked formidable, Wolseley's days of reconnaissance, which had made his leg wound flare up once more, had convinced him otherwise. The position was a large conical hill which was honeycombed with caves, ideal for defence and concealment. Numerous defensive stone breastworks had been constructed and these combined with thick thorn fences seemed impregnable to a frontal attack. However, Wolseley was convinced that the very steepness of the hill and the roughness of the approaches would provide ample dead ground over which the troops could advance. Wolseley ordered a dawn assault on the morning of 28 November. His plan was for troops under Baker Russell's command to advance from the north, to take the lower slopes where the town of Tsate had been fortified, whilst Bushman's column, principally of Swazi warriors, would descend from the south-east, with both columns converging on the final stronghold of the 'fighting kopje'. Wolseley personally rode to explain to the Swazi chief what was expected of his warriors, not just in battle, but also in their behaviour towards Pedi women and children.

The early morning attack began with artillery fire from four British guns upon the kopje, which Wolseley himself described as 'bad at first and indifferent all day although the range was only 450 yards'.[17] The initial salvos did little more than bring down an intense rifle fire from the Pedi defenders, which fortunately was as ineffective as the efforts of the British artillery. Although confident of success, Wolseley was concerned that his force would suffer high casualties for he knew the roughly 4,000 Pedi, of whom around half were armed with percussion rifles, were determined to make a stout defence but thought that a rapid assault would lessen any losses. Fortunately, Wolseley had chosen the officers of his assault force well. On the right the attack was led by Colonel Ferreria of the Colonial Horse, who Wolseley described as 'ruthless' in his journal of the campaign and stated that Ferreria '... did not regard killing a native as killing a human being: he [Ferreria] is most anxious the town should not be burnt until it is well looted'.[18] On the left the force was led by Major Frederick Carrington, who had served with such distinction against both the Xhosa and the Zulus. He was tasked with capturing the lower town, clearing the hills above and then joining with Ferreria's colonials in the big kraal before both units combined with the main body of British regulars, under Colonel Murray, for a final assault upon the fighting kopje.

Wolseley sat under a tree to watch the initial assault and was delighted to see the right and left columns spring from boulder to boulder as they rushed up the slopes. Both Ferreria's and Carrington's men met strong resistance with the Pedi fighting for every inch of their homestead and Baker Russell had to reinforce Ferreria's column with troops from the 94th. The most senior officer lost in this assault was Commandant J. Macaulay who was instantly killed when hit in the head by a Pedi slug. His brains were splattered over the nearby Carrington. Meanwhile Bushman was having difficult persuading the Swazis to advance for they seemed reluctant to move forward until they were sure that the British were committed to the fight. Once Murray's infantry was engaged the Swazi rose and on seeing Bushman's column break the skyline of the mountain Wolseley was able to write that this sight 'rejoiced my heart very much'.[19]

The fighting went on in and around Tsate until around 9am and was fierce, intense and brutal, but with the lower town finally in British and colonial hands Baker Russell could follow Wolseley's orders for the assault upon the 'fighting kopje'. This final attack was signalled by the firing of two rockets and when these were unleashed the kopje was assailed on all four sides with all troops now engaged. Wolseley, writing in his private journal, stated that the assault was made in the 'most gallant style: the first men I saw on the Koppice were our own red coasts: the 21st advanced with their pipes playing: I never saw a prettier sight in my life'. Wolseley wrote candidly of his views on Baker Russell's abilities, as well as that of the British troops and even in his private journal he could not resist making a jibe against the Duke of Cambridge;

> Baker Russell ... was always brave. He is a splendid fellow in action and would make a first rate cavalry General, but he is good all round, quite good enough for me, and such a relief after the sort of useless men the Duke [Cambridge] give command of Regt and selects for command of troops in the field ... The young soldiers that HRH [Cambridge] is never tired of abusing behaved well. He [Cambridge] and most of those who abuse our young soldiers have little or no war service and many of them have never seen these same young soldiers in action.[20]

Although the British and colonial troops were heavily engaged, it was the Swazis whose hatred of the Pedi and desire for bounty saw them close on their old enemy with their traditional assegais. The slaughter between the two tribes was fierce and brutal. With the help from British rifles, Sekhukune and his surviving followers, including women and children, were dislodged from their stronghold and they sought refuge inside the numerous caves which littered the mountain. Wolseley would not let them rest and rather ruthlessly ordered his engineers to blow up the caves with gun cotton, otherwise known as the highly explosive nitrocellulose. Although this act must have resulted in several casualties, the surviving Pedi could not be dislodged. Wolseley ordered the caves to be ringed by his troops but during a very wet and dark night the survivors, including Sekhukune, managed to slip through the cordon.

Wolseley quickly recovered from the frustration of losing his prey and ordered Ferreria, with his command and two companies of the 94th, to pursue and capture Sekhukune. This did not prove too difficult for the chief feared the Swazis more than the British and offered to surrender as long as the Swazis were disbanded. Wolseley duly agreed to this and on 2 December 1879, Sekhukune was brought into the British camp and from there to prison in Pretoria. Wolseley wasted no time in dismissing the Swazis who left with Pedi cattle and dogs, although Wolseley refused to let them take Pedi women with them.

Once again Wolseley had demonstrated that he was the master of planning and operating a campaign in the harshest of terrain and against a determined foe. Despite his initial fears that the 'butcher's bill' would be high, British losses were three officers killed and seven wounded, with four other ranks lost and thirty wounded. This was primarily due to the fact that the Swazis were engaged in the fiercest fighting and that the percussion rifles of the Pedi were largely ineffective. Lord Beaconsfield, troubled as he and his government was by the conflict in Afghanistan, was delighted that the campaign had been successful and brief and the cost low both in terms of casualties and finances, at just £383,000. Writing to his friend and confidant, Lady Bradford, the Prime Minster provided Wolseley with one of his most famous labels when he wrote, 'Sir Garnet Wolseley has not disappointed me. He is one of those men who not only succeed but succeed quickly. Nothing can give you an idea of the jealousy, hatred, and all uncharitable-ness of the Horse Guards against *our only soldier* [author's italics]'.[21] This jealousy and dislike of Wolseley by those who supported Cambridge was to plague Garnet for most of the remainder of his career, although sometimes his own tactlessness was to exacerbate this.

With the ending of operations against the Pedi, Wolseley was determined to leave South Africa and return to England. Conversely his military success had made conflict with the Boers more likely. Both he and the British government had hoped that the capture of Sekhukhune and the ending of the military threat from both the Pedi and Zulu peoples might impress the moderate Boers of the Transvaal and quieten the dissenters who aimed for independence from Britain at whatever cost. In reality the opposite was true for having destroyed the powers of the indigenous peoples the British military presence was no longer required or desired. As Wolseley was marching triumphantly back to Pretoria, 3,000 armed Boers congregated at Wonderfontein, just 70 miles from the capital, in contradiction of Wolseley's ban on such a mass armed meeting. A week of angry debate followed during which a resolution was passed demanding a restoration of Boer Transvaal independence, with some of the more hardline delegates calling for military action. A further meeting was agreed for April 1880.

Wolseley, ever the good imperialist, was determined that the Transvaal would not leave the Confederation. He wrote a clear and frank assessment of the political and military situation for the Colonial Secretary, Sir Michael Hicks Beach, in which he stated that in his opinion the Boers, in the near future, would fight for their independence and that 'the great bulk of the Boer population is hostile to our rule'.[22] In addition, again writing to Hicks Beach, Wolseley laid out solid economic reasoning as to why the Transvaal should remain within the Empire for the area was rich in minerals, gold had already been found, and it was likely that further resources would be discovered which would entice British emigrants to the area and lessen the political sway of the Boer population. For this reason alone, Wolseley argued, the maintenance of a strong military presence in the region was essential. With rhetoric rising from the Boers, Wolseley made military preparations so that the British would not be caught unawares by a surprise uprising. Positions in and around Pretoria were strengthened and eight fortifications were constructed at strategic points, with thirty days' supplies and roughly a company of troops each. Yet despite these precautions Wolseley was contemptuous of the military threat from the Boers and even expressed the opinion that the Boers were cowards who 'go on playing at soldiers and blustering, knowing in their hearts they would bolt at the sight of the first Dragoons they saw'.[23] Wolseley was not to be the first or last British general to underestimate the fighting capabilities and resolve of the Boers, but these words suggest that Wolseley's determination to return to London, and his frustration that he was being delayed in South Africa, was dominating his thinking at the expense of more rational and considered military thinking. It seems clear that Wolseley viewed the Boer threat not as his own problem but for others to deal with at a later date.

Throughout Wolseley's career he was bedevilled by tactless moments in which his forthrightness overwhelmed both common and political sense and in South Africa he was again guilty of such a moment. In conversation with a group of senior Transvaal Boers he declared that the Vaal River would flow backwards before Britain gave the Transvaal back to the Boers. This was an ill-conceived and foolish remark at a time when his government was aiming to be conciliatory towards the Boers and certainly increased the tension at the time. This moment was probably driven by his own personal frustration. After the ending of the campaign against Sekhukune Wolseley felt time hanging heavy in South Africa. In his own mind he had been sent out to resolve the then Zulu crisis, eradicate the Pedi threat and place the region on a secure military footing. In all these things Wolseley felt he had achieved his goal and now wished to return home. Writing to Lady Wolseley from Pietermaritzburg on 23 February 1880 he penned, 'I never thought that I should have been so treated. If I had come here to be a Civil Governor I should have no ground for complaint, but I came to bring the Zulu War to an end and settle the native disturbances in the Transvaal, and having completed my mission I should be allowed to return home'.[24] He still longed for senior command in India and felt that once again he needed to be back in London to influence his own career.

Yet Wolseley became a victim of a political hiatus which centred on the General Election of April 1880. Both the Zulu and Afghan conflicts had lessened public support for Beaconsfield's government and with it, its firm stance on imperial expansion. The Liberal leader of the opposition, William Gladstone, had seized this moment of discontent and in his famous 'Midlothian Campaign' of early 1880 used his oratory skills to denounce the Government's foreign policy. At such a moment the Colonial Secretary was not going to upset the status quo in South Africa and allow Wolseley, as the standing High Commissioner, to step down and return to Britain. The Boer leadership was very aware of the coming election campaign and knew that if Gladstone triumphed then his new executive would take a more conciliatory view towards Boer independence and that Wolseley, whose military skill and reputation they both feared and respected, would likely be replaced. For the Boers the early months of 1880 were a waiting game.

Wolseley, however, was tired of waiting and he was certainly not going to put his name to a policy of troop withdrawal or independence for the Boers. Although he received news that he would finally be replaced by his old comrade George Colley, Wolseley's departure was dependent on Colley's arrival from service in India and no date seemed imminent. In addition, Hicks Beach, who now Wolseley referred to contemptuously as 'Higgs Bitch' who he hoped '... never again to have any official dealings with ...',[25] insisted that Wolseley had to remain in place until after the meeting of malcontent Transvaal Boers sent for April 1880. With these delays, Wolseley had resigned himself that he would now not get his desired senior command in India and somewhat reluctantly agreed that on his return to London he would accept the position of Quartermaster-General.

By the middle of March, Wolseley's frustration had reached new heights. He loathed Pretoria, for both its climate and dullness, and he complained that he had little to do. His days were filled with morning horse rides, tennis, and mind-numbing social gatherings. Finally, towards the end of the month he received the cheering news that Colley was on his way and that the proposed Boer gathering had been cancelled. The Boer leadership, with Paul Kruger at its head, had clearly foreseen a Liberal election victory and he and his comrades were happy to wait until Wolseley had departed before they decided to act. Finally, on 5 May, the new Liberal Government officially recalled Wolseley to London. However, Wolseley had already pre-empted his recall for he had departed from Pretoria two weeks before his departure had been officially sanctioned and this act alone says much for his state of mind at the time. Just before he departed South African shores for his last time Wolseley, writing of his new appointment to his brother Dick, stated, 'I don't care a straw to be Q.M.G. for I cannot pull with the Duke [Cambridge] and we shall have continued rows and he will hate me more than before if indeed that be possible'.[26]

Following Wolseley's departure from South Africa the tensions between the Boers and the British increased. This was especially the case after the new Gladstone administration confirmed that independence for the Transvaal would still require the Boers to accept that they were part of the wider South African Confederation. Matters came to a head on 13 December 1880 when a meeting of over 4,000 Boers proclaimed the reconstitution of the South African Republic and appointed a provisional government. A formal declaration of the new republic was declared three days later, and military action began with the siege of British troops at Potchefstroom. The High Commissioner, George Colley, clearly had to act to restore order, but like Wolseley before him, seemed disdainful of Boer military capabilities. A series of disaster fell upon the British forces in the field as the Boer's superior marksmanship and ambush tactics proved to be decisive. The defeat at Bronkhorst Spruit on 20 December 1880 was the first of a series of humiliations for the British. Colley assumed command of British forces in the field and was roundly defeated at both Laing's Nek on 28 January 1881 and then again at Majuba Hill on 26 February 1881. In this last engagement Colley was killed and command of the remaining forces passed to another veteran of the Asante Expedition, Sir Evelyn Wood.

Whist Wood prepared for a further offensive, London dispatched reinforcements under the command of Wolseley's great rival Sir Frederick Roberts. To buy time until further troops arrived Wood entered peace talks with the Boer leadership, although it appears that he always intended to renew the offensive. However, once the talks had begun, both the Foreign Secretary, Lord Kimberley, and Gladstone were impressed by the Boer willingness to be conciliatory, and Wood was instructed to continue peace negotiations. These successfully concluded on 21 March and were confirmed by the Pretoria Convention of 3 August 1881. The Transvaal was granted internal independence under British suzerainty and British control of foreign relations, but even these requirements were removed by the London Convention of 1884 by which the Transvaal gained full independence.[27]

Wolseley found the death of his dear friend and colleague Colley a difficult loss to bear. He wrote to Frederick Maurice that he thought Colley was 'the ablest man I knew in any walk of life, and although I am well aware that he underestimated the fighting power and strength of his enemy, I still think so'.[28] Yet Wolseley's sadness at the loss of his friend was outweighed by the disgust he felt towards another member of the 'Asante Ring', Evelyn Wood. Wolseley was to bitterly claim that if Colley had had 10,000 men at his command, as Wood had done, then he would never had made peace, and he furiously declared that by signing the peace treaty Wood 'has injured our national renown most seriously abroad'.[29] Wolseley felt that the 1881 settlement had allowed the Boers to remain a strong force which was more than capable of challenging British authority in South Africa and that the peace treaty had made future conflict more likely. Within 20 years Wolseley's foresight was to be proved correct and he was then tasked with overseeing a conflict from a desk in Horse Guards. Wolseley was always slow to forgive and forget and he saw Wood's involvement in the peace negotiations as little more than a betrayal and his patronage of Wood was lessened in future conflicts.

Wolseley had returned from South Africa at the end of May 1880 and after a brief holiday took on the role of Quartermaster-General on 1 July. He returned to a much-altered political situation and it took him a few months for him to realize that the change of administration from a Conservative to Liberal government would work in his favour. Due to his reforming nature many, including the Queen, saw Wolseley as a Radical. This could not be further from the truth for he was a true imperialist and privately he described himself as 'a Jingo of the Jingos',[30] which was a reference to the expansionist imperial views of the former Prime Minister, Beaconsfield. Wolseley initially viewed the Liberal general election victory as both a national and potentially personal disaster. He feared for his own aspirations for future command as he saw the new Prime Minster as a reluctant imperialist. Wolseley even scornfully remarked that Gladstone would not fight for the Isle of Wight if it was seized by an enemy. Yet over the next years Wolseley was more actively involved in army reform and service abroad than when under the Conservatives, who for their outward signs of imperial ambition had largely avoided army reform, which was unpopular with royalty and the elite of society.

Wolseley had worked successfully with the former Liberal Secretary for War, Edward Cardwell, and he was now to form an equally strong relationship with the new Secretary, Hugh Childers. Wolseley returned from South Africa to discover that the traditionalists at the War Office had used his absence to attack the Cardwell reforms, especially the short-service system, of which Wolseley had been a major advocate. Although the decade would see Wolseley on active service in two more significant campaigns, whilst at home, in his roles of Quartermaster-General and then Adjutant-General, he would continue to push for army reform and in many ways this fight would be the most difficult and exhausting of his long army career.

In 1878 General Sir Richard Airey had been tasked with forming a committee to look at the organization of the army and the effect of the Cardwell reforms upon it. Intriguingly, it had been called whilst Wolseley was away in Cyprus, and it deliberated when he was serving in South Africa. The committee members were largely 'old school conservatives', holding views similar to those of the Duke of Cambridge, who held a prejudiced view of the Cardwell reforms. The committee reported its findings in early 1880 and Wolseley first read the report in March of that year. He was outraged for the committee had recommended the abolition of the linked battalion system, the cornerstone of the reforms. On his return to London, Wolseley angrily argued that the changes had not had sufficient time to bed down and that insufficient funds had been provided to raise the establishment of the depots so as to compensate if both battalions of a regiment had to serve abroad at the same time. Fortunately, Wolseley had an ally in Childers who also disapproved of the committee's recommendations. His disapproval of , if not disdain for, the work of the committee was clearly seen during a House of Commons debate on 31 May 1880. When asked by Colonel Owen Williams when the government intended to publish and act on the Airey commission's recommendations, Childers responded by stating:

> Sir, I have to point out to the hon. and gallant Member that the body presided over by Lord Airey was not a Royal Commission, nor a Departmental Committee, but a Committee consisting solely of military officers, with whom no civilians were associated, whose opinion on certain professional questions was sought by the Secretary of State. Their Report was only presented, in a complete form, since I took Office; and as soon as Her Majesty's Government have come to conclusions on the very important questions discussed by the Committee, ranging as they do over the whole organization of the Army, and affecting the interest of almost every class in it, I will lay on the Table the Report; or, at least, so much of it as may be given consistently with the public interest. I am bound to add that the Committee was far from unanimous, and that this divergence of opinion makes it the more necessary to guard against any premature publication.[31]

Undoubtedly with Wolseley's views ringing in his ears, Childers, to a significant degree, ignored the Airey Committee's recommendations and both men largely completed Cardwell's work regarding the linked battalion system. The two men were to work together effectively in other areas of reform, such as improving the conditions of service, although they failed to increase army pay, which seriously hindered recruitment. Wolseley and Childers also worked together for the abolition of flogging whilst on active service. Writing in 1881, after flogging had passed into history, Wolseley stated that now the private would not wear stripes on his back as the sergeant wore them on his arm. Perhaps Childers' biggest contribution, and that which benefitted Wolseley the most, was his stand against the conservative influence of both Cambridge and the Queen. This ranged from their opposition of removing the numbers attributed to specific regiments to promotion on merit, rather than seniority or family connection. In the latter argument both Childers and Wolseley advocated that promotion beyond the rank of Lieutenant-Colonel should be merit-based and in this Wolseley particularly clashed with the Duke.

The matter was further inflamed by Wolseley's desire to constantly appoint and promote men of his choosing when on campaign. As early at the Red River Campaign Wolseley had favoured certain officers; men such as Henry Brackenbury, Redvers Buller, Baker Russell and Evelyn Wood and this became so pronounced after the Asante Expedition that these men, and others, became known as the 'Asante Ring'. Many of these officers were graduates of the Staff College, which Wolseley favoured. He had taken an interest in its revitalisation under Edward Hamley in the 1870s, after its reputation had suffered in the previous decades. It is easy to understand why Wolseley promoted the careers of these specific individuals. They had served him well, they understood what was expected of them and they had great respect, if not a love, for their commander. For Wolseley his consideration was in not tampering with a winning team. In an interview with the reporter Archibald Forbes Wolseley laid bare his thinking as to the men of the 'Ring': 'I know these men of men and they know me. I selected them originally because of my discernment of character, not at the behest of interest or from the dictates of nepotism. We have worked long together; their familiarity with my methods and my just reliance on them relieves me of half the burden of command.'[32] Furthermore, Wolseley was always on the lookout for fresh talent especially as he considered that such men were not plentiful in the British army at that time.

For the detractors of the 'Ring', who included Cambridge, they disdainfully referred to it as the 'Mutual Admiration Society'. They saw Wolseley's patronage as affecting morale elsewhere and the existence of the Wolseley 'gang' encouraged emulation by his great rival, Sir Frederick Roberts, who formed a similar cohort of favoured officers in the Indian Army. For an officer not part of either of these 'Rings', and for one who was not motivated to attend Staff College, they must surely have viewed their prospects for active service as limited. It is understandable that Cambridge said the existence of the 'Ring' dented morale and he fought against Wolseley on this point. For Wolseley though such officers as favoured by Cambridge were an enigma to him. While Wolseley was successful in war, the politicians and the public supported him and to Wolseley that was what truly mattered.

Wolseley found his role as Quartermaster-General unsatisfying. The work was routine and included the transportation of troops abroad, issuing of stores and equipment and ensuring that the home garrisons were supplied. He was left with plenty of free time and Wolseley used this to promote his own ideas of army reform, away from the War Office. As well as there being an element of self-publicity, and perhaps even vanity, in his pronouncements in speeches and articles, Wolseley strongly felt that it was his duty and responsibility to point out perceived failings in the army and suggest remedies. Cambridge saw things very differently and indeed viewed Wolseley's public musings as insubordination and an undermining of his own position as Commander-in-Chief.

Wolseley's candid use of the pen particularly distressed the Duke for it was clear who Wolseley was targeting with his words. For example, in the *Nineteenth Century* magazine in 1881, Wolseley informed the reader that there existed a group of officers for whom the world stood still. Whilst the Industrial Revolution had wrought huge changes in the economy and society, and had transformed manufacturing, Wolseley described these officers of being ignorant and 'unconscious of the fact that all such discoveries and inventions react upon armies and military science'.[33] This was clearly seen in the technical developments that had resulted in most modern armies adopting the breech-loading rifle, which had dramatic increased and improved the range and accuracy of rifles and had transformed the battlefield, in both defensive and offensive terms.[34] In the same article Wolseley debated the advantages of short service over long service in the Army and to do so in such a public forum seriously increased the Duke's angst. Wolseley had already angered Cambridge when speaking on this subject in a speech at the Mansion House in which he blatantly called for help to stop Horse Guards 'sabotaging' short service. Wolseley used a rather bizarre analogy to seek support when he asked for the press and public to enable him 'to put new wheels on the military coach, which by its creaking tells us of its present dangerous condition, and which is only with difficulty maintained in an upright position at all'.[35]

Such words outraged Cambridge, who, correctly, saw them as a personal attack upon the Commander-in-Chief. Victoria energetically defended her cousin Cambridge during his tenure and was an ultra-conservative when it came to army matters and there is no doubt that the monarch viewed Wolseley as impertinent and something of an upstart. To make foes of such prominent people was always going to have a consequence and when Gladstone pressed for Wolseley to be made a peer and become the spokesman on army matters in the House of Lords, both Cambridge and the Queen recoiled in horror. The Duke was particularly concerned that Wolseley would use the privilege of the House to make unbridled attacks upon him and Horse Guards. Whilst using the argument that Wolseley as Quartermaster-General had to be seen to be apolitical, both the Duke and Victoria simply flatly refused to sanction a peerage, despite the efforts of both Gladstone and Childers. For once Wolseley kept his thoughts to himself during the 'discussions', but he was particularly upset that the Queen had so adamantly opposed his peerage.

Having lost the peerage battle, Wolseley then faced a similar fight when Childers pressed for his promotion to Adjutant-General, second only to Cambridge in the army hierarchy. With Adjutant-General Charles Ellice due to retire at the end of 1881, Childers put forward Wolseley's name as the government's preferred replacement. The Duke reacted quickly and firmly for if Wolseley was appointed to the role, it would provide him with great influence as he would oversee training, recruitment, discipline and education. Significantly the position of Adjutant-General was also the traditional channel for communication between the Queen and the army and Victoria was reluctant to see Wolseley become the Army's spokesman on such important matters and again wished to protect her cousin's influence.

Cambridge argued that Wolseley was not the best qualified candidate for the position and promoted Sir Lintern Simmons instead. However, Simmons had demonstrated his conservative nature when serving on the Airey Committee and for this reason alone was unsuitable to Childers. Writing to the Queen's Private Secretary, Sir Henry Ponsonby, Cambridge candidly outlined why he opposed Wolseley's appointment and demonstrated how little trust the Duke had in Wolseley. Cambridge stated:

> :... I think the Army wants *rest*. Such great changes have been introduced, that time should be given to allow matters to settle down. Sir Garnet Wolseley's great object seems to be to go further and further, and to upset the little that is left of the old spirit of the officer by indiscriminate section, carrying education to the extremist limit, by letting men go the Reserve after three years' service, and in a variety of ways intensifying the sweeping changes that have already been effected.

The Duke continued, and this was perhaps the crux of his objections:

> ... I think the mode of his introduction into the office of A.G. would be a slur and imputation upon me, and on the manner in which I have performed my Departmental duty as military adviser to the Secretary of State, and as such a serious insult would be offered to me in my official position. Lastly Sir Garnet's close connection with the Press, and his strong expressions on military matters in speeches and writings, are of that character as I believe would prove most detrimental to the interests of the Army, and would certainly turn military matters into subjects for political discussions ...[36]

Again, Wolseley managed to suppress his own upset during the appointment process but wrote candidly to his wife of his hurt and cruel treatment at the hands of the Royal Family. Whilst Cambridge felt so strongly on the matter of Wolseley's appointment that he even considered it a resignation issue, eventually tempers cooled and rational thought won through. The Duke realized that Childers was determined to see Wolseley promoted and Childers might even resign if he did not prevail. Cambridge feared that Childers' replacement might be even more radical in his reforms. Thus, a compromise was sought in which Wolseley promised Cambridge that going forward he would refrain from writing or speaking on military matters away from the War Office. Whether Wolseley truly believed this at the time is unclear, but it was a promise he would soon break and once again the Commander-in-Chief and the new Adjutant-General would be on a collision course. But before this battle could commence, Wolseley would be called upon again on active service, once more in Africa, and this latest campaign would be crowned by arguably his greatest personal triumph.

British interests in Egypt centred upon the Suez Canal, which had been built by the French engineer Ferdinand de Lesseps between 1859–69 and largely financed by loans from British and other European banks. The Canal was perhaps the grandest manifestation of the many projects undertaken by the Khedive, Ismail, who ruled as governor of Egypt under the suzerainty of Ottoman Turkey. Through the 1860s and into the following decade Ismail borrowed huge sums to modernize Egypt and improve its infrastructure. Railways, harbours, a telegraph system, and other amenities were built which transformed the cities of Alexandria and Cairo whilst improving the country's agricultural production. Unfortunately, Ismail's government was inefficient as well as corrupt and the monies borrowed from European banks saw the national debt rise to a staggering £100,000,000 (equivalent to over £15 billion in 2023). Within a matter of a few years Egypt's finance were in such dire straits that it was unable to meet interest payments on its colossal debt. The inevitable default was delayed when, in 1875, the Disraeli government took advantage of the perilous situation to purchase Ismail's shares in the Suez Canal and effectively made the Canal, an essential highway to India, British owned. The following year Ismail was forced to admit bankruptcy and dual Anglo-French control was established over Egyptian finances.

Egypt remained, nominally at least, part of the Ottoman Empire. When in 1879 Ismail tried to push back against some of the bondholders and financiers' demands and restrictions, both the French and British placed pressure upon the Ottoman Sultan to dispose Ismail and replace him with his more pliable and obliging son, Tewfik. Although this usurpation solved the immediate problem it caused another as many Egyptians began to fight against foreign intervention and political unrest ensured. The loudest voices of protests came from within the Egyptian Army and 'Egypt for the Egyptians' became a rallying call. Many officers had been dismissed as an economy measure, which of course inflamed dissent, and one prominent Colonel, Ahmed Arabi, became the figurehead for national unrest. Arabi was a strong, tall, sturdy intelligent man with a skill for oratory who quickly marshalled a strong nationalist movement into a political and military force. Arabi at first won some concessions from the weak Tewfik, who was forced to appoint him War Minster. In May 1882 Arabi acted and seized power with the support of the miliary and Tewfik was made a prisoner of his own government.

The British and French governments were appalled by developments and military intervention looked to be the only option to secure its loans and access to the vital transit of the Suez Canal. In addition, there were over 100,000 foreign nationals living and working in Egypt whose lives were potentially at risk. With the situation clearly deteriorating in Egypt Wolseley had spent some time assessing the possibility of military intervention. In the autumn of 1881 his old colleague, Colonel Richard Harrison had holidayed with his wife in Egypt and had used the opportunity to 'spy' on Egyptian fortifications and the Suez Canal. On his return to London in January 1882, Harrison called on Wolseley at the War Office with his sketches and first-hand accounts of unrest from which Wolseley concluded that military intervention looked a real possibility. The Adjutant-General asked Major Alexander Tulloch of the Intelligence Department to begin to compile a dossier on Egypt and its military strength whilst Wolseley began to formulate his own plans for a possible campaign.

Even as late as March of 1882 Wolseley believed that the Egyptians would not resist if British and French forces intervened to restore political and economic stability. Writing to Wilfred Blunt, a supporter of Egyptian nationalism, Wolseley stated that the 'occupation of Egypt would be most unpopular with the army, and that he himself should be sorry to have to go there'.[37] Yet Arabi's actions against Tewfik just two months later made intervention inevitable.

With Turkey reluctant to act against Arabi's 'coup', both Britain and France sent warships to Alexandria which played straight into the hands of the nationalists stirring up further discord, which spilled over into rioting in the city on 11 and 12 June. This resulted in around fifty deaths and the British Consul was forcibly dragged from his carriage and badly beaten in the street. On 24 June, the British and French officials who had sat on Egyptian Council meetings which had, in effect, ensured the allies' interests came before those of the Egyptians, were informed that their presence was no longer welcome or required. Thus, with this pronouncement, Arabi's nationalist movement had regained self-government.

Within the British Cabinet pressure mounted upon a reluctant Prime Minster to intervene. When Admiral Sir Beauchamp Seymour, who was in command of naval forces in Alexandria harbour, reported that Arabi had ordered the construction of shore batteries, which could threaten the British warships, Gladstone could procrastinate no longer, and two infantry battalions were ordered from Malta to Cyprus to be ready to protect the Suez Canal. A preliminary meeting to discuss the military response was held in the War Office on 17 June but it was not until 28 June when the first official steps were taken. Then the Commissariat Department supplied Wolseley with a detailed account of transport, horses, mules and carts that were available at home and in Cyprus, Gibraltar and Malta along with details of what would be required if a corps of 24,000 troops were to be sent to Egypt. On 30 June a committee of both Navy and Army officials met for the first time to start detailed planning for military intervention. Thanks to the work of Tulloch and others Wolseley was able to astound those present with how much intelligence had already been gathered. Three days later much of what Wolseley had reported was used as the basis of a memorandum circulated to Childers and Cambridge and this formed the bases of Wolseley's subsequent plan for the campaign against Arabi. It envisaged that two divisions of infantry and one cavalry brigade would be sent to Ismailia and from there an advance on Cairo would follow along the railway line. Locomotives and at least 10 miles of steel rails would be needed to keep the army supplied as it advanced and of course these would have to be shipped to Ismailia. Wolseley predicted that the enemy would make a stand somewhere along the line of march and he considered that the fortification at Tel-el-Kebir would be the most likely spot. Wolseley thought that the Egyptians might then make a further stand before Cairo, but he stated that if they could be decisively beaten in the first engagement then this was unlikely.

The memorandum was an astonishing document, not just for its clarity and detail, but also its vision for the eventual campaign that did indeed play out much along the lines that Wolseley had envisaged. As in Asante and Canada Wolseley saw the main challenge to be a logistical one and like in Asante the troops would be battling both the enemy and the climate, and it was the latter that Wolseley feared the most. The men would be required to advance through the tremendous heat of the Egyptian summer, with no time for acclimatization, and Wolseley hoped that his soldiers could spend the least amount of time exposed to this threat.

Childers and even Cambridge were impressed by Wolseley's advanced planning, although all realized that any campaign would empty Britain of its troops and even the Queen's personal bodyguard, the Household Cavalry, would have to take part. This was another reason why all those involved at the planning stage wished for the campaign to be a short one. Wolseley feared that a naval action might prematurely force his hand, before he could assembly his force. This indeed happened when on 11 July Admiral Seymour ordered the Egyptian batteries in Alexandria to be bombarded. Seymour had given Arabi an ultimatum to surrender the forts and batteries that ringed the harbour, which Arabi simply ignored. The French refused to join Seymour in his actions and withdrew in some anger. Whilst the perceived threat from the batteries was extinguished damage was also inflicted upon the town and there were some civilian casualties. Wolseley was furious for not only would the damage impede any British landing, but Seymour's action had inflamed still further the nationalist movement and more rioting occurred, for which Seymour had too few men to control.

On 20 July Childers officially announced in the House of Commons that Wolseley was to be appointed to command a British expedition to Egypt. Cambridge advised the Queen to sanction the appointment for Wolseley had public support and it would remove the troublesome Adjutant-General from the War Office for a few months at least. Cambridge did reluctantly admit to Her Majesty that Wolseley was 'very decidedly as able a man for the field as we have got'.[38] On 22 July Gladstone rose in the House of Commons asking for £2,300,000 to finance an expeditionary force. In seeking the funds, he declared, 'The insecurity of the canal is a symptom only and the seat of the disease is in the interior of Egypt, in its disturbed and its anarchical condition. We feel that we should not fully discharge our duty if we did not endeavour to convert the present state of Egypt from anarchy and conflict to peace and order.'[39]

Gladstone went onto say that Arabi and his supporters were anti-Christian militarists who cared nothing for the rights and liberties of the ordinary Egyptian. The vote was carried 275 for to 19 against. Yet some historians, such as Peter Mansfield, claim that the situation in Egypt was far from anarchy. Immediately after Seymour's ill-advised bombardment there were serious riots in the three Delta towns of Tana, Mehella and Damanhur in which around 100 Greek and Syrian Christians were killed, but these disturbances were quickly quashed by Arabi's followers and there was no recurrence of such violence, during the remaining months of the administration. The Europeans who remained in Egypt were unmolested and those wishing to leave the country were escorted under the protection of Arabi's troops to Alexandria. Either Gladstone was being disingenuous in his claims of anarchy and violence or the hysteria that was flowing around the possible loss of the Suez Canal had led many to believe what they wanted to hear to ease their minds over British military intervention.

The Queen signed the Proclamation calling out the Army Reserves on 25 July and just two days later the first British troops, including Royal Marines, had sailed from Portsmouth. Within a further three days the Guards had left their London barracks and by the middle of August two divisions, each of two infantry brigades, with cavalry and artillery were on their way to Egypt from Britain, Malta, Gibraltar, Cyprus, Aden, and Bombay. The total of all ranks under Wolseley's command was 40,560. The size of the logistical undertaking is reflected in the fact that sixty-one steamers were employed to carry the troops and 41,000 tons of supplies to Egypt.

Whilst Wolseley's plan had been approved and he had been given the troops he had requested, he was not to get everything he wanted. Once again, Wolseley had managed to upset Cambridge by appointing many of his indispensable 'Ring' of officers to his Staff and key positions. These included Buller (Intelligence Department), Wood (command of an infantry brigade), Baker Russell (command of 1st Cavalry Brigade), Maurice (Headquarters Staff), McCalmont (cavalry) and Herbert Stewart (also cavalry) as well as others. Stewart was becoming a firm favourite of Wolseley who appreciated his intelligence, humour and above all his ability to quietly get on with the job. He even, in a letter to Louisa, described Stewart as 'a real brother', which for someone who was often critical of his colleagues in his campaign letters to his wife meant Stewart clearly had made a positive impact upon Wolseley.

However, Cambridge insisted that Wolseley accept his recommendations for chief commanders, both divisional and at brigade level. Wolseley was to complain both during the campaign and after about many of these senior men, and hangers-on, that he felt had been unwisely foisted upon him. The divisional commanders were those who had already been chosen to command in the planned autumn manoeuvres. Neither Lieutenant-General Frederick Willis, who was to lead the 1st Division, and Lieutenant-General Edward Hamley, commander of the 2nd Division, had seen active service since the Crimean War. Wolseley was to find both men frustrating to deal with and slow to act, whilst in Hamley he was, before the end of the campaign, to make a lifelong enemy. Wolseley was to later write that both Hamley and Willis had 'an overwhelming opinion of their own importance'.[40] This was perhaps rather rich of Wolseley who was certainly not shy to promote his own abilities.

In addition to the divisional commanders, Wolseley had to accept General Sir John Adye, then the Surveyor General of Ordnance at the War Office, as his Chief of Staff. Wolseley was happier to accept the then of Head of the Intelligence Department, his old colleague from the Asante Expedition, Sir Archibald Alison. As in Asante, Alison was to lead the Highlanders within the 2nd Division. Such appointments denuded the War Office of most of its senior officials. Wolseley was also forced to accept several royal appointments. The Duke of Connaught, the Queen's favourite son, joined the 1st Division as a brigadier, whilst Cambridge's own son Major George Fitzgeorge (who Wolseley described to Lady Wolseley as a terrible snob and quite useless) and the Queen's cousin, the Duke of Teck were 'found' positions. Wolseley must have feared a repeat of the incident when the Prince Imperial had been killed whilst on service in the Zulu War, but unlike the British commander then, Lord Chelmsford, Wolseley had the sense to ensure that those royal personages in his charge were kept, as much as possible, far away from danger. Fortunately, the Queen herself vetoed the Prince of Wales's desire to join the expedition and Wolseley was at least grateful to the monarch for saving him from the responsibility of ensuring the safety of the future king. Wolseley did have the satisfaction of refusing the services of some individuals who simply arrived expecting positions, and these included Captain Charles Beresford, RN, who had taken part in the bombardment of Alexandria, and the well-connected pseudo-war correspondent St Leger Herbert who was given only a position as a private in the mounted infantry.

Wolseley left London on 1 August on the *Calabria* along with the Household Cavalry. He had been forced to take this course rather than the quicker overland route to Brindisi and then on to Cyprus and from there to Alexandria, for he had caught a chill whilst visiting the Queen at Osborne House which had developed into a painful case of erysipelas. His doctors advised him to take the longer transit to allow him time to recover and rest. Although frustrated that many of his senior staff, including Adye and Alison, would be arriving before him Wolseley used the extra time to firmly formulate his plans for the forthcoming campaign. Whilst he still focused on the need to advance from Ismailia he realized that the protection of the Suez Canal was of paramount importance, not just for the logistical success of the expedition but also for Britain's long-term economic benefit. Wolseley thus knew that deception and deceit of the enemy would be vital for his plans to succeed. Therefore, he instructed Alison that on arriving in Alexandria he was to advance a few miles outside and establish a defensive line upon the Ramleh ridge to tie down the enemy forces there and to confuse Arabi of his true intentions. On route the *Calabria* called into Malta where Wolseley received the report that Arabi had despatched forces to the town of Nefiche, just a few miles from Ismailia. Concerned that Adye might react to this news and send forces prematurely to Ismailia Wolseley telegraphed an urgent order to Adye that he was not to take any action until Wolseley had arrived.

On 15 August Wolseley duly sailed into Alexandria. Here he became angered at the sight of what he considered to have been the unnecessary bombardment carried out by Seymour, but he kept his displeasure from the Admiral for he now needed the naval commander's full support in his plans to deceive Arabi as to his real intentions for the campaign. Wolseley was to make several bold command decisions over the next few weeks and perhaps his night march upon Tel-el-Kebir has overshadowed others, but his plans for the initial stages of the campaign were absolutely central to its final successful outcome. In hushed tones Wolseley informed Seymour of his audacious idea; he intended to secure the Canal by a secret move of most of his available force to Ismailia whilst at the same time deceiving the enemy, the press and some of his senior officers to believe that his real intention was a combined naval and army attack from the sea at Aboukir Bay. Wolseley stressed that as few naval officers as possible should know of his true plans and Seymour promised his full cooperation.

Wolseley rode out to inspect Alison's position at Ramleh and made himself as conspicuous as possible, knowing that Arabi's spies would be everywhere. To keep up the pretence of an attack at Aboukir Bay and the Egyptian lines at Kafr-ed-Duer he instructed Hamley and Alison to draw up plans for the assault and he even made amendments to it before endorsing it. Wolseley loathed the presence of newspaper correspondents whilst on campaign, but he cleverly decided to use them to his own advantage. On 17 August he instructed one of staff officers to brief the gathering pressmen that Aboukir Bay was to be the target for assault and censorship was removed so that this news could be widely circulated. Wolseley even instructed Major Tulloch to telegraph the *Standard* in London pretending to be their correspondent and spread the story that rumours of a British occupation of the Canal were false. Arabi and his commanders were completely deceived and whilst Egyptian troops were rushed to oppose the assault at Aboukir Bay, troops of the 1st Division boarded transports and at noon on 19 August the powerful naval squadron headed east, making as much conspicuous noise and smoke as possible.

Hamley was left behind with sealed orders that he was not to open until 20 August. As Wolseley sailed passed Aboukir Bay under cover of darkness, a few small craft were sent close to shore to loose off a few rounds to deceive both the enemy and the press that the expected assault was under way. The rest of the squadron sailed on to Port Said and the Canal. By sunrise the Egyptian gunners at Aboukir Bay saw an empty horizon, whilst their colleagues guarding the Canal had awoken to the British assault which had taken all by surprise. Sentries were disarmed and the garrison at Port Said surrendered en masse. The Suez Canal Company's telegraph was seized to prevent the enemy knowing of Wolseley's successful coup. When news of Wolseley's audacity reached London the Secretary of State of War, Childers, was at first annoyed that he had not been party to the plan but soon offered his congratulations on Wolseley's success. Cambridge and the Queen questioned whether it was ethical to deceive the press in such a fashion. Editors largely, and quickly, forgave Wolseley and cheered his ruse. Hamley, however, was furious with Wolseley for duping him and not taking him into his confidence. Either Wolseley was insensitive towards one of his senior commanders or he already had no trust in Hamley's ability. This deceit was to be the beginning of a lifelong feud between the two men.

By 23 August the majority of troops were ashore at Ismailia but already Wolseley was becoming aware of the scale of the task that now lay ahead. Not only were his men to battle the enemy but also the unrelating sun that beat down upon them from a cloudless sky. Added to this burden was the supply problems which were already apparent. The facilities at Ismailia were totally inadequate to unload the huge amount of stores needed to feed and supply the advance. There was no railway line between the river and the town, so trains had to be unloaded at Suez and furthermore the track to Suez had been damaged and the Royal Engineers had to work frantically to repair the line. This was coupled with commissariat officers and port officials who were completely overwhelmed by the task given to them. With all these elements conspiring against Wolseley, it is perhaps not surprising that the Egyptian campaign was hindered by supply problems, unlike both the Red River and Asante expeditions.

Yet Wolseley's most immediate concern was to supply his men with sufficient water. Within hours of disembarking at Ismailia Wolseley noted that the level of the nearby Sweetwater Canal, the primary source of drinking water in the area, was steadily falling. Wolseley ordered a forward reconnaissance and the intelligence gathered established that the Egyptians had not been idle. Although the deception of an attack at Aboukir Bay had meant that most the enemy's forces were positioned there, engineers had built a dam at Magfar, six miles away, and were attempting to restrict water to the invading force. Wolseley reacted swiftly and, on 24 August, he accompanied Generals Drury Lowe and Willis to Magfar with a contingent of cavalry and mounted infantry, along with infantry from the York and Lancs Regiment, commanded by Major-General Gerald Graham, who was to play a major part in the subsequent advance to Tel-el-Kebir. In the early hours of the morning Wolseley discovered only a handful of Egyptians protecting the dam at Magfar, who offered no resistance and even informed him that a further dam, protected by a substantial infantry force, had been constructed at Tel-el-Mahuta. Ordering the dam at Magfar to be destroyed, Wolseley carried on to see the next Egyptian position.

Arriving at Tel-el-Mahuta Wolseley realized that he would need to make a quick decision for through his binoculars he could see locomotives arriving and unloading substantial supplies for an enemy force which he calculated to be in the region of 8,000–9,000 strong. The enemy was increasing and would be larger than he could then put into the field against them. Wolseley knew that he would have to push onto Kassassin Lock for it was only by capturing the Lock could he secure sufficient water supplies for his troops. He also intended to use the Lock as a base to assemble his force before launching an attack upon the strong enemy position at Tel-el-Kebir. Wolseley realized that he needed to gamble.

Without hesitating Wolseley ordered Graham's infantry forward and called for Drury Lowe to advance with his cavalry in support. Command of the force was given to Willis who moved the two artillery pieces that had accompanied the reconnaissance in force to a position to challenge the Egyptian artillery. The enemy was armed with Krupp artillery, superior in firepower and numbers, six to the two British pieces, but in the subsequent artillery duel fate was on Wolseley's side for the Egyptian shells were percussion, rather than shrapnel, and most buried themselves into the sand without denotating.

Wolseley was conspicuous to both his men and the enemy gunners who soon targeted him. A shell passed just a few feet over his head and even Wolseley considered prudence to be better than valour and withdrew behind a sand dune to observe events. Butler recorded that throughout the day Wolseley was cheerful and encouraging to those around him yet at the same time his mind and eyes were never far from the battle, whether he was engaged on the immediate front or keeping watch on his flanks. The Egyptians were deterred from advancing to engage the British, for the superior range of the British

Martini-Henry rifle, as compared to the Remingtons of the Egyptians, did check the enemy infantry. However, as the morning wore on the Egyptian commander, Rashid Pasha, attempted to outflank the British on the right. Fortunately, the timely arrival of Baker Russell with over 300 troopers from the 4th and 7th Dragoon Guards, as well as two Gatling guns manned by sailors from HMS *Orion*, stopped any further enemy advance and the engagement became static.

Whilst the enemy might not have offered any immediate danger, the British were suffering from the overpowering heat. Before handing over battlefield command to Willis, Wolseley had hurriedly sent for reinforcements from the Guards and the Duke of Cornwall's Light Infantry (DCLI). Both units battled through the heat of the day and when they did arrive at Tel-el-Mahuta in the afternoon they were so exhausted that they could not possibly close on the enemy. This was a sobering lesson for Wolseley who realized, as the morning turned into the heat of the afternoon, that he could not expect his troops to be effective in these conditions. He himself, after 16 hours in the saddle, suffered from sunburn, and intolerable pain from tight boots which had to be cut off him, whilst Willis joined over fifty troops who collapsed from sunstroke. Wolseley decided to abandon all thoughts of an advance and as the Egyptians retired to their entrenchments, he returned to Ismailia leaving the now recovered Willis with instructors to attack at daybreak. Even in great discomfort, before Wolseley left the men deployed at Tel-el-Mahuta, he made the time to visit each position to thank the men personally for their bravery and determination. It is easy to view Wolseley as somewhat hard-hearted towards the rank and file, viewing them as a means, or a tool, to his own personal success. However, acts such as this demonstrate that this was far from the case. According to a Corporal Philip, Wolseley stopped every 12 paces or so to chat with individual soldiers and Philip recorded that Wolseley spoke softly with the words, 'Men you have the place of honour; the safety of your comrades and the glory of your country is in your keeping; you must stand or fall where you are now even though the whole army of Egypt come against you'.[41] Ever the true imperialist, Wolseley did certainly know how to inspire his men.

As daylight broke on the morning of 25 August the British discovered that during the night Rashi Pasha had decided to abandon his position at Tel-el-Mahuta and had pulled his forces back towards Kassassin. Despite the exhaustion of yesterday and the fact that the horses of Drury Lowe's contingent were far from acclimatized after their sea voyage, Wolseley did not hesitate, and he ordered his cavalry commander to spur on his men to intercept the retreating Egyptians, many of whom had boarded locomotives.

Wolseley even sent an order to Drury Lowe to attempt to capture one of the departing trains, but the horses were simply not strong enough for such a task and despite Wolseley's enthusiasm the British were unable to catch the enemy on their line of march. Wolseley had earlier ordered Drury Lowe to swing his mounted force to the right in a great arc to bring it, hopefully, back to the Canal in a position behind the retreating Egyptians and thus capture them. Although this did not happen quite as envisaged by Wolseley, his mounted infantry were placed in an advantageous point to later charge the enemy.

Forward British reconnaissance found that Rashi Pasha had ordered his rear retreating units to occupy a position roughly 10 miles further on from Tel-el-Mahuta, along a ridge line at Mahsama. In the town itself were mountains of supplies and British mounted units were able to seize much of this bounty but in doing so provoked the enemy's gunners and seven Krupp guns located near the station began to lob shells at the advancing British units. On arriving at the scene, from his 'arc' into the desert, Drury Lowe acted decisively by first deterring a force of enemy cavalry from attacking the British left flank and then moving the bulk of his cavalry force to the rear of the Egyptian position to attack them from behind. The infantry supporting the Krupp guns were just able to form a line and unleash one volley at the charging cavalry before the British were upon them. Cavalry sabres were ruthlessly used and both the Egyptians who made a stand and those who dropped their Remingtons and fled were cut down.

Although once again the British were unable to stop the last departing locomotive escaping from Mahsama station, overall, this brief chase and action had been a great success. Taking the enemy off-guard the British had captured the seven Krupp guns, large amounts of mumitions and seventy-five railway carriages full of food and other essential supplies. Drury Lowe had lost five killed and twenty-five wounded during this cavalry action and of course his command had advanced without infantry support. Fearful of an Egyptian counter-attack, Willis initially ordered Drury Lowe to destroy the captured supplies and withdraw, but Wolseley overruled this and instead told Drury Lowe to remain at Mahsama and instructed Graham to march with his infantry brigade in support. Despite their suffering of the previous day the troops accomplished the march and arrived under cover of darkness to feast on the enemy's supplies.

Wolseley had spent 12 hours in the saddle and after his exertions of the previous day this was a herculean effort. He returned that night to the former's Governor's House at Ismailia to reflect on what had been achieved. Before departing his last order was that on the following morning British forces should advance a further 2½ miles west to occupy Kassassin Lock. As he rode back to Mahsama, in the early morning hours of 26 August he was informed by Stewart that forward reconnaissance had reported that the Lock had also been abandoned by the enemy and cavalry units were securing the position. Later in the day Graham's infantry occupied Kassassin Lock and the cavalry retired. Wolseley was now able to boast that by occupying the Lock British forces had secured the upper reaches of the canal and had, by doing so, neutralised any Egyptian attempts to cut off the British from their only water supply. This was a significant tactical victory and Wolseley could assess the achievements of the previous week as not only a personal success, but also as a statement of the tenacity and resolute work of his troops.

Although Wolseley was a full week ahead of his own demanding timetable to attack Tel-el-Kebir, his success was not all that it seemed. The British held the railway, Canal and telegraph as far as Kassassin Lock and were just nine miles from their military objective, yet, despite securing much needed Egyptian supplies, food was becoming a major concern for Wolseley and his men. The advance had been so rapid that it had overstretched the already struggling commissariat at Ismailia. Those men of Graham's brigade, the furthest west of all Wolseley's troops and the nearest to the enemy, were suffering from lack of food and shelter and to make matters worse the Egyptians had thrown the bodies of animals as well as dead soldiers into the Canal west of Mahsama. The risks were obvious but many men, tortured by thirst, the Duke of Connaught included, could not resist, and suffered with debilitating dysentery as a result. Still Wolseley felt that with his rapid advance and the lack of fight shown by the enemy, he should continue, but was realist. In a letter to his wife Wolseley admitted that the last two days, although achieving much, had been hard and he 'had been very fortunate' and that was now in 'a position far in advance of what I expected', but 'I cannot, however, go further for ten days or a fortnight yet …'.[42]

The delay, despite Wolseley's eagerness to press on to Tel-el-Kebir, was forced upon him for many of his troops had not reached the front line and those that were there were lacking food and supplies, and many were in great discomfort. Writing to Childers Wolseley admitted that the troops were exhausted, and the cavalry and artillery horses were 'well pumped out, so that I cannot use them again for some days'. Wolseley went onto say that 'Circumstances have pushed me forward sooner than I had intended and consequently the difficulty of feeding and forwarding camp equipment to the front had been very great. As usual transport has been our difficulty, and until we have an engine or two working on the line, I cannot move forward again.'[43]

Earlier, in a letter to Childers of 19 August, Wolseley had indicated a certain scorn of the enemy he was to face. Wolseley wrote, rather egotistically, that 'with our two divisions and the Indian contingent, the whole of Egypt assembled at Tel-el-Kebir would be made short work of'.[44] The engagements at Mahsama, and Tel-el-Mahuta in which the Egyptians, both cavalry and infantry, had been reluctant to engage and quick to run, had reinforced in Wolseley's mind that the enemy had no stomach for a fight. However, the surprise Egyptian attack at Kassassin would snap Wolseley out of any complacency he may have still held and made him realize that Tel-el-Kebir would be a much harder proposition to take than he had first envisaged.

After securing Kassassin Lock Wolseley left Willis in overall command of the forces there, primarily Graham's 2nd Infantry Brigade, and he returned to Ismailia with the intention of assessing and improving the supply log-jam issues, which were blighting the campaign. In the afternoon of 28 August he heard the sound of heavy firing from the west but, as he later wrote to Louisa, he had not paid '... much attention to it, especially as I knew we had plenty of troops to hold their own against any number the enemy could bring against us'.[45] At around 7pm Wolseley received news that Graham had been attacked and an hour later a startling telegram from Willis which claimed that Graham had been defeated and the enemy were advancing on Mahsama. Rather than immediately heading for the front, Wolseley thought on the news, ate his dinner, and retired at around 11pm with orders for him to be called at 1am when he planned to head to Kassassin to assess the situation for himself. It is surprising that Wolseley did not immediately head westwards on hearing the firing in the afternoon and when he then received the alarming news of a defeat why was he so apparently indifferent? Perhaps there was a small element of complacency on his part for he was certainly disdainful of the enemy's willingness to fight, but it seems clear from a letter written to Louisa that he had faith in his commander of the 2nd Infantry Brigade, if not of Willis. He wrote, 'I have known Graham all my life [the two men had served alongside each other in China in 1860]. I have seen him under the heaviest fire as stolidly and as cool as if he were at a review. I felt as confident that he would never retreat before any number of Egyptians as I should myself.'[46] Wolseley did confess though that he had begun to worry at what might have happened if Graham had been killed, yet Wolseley's relative inaction demonstrates that he was able to delegate to those officers with which he had confidence. Willis was not to be one of these men.

Fortunately, what concerns Wolseley may have had over the fate of his friend Graham and the action at Kassassin were laid to rest with the arrival at Ismailia of the special correspondent of the *Daily Telegraph*, Godfrey Lagen, who told of a stunning victory. Wolseley left the Governor's House at 2am and by 8am he was at the scene of the battle listening to various accounts.

Wolseley learnt that Arabi himself had led out 12,000 troops from Tel-el-Kebir to attack Graham's strong defensive position at Kassassin Lock. Despite suffering from lumbago and dosed with morphine injections to enable him to move around the battlefield, Graham reacted as Wolseley knew he would and countered every move that Arabi made. Even though Arabi was in command the Egyptian troops demonstrated a reluctance to engage and once again the longer range of the British Martini-Henry rifle kept them at a distance. Graham ordered Drury Lowe, who was at Mahsama to remain on standby ready to advance in support when ordered. Hours went bye in the which the British suffered from the effects of the penetrating sun. At 3pm it appeared that the stalemate was coming to an end with news that the Egyptians were retiring. Drury Lowe ordered his exhausted troops to stand down and for them to seek out a meal. This was rudely interrupted and hour and half later when the Egyptians rallied and began to advance with renewed purpose. Still in terrible pain, Graham used the lay of the ground on his left to great advantage, skilfully concealing his weak position there whilst enticing the Egyptians to his right flank where he intended Drury Lowe to pounce. At around 5.30pm Graham sent his aide-de-camp, Lieutenant Pirie of the 4th Dragoon Guards, with an order to Drury Lowe which stated 'Take the cavalry round by our right, under cover of the hill, and attack the left flank of the enemy'.[47]

However, Pirie had difficulty in finding Drury Lowe, for he and his command had retire back to camp to enjoy a much-needed meal and rest and were thus not where Pirie had expected them to be. Pirie exhausted one horse and was forced to obtain another from an artillery battery and by the time he did locate Drury Lowe, Pirie was nervous, tired, and excitable. Having delivered the order, he incorrectly added that Graham was 'only just able to hold his own'. These words became magnified in importance and when they reached Willis he reacted and sent his panicky telegram to Wolseley, which later resulted in Willis being castigated by his General. Although delayed in his advance, Drury Lowe rapidly headed forward to follow Graham's orders and in fact his timing was fortuitous. The cavalry force arrived as the Egyptians were retreating once more. Arriving as the moon bathed the desert Drury Lowe charged into the right flank of the enemy, catching them in the open. Simultaneously, Graham ordered a general advance of the infantry and the Egyptians fled back to Tel-el-Kebir in some disorder. Drury Lowe was supported by Baker Russell who led the 7th Dragoons into the melee. Egyptian troops were ridden over and slaughtered in the charge as the British advanced over two miles in their pursuit. By 8.45pm Graham called a halt and ordered the troops back to their camp at Kassassin. Graham estimated the enemy's losses to be in the region of 400 dead and the day had cost the British

16 dead and 79 wounded, yet the victory was complete. Surely nothing could stop Wolseley from pushing onto to his final objective.

Mindful of soothing the egos of both the Queen and Cambridge, Wolseley ensured that he was fulsome in his praises of the efforts of the Household Cavalry and of Baker Russell who led them in the charge. Cambridge was furious with Wolseley for appointing Baker Russell a brigadier without consulting him. So, Wolseley was delighted to convey how nobly Baker Russell had command the Dragoons and how brave he had been, even having his horse shot under him. He mollified the Royals by also praising the efforts and fortitude of the Duke of Teck. It appeared that Wolseley was finally learning that whilst on campaign at least he needed to keep both the Monarch and the Duke well informed. Wolseley was now not reluctant to be colourful in his reports if that eased the pressure on him from Horse Guards and Windsor.

After the victory at Kassassin both the press and the War Office were expecting Wolseley to press his advantage and move on Tel-el-Kebir. However, all was not as it seemed for the logistical shortcomings were now seriously hampering Wolseley's ability to move forward. It seems clear that Wolseley's brief illness before he had departed from England had incapacitated him at a crucial moment for it resulted in him not giving his usual attention to the issue of logistics. Indeed, this area had been largely left in the hands of Wolseley's Chief of Staff, Adye, who certainly did not regard such mundane matters of much consequence. The results, once at Ismailia, were predictable and although Wolseley cannot be blamed for his inability to involve himself in the supply issue when he was ill, it is somewhat surprising that it was not until the problem was acute that he threw his energies at assessing and resolving the lack of supplies at the front.

Adye made two crucial errors in the early stages of planning. First, despite Wolseley telling him of the importance of regimental transport, Adye did not insist on each battalion embarking with its own equipment and regimental transport; the result was that men were embarked on one ship whilst their stores went in another vessel. The situation at Ismailia, once men and stores had arrived, was at best chaotic, at worse shambolic. In addition, Adye foolishly, if perhaps naively, relied on the Ottomans to supply the force with sufficient transport mules to move supplies forward from Ismailia to the front line as the British advanced along the Sweetwater Canal. The Sultan of Turkey, however, decided to play politics and rather than help the British he placed an embargo on the exportation of all animals until the campaign was nearly over. The result was that the expedition had to turn to other sources. Mules were ordered from Spain, Italy and even America, but all arrived too late and although some mules were received from Cyprus, they were not in sufficient numbers and of those which did arrive nearly a quarter were found to be useless for any sort of work. Furthermore, the expedition really struggled to obtain the right number and quality of mule drivers, and all this meant that it took an excessive amount of time to organize an efficient train of mules to move supplies forward. Wolseley was to write to his wife that the purchase of thousands of mules did not constitute a transport service whilst the Commissary-General, Sir Edward Morris, was far more damming when he wrote, 'Drivers, collected anyhow, under varied or no agreements, on different rates of pay, without clothing, equipment of regulations: mules, unfit for immediate service, unmarked, unregistered, unshod, without fitted harness or saddles, and in some instances without head collars, are worse than useless; they are an embarrassment'.[48] Wolseley was disdainful of the troops from the Indian contingent, but fortunately they did bring with them 2,500 mules which were at least able to move their own supplies forward. The result of all these failings was that supplies sat at the dockside at Ismailia.

All these problems resulted in the expedition not only experiencing unnecessary delays but also hardships for the troops further forward suffered from shortages of both food and supplies. Wolseley was forced to throw his energies into the only two other means of transporting stores forward: those being the Sweetwater Canal and the railway. Yet the enemy had built dams at Magfar and elsewhere and the destruction of these substantial barriers delayed the ability of the British to use the Canal to move supplies. Throughout the campaign Wolseley was only able to use the Canal to move 75 tons of supplies per day, which was insufficient to build up supplies at Kassassin. To compound the problem, the Egyptians had damaged the railway line and the British struggled to get the line up and running again. The Railway Company was put in the hands of Major W.A.J. Wallace, RE, who was the only railway expert available. The Royal Engineers cleared damaged track, constituted trains, and even built two short lines from Ismailia station to the wharf, where most of the supplies were being held up. However, it was not until 28 August that the railway began to deliver supplies forward in large quantities and hence Wolseley was forced to delay any further advance until sufficient men and supplies had arrived at Kassassin. By 6 September 250 tons of supplies per day were being transported by train and over the whole campaign the railway moved 9,000 tons of supplies to the front in less than a month; without this effort it is certain that the campaign would have dragged on for many more weeks.

Ever keen to learn lessons, Wolseley was to write after the campaign, 'The next time I come on any expedition I shall insist upon having a full staff of engine drivers, traffic-managers etc. The R.E. are most willing and anxious, but railway management is a trade in itself; it cannot be learnt in a day, and special knowledge will not serve as a substitute for it.' Despite these words, it is apparent that Wallace and his small team had managed a miracle for on 7 September Wolseley was able to write to Cambridge that,

> ... I have now seven locomotives at work, and the army front is consequently well supplied, and the foundations of a reserve depot have been laid down. I am consequently about to bid farewell to Ismailia and form my camp at Kassassin ... Everyone will be in motion for the front at the same time and by the time I have pushed my reconnaissances sufficiently well home and made my first plans, all will be concentrated and ready for an advance upon the enemy.[49]

It was not just in the matter of logistics that some criticism can be directed towards Wolseley, for the medical facilities were in no way near the standard Wolseley would have wished for, nor had been delivered in his earlier campaigns. Again, some of the problems can be attributed to Wolseley's incapacitation at a critical moment in the logistical planning of the expedition but the problems were real and there is no doubt both British wounded, dying and sick suffered unnecessarily during the campaign, as did the medical staff themselves, as described by Dr Alex S. Rose to his father. Rose wrote of how the medical department lacked double-lined tents to keep the worse effects of the heat from their patients and both staff and patients had to endure appalling food and water. He went onto state that the shortage of transport animals hindered the movement of hospital stores, left the staff exhausted after moving camps and impaired the care of the mounting toll of those sick from heat exhaustion and other illnesses. Rose claimed that 'The transport service had somehow broken down, the result being that we were much hampered in all our movements, and sometimes left quite helpless'.[50] After the campaign the logistical and medical failings were the subject of a War Office enquiry in which Wolseley was to testify. Although lessons, such as the need for trained railway staff in future campaigns, were learnt, little blame was attached to individuals, least of all the expedition's militarily successful commander.

The government was under increasing pressure from both Parliament and the press as to why Wolseley had not advanced upon Tel-el-Kebir. Even Childers, such a supporter of Wolseley, gave broad hints in his telegrams to Wolseley of the need to move forward. Yet Wolseley remained steadfast and refused to be drawn into action until his supplies and men were in place. By the end of August, the Indian contingent, which included Wolseley's brother Colonel George Wolseley, was in place and Alison's Highland Brigade, under the command of the still disgruntled Hamley was due to arrive soon. With the railway now delivering sufficient supplies, Wolseley was at last in a position to consider his plan of attack, although he was upset and disappointed to have to leave Evelyn Wood and his force outside of Alexandria, for he could not risk leaving the city open to assault. On 7 September Wolseley even wrote to Lady Wolseley informing her of his resolve upon '… fighting Arabi next Tuesday or Wednesday, perhaps on both days, for he has two lines of entrenchments, and he may take two days of hammering'.[51] However, a new Egyptian assault upon the British position at Kassassin provided Wolseley with not only a fresh opportunity but also a radical plan for his final assault.

Whilst Wolseley had been building up supplies and moving troops to his forward base at Kassassin, the enemy had remained behind the fortifications of Tel-el-Kebir. Arabi had not taken any offensive action against the British supply lines and had made no attempt to disrupt fresh water supplies. Instead, Arabi had relied on intelligence reports from Bedouin scouts that the enemy's position at Kassassin was weak and vulnerable to an early morning surprise attack. The truth was that Wolseley already had 8,000 troops there, with the Guards, artillery, and cavalry nearby and able to reinforce Kassassin if required. So, with his faulty intelligence Arabi, in the early hours of 9 September, launched a two-pronged attack against the British, with troops from Tel-el-Kebir and from a smaller base at Saliheen to the north. In total Arabi's force was comprised of eighteen battalions of infantry, thirty artillery pieces and a substantial mounted force.

The British first discovered the surprise assault at around 5am when forward outpost patrols of the 13th Bengal Lancers first made contact. As riders rode back to Kassassin, to warn of the impending assault, the remaining Lancers made a fighting retreat. Arabi continued to move forward heading for the British right flank held by Graham and his now seasoned troops. Forewarned, the British were in full battle order by around 7am and ready for the Egyptian attack. This was first seen in an artillery bombardment of the British camp, which, fortunately, caused few casualties. Drury Lowe utilized the whole of the Indian Cavalry Contingent, as well as Baker Russell's 1st Cavalry Brigade, along with Royal Horse Artillery (RHA) to hamper the Egyptian advance and prevent the enemy from outflanking the British position.

The Egyptians advanced on each side of the railway and canal and moved to within 800 yards of the British front line but were stalled here by British artillery and rifle fire, which also silenced Arabi's guns. A large body of the enemy sought cover behind the sandhills from where they directed a heavy fire upon the British. At 7.45am Graham, in consultation with Willis, ordered a general advance. The Royal Marine Light Infantry (RMLI) and the Royal

Rifle Corps attacked along the line of the canal and railway whilst the Yorks and Lancs moved against the concentration of enemy infantry on the sandhills. Although outnumbered, the superior fire of the British soon dislodged the Egyptians and Graham pushed his forces on and by 10.30am the enemy was in full retreat back to the lines of Tel-el-Kebir. Indeed, it was a total rout with many of the Egyptian infantry discarding their boots so as to run faster across the sand. British casualties were three dead and seventy-seven wounded whilst the Egyptian losses ran into the hundreds and a further three artillery pieces were captured by the British.

Wolseley was informed by Willis early on the morning of 9 September of the unexpected Egyptian attack and that he had ordered up the Guards Brigade to support Graham's position. Clearly Willis had learnt from the wrath that Wolseley had directed towards him after his panicked response to the first enemy assault upon Kassassin. On hearing the news Wolseley and his staff immediately boarded a train from Ismailia, travelling in an open cattle truck, to travel the 22 miles to the front line. On arrival, Wolseley discovered that the enemy had been beaten and was already being driven back to Tel-el-Kebir. For many of his officers, including Buller and Adye, this second success at Kassassin offered the British a great opportunity to continue the attack and assault Tel-el-Kebir that day. Willis was dawdling on whether to attack, stand his ground or return to Kassassin, but Wolseley put an end to any debate and to the disgruntlement of many, including the accompanying press, called a halt to the pursuit at 5,000 yards from the Egyptian fortifications and just out of range of the enemy's artillery. He quickly ordered outposts to be stationed in the hills whilst the remainder of the army returned to camp. Whilst Wolseley felt it was likely that an assault on the afternoon of 9 September would have been successful, he feared it would be at a high cost in British dead. In addition, when the Guards Brigade under the Duke of Connaught arrived late in the day all the men, including the Duke himself, were utterly exhausted by their march due to the heat and badly required rest. Finally, Wolseley did not think his force was strong enough at that moment to prevent Arabi fleeing from Tel-el-Kebir with a substantial force that might then deny or delay Wolseley's entry into Cairo and thus prolong the war. Wolseley knew that he would need to not only take Tel-el-Kebir but also have enough troops, both infantry and cavalry, with which to surround the fortification to be able to claim a complete victory. This, he felt, was the only way to ensure a quick end to the war. Thus, despite yet more pressure placed upon him Wolseley refused to move on the Egyptian position until he had a sufficient force and adequate intelligence on what he might encounter.

Wolseley used the opportunity given to him on the afternoon of 9 September to take a view of Tel-el-Kebir, or 'the big hill' as it was known by the locals for even though it was only on a slight elevation it held a commanding position. Wolseley was impressed by how strong and well-constructed the fortifications looked. Using a telescope, he surveyed the earthworks over which thousands of 'fellahin', or peasants had worked for weeks. These men had constructed gravel sand parapets to 4 to 6ft in height which were surrounded with ditches, many over 10ft wide. Wolseley could not make out how deep these ditches were, but they extended from the Sweetwater Canal for nearly four miles into the desert. At intervals there were salient redoubts which provided a commanding view on each flank. Behind these defences were interior works, which ran for two miles of shelter trenches, rifle pits and artillery pieces. British intelligence was that Tel-el-Kebir was held by 20,000 regular Egyptian troops, supported by 6,000 irregulars, mainly Bedouin tribesmen, 2,500 cavalry and around 75 artillery pieces. Although the defences were not yet finished in the northern section, in the few weeks Arabi had been given the works were truly a remarkable feat of engineering and human toil.

The day after the second battle of Kassassin, 10 September, Wolseley's position was strengthened by the arrival of a Naval Brigade, consisting of 15 officers, 199 sailors and six Gatling guns. The following day the Indian infantry and the 1st Battalion of the Seaforth Highlanders marched into camp to complete the Indian Contingent. Finally in the late afternoon of 11 September Alison and Hamley arrived with the Highland Brigade of the 2nd Division. Hamley, still irritated by being used as a dupe by Wolseley outside of Alexandria was now furious that his men had been forced to march during the heat of the day and he sought out Wolseley to berate him. At first Wolseley allowed the subordinate Hamley to have his rant, but he soon became annoyed at Hamley's tone and abruptly ended the conversation by stating to Hamley he would now not have Macpherson's Indian troops under his command for the two units would be positioned either side of the Sweetwater Canal. Outraged Hamley took his angst to Sir John Adye in his capacity as Chief of Staff, claiming that to lose Macpherson's troops was yet another slur upon him and Hamley claimed that he felt Wolseley was treating him shamefully. Adye raised Hamley's objections with Wolseley, who did alter his plans for the assault to somewhat accommodate Hamley but the whole incident had left further ill-feeling between Hamley and Wolseley, and their relationship never recovered. With the new arrivals Wolseley now had over 17,000 troops at his command, including artillery and cavalry units. It was a force substantially smaller than that of the enemy's, but Wolseley knew that with Wood's command destined to remain positioned outside of Alexandria the force at Kassassin would now not increase. He would have to work with what he had, and he knew the time for an attack on Arabi's stronghold was imminent.

Wolseley realized that any assault upon the Tel-el-Kebir defences, across the flat, open, desert ground which was devoid of any natural cover, would be met by a thunderous response and a likely high cost in British lives. With much to ponder as he retired to bed on the night of 9 September, Wolseley resolved to make a very early start the next day to view his objective once again. Over the next two mornings Wolseley rose well before dawn and with a small contingent, or bodyguard, of Bengal Lancers, along with a few trusted comrades, including his brother George, he rode out to survey the Egyptian lines. What was soon apparent to Wolseley's one good eye was that the first mounted sentinels left the Egyptian position to go on forward reconnaissance each day just after dawn and crucially there were apparently no outriders at night to warn of a British advance. This fact alone decided Wolseley's plan for he now resolved upon a night march across the intervening desert, a distance of six miles, with his full force so to arrive at the parapets of Tel-el-Kebir just before dawn. This was perhaps the biggest military gamble that Wolseley made in his lengthy career for to successfully coordinate a night march of a large body of troops was notoriously difficult and prone to error, confusion and potential disaster and under the current Commander-in-Chief, the Duke of Cambridge, night marches were not even practised. Yet his mind was made up and on the morning of 12 September Wolseley once again rose early and with his Staff and brigade commanders rode into the desert to a position Wolseley christened Ninth Hill, a sandy mound which had been at the centre of the fighting of 9 September. Here all his officers convened by 4pm and from there they galloped, undetected, to within 800 yards of the enemy's lines and waited patiently for the dawn to appear.

At 5.45am the first streaks of light could be seen in the east and through the early morning gloom the first stirrings of the Egyptian sentries were visible. Turning to his commanders Wolseley said, 'Note the time! Our attack must be delivered before this hour tomorrow morning, otherwise those vedettes [sentries] will detect our presence'.[52] Although many, including Adye and Hamley, were shocked, if not appalled to hear of Wolseley's plan, at that moment they kept their counsel, probably fearful of Wolseley's wrath. Others, such as Buller, would later privately share their concerns with Wolseley for there was a general and shared belief that inexperienced young soldiers would not be able to maintain order and discipline on a night march. Wolseley thought a night march and a surprise dawn attack were his only option for he felt that he did not possess enough troops or artillery for a sustained attack, and he was very fearful that a daylight assault would result in hundreds of British dead and wounded. He was mindful that the medical facilities were already struggling, and large numbers of casualties would undoubtedly place the Army doctors and their staff at breaking point. Finally, Wolseley also knew that the military reforms, of which he had been such an advocate, would be under the microscope for it would be the first time battalions would march into battle with men of the Reserve, and he strongly felt that he had to back not only the reform but also his men. Wolseley shared his thoughts with his wife two nights before the impending battle when he wrote, 'If my plan succeeds, it will be the end of Arabi, and my losses will be light. Everything depends upon the steadiness of the infantry. If they are steady in the dark – a very crucial trial – I must succeed. Otherwise, I might fail altogether, or achieve very little. You can fancy that this responsibility tells a little upon me, but I don't think any soul here thinks so.'[53]

As the sun began to come up in the sky more of the Egyptian defences became visible and Wolseley admitted to the collection of his commanders that he had no idea how deep the ditches were and that he had no firm intelligence on the number of the enemy's artillery pieces. However, he surmised that he thought most would be positioned on the right near the Canal, stating that he thought it unlikely the Egyptians would have move heavy guns across the desert to cover their left flank, and in this judgement, he was proved to be correct. Wolseley then, displaying his usual determination and stoicism, went onto explain his plans for the forthcoming attack and each man's role within it. He stated that the attack would be concentrated on the left centre of the enemy lines. The Indian Contingent, including the mobile Bengal Lancers, were to advance further to the left of the British, beyond the Canal and swing round behind Tel-el-Kebir, to not only stop the retreat of any Egyptian units but also to seize the important rail junction at Zagazig, which led directly to Cairo. Wolseley knew that he had to follow up a successful action with the greatest rapidity in order, for both political and military reasons, to seize Cairo. By doing so it would prevent the still sizeable enemy units stationed in Cairo, Kafr ed-Dauar, Damietta, Rosetta and Es-Salihiyeh from unifying and offering a formidable force in the field. Thus, the task given to the Indian Contingent was of the upmost importance for Wolseley to achieve a quick end to the war.

Of the remaining troops, Wolseley explained the 1st Division, under Willis's command, would be on the right with Graham's brigade leading and the Guards behind. Wolseley was reluctant to place the Guards at the forefront of the attack, even though he considered them his best troops, for he could not risk the life of the Queen's favourite son, the Duke of Connaught, in the assault. To the rear of the 1st Division Wolseley placed mounted troops and two batteries of Royal Horse Artillery who were ordered to swing around the enemy's left and threaten the defenders from the rear and to pursue any retreating Egyptians. The 2nd Division would be on the left with Alison's Highlanders in the front.

As a sop to Hamley's ego, Wolseley did concede that the King's Royal Rifles and the DCLI Battalions, as well as the Naval Brigade would be moved to Hamley's command and would be in the rear of the Highlanders to support their advance. Wolseley pointedly, in front of all present, spoke directly to Hamley and told him firmly that once his Highlanders had scaled the Egyptian parapets, they were to halt their advance until the reserve infantry could be brought up to support a push into the interior defences. Wolseley's disdain for Hamley was such that he even stated to the commander of the 1st Brigade that, 'Alison will be with his brigade. You go where you please.'[54]

The troops were to cover the night march in their order of battle for no adjustments could be made as their neared the enemy position. Wolseley deliberately placed Brigadier-General Goodenough's forty-two artillery pieces in the centre, between the troops of the 1st and 2nd Divisions and this seems to have been Wolseley's once concession to a consideration that some troops might panic whilst on the night march. If this was to occur the positioning of the artillery would, it was hoped, stop the panic spreading between the two divisions. Wolseley left the exact formation of the infantry march to the divisional commander's discretion with Willis deciding upon the drill-book formation of half battalions in columns of companies, whilst Hamley decided to advance in half-battalions of double company columns. The formations are shown below. This would result in each division being unaware of the other as they reached the point of attack, but this was yet to be realized as the plans for the line of march were agreed upon.

| Hamley's 2nd Division | Willis's 1st Division |
|---|---|
| —— —— —— —— | —— —— |
| —— —— —— —— | —— —— |
| | —— —— |
| | —— —— |

Specifically, within Hamley's division the Highland Brigade was placed in the following formation:

| HIGHLAND LIGHT INFANTRY | BLACK WATCH | CAMERON HIGHLANDERS | GORDON HIGHLANDERS |
|---|---|---|---|
| Left Half Battalion | Left Half Battalion | Left Half Battalion | Left Half Battalion |
| Deploying Interval | | Deploying Interval | Deploying Interval |
| Right Half Battalion | Right Half Battalion | Right Half Battalion | Right Half Battalion |

Wolseley concluded his briefing with the words 'Well gentlemen, don't talk about it [the plan of attack] until the orders are issued. I wish you all luck.'[55] There was no debate and Wolseley made it clear that his words were final. Despite the outward show of confidence Wolseley did confide later that day to Major Neville Lyttelton, an aide to Adye, that he expected to win the battle but expected to lose 1,200 men. The remainder of the day was spent issuing orders to the various units and explaining the order of march and Wolseley specifically focused on how he would navigate with his army through the night. He had earlier ordered the Royal Engineers to erect a line of telegraph poles to act as guideposts which ran west for 1,000 yards from 'Ninth Hill', just above the Kassassin camp and these would be utilized to assemble the troops and then direct them in the first stage of the night march. Wolseley also turned to 29-year-old Lieutenant Wyatt Rawson RN, the Royal Navy *aide-de-camp*, who despite his young age had already lived a full and adventurous life. Rawson had served with Wolseley in the Asante Campaign where he had been shot in the leg on the march to Kumasi. The previous year Rawson had achieved national fame when he made an unsuccessful attempt to reach the North Pole and had received many plaudits for his action in trekking across ice to rescue a Danish dog-driver. Earlier reconnaissance had charted the stars necessary to guide the army to Tel-el-Kebir and Wolseley now tasked the Royal Navy officer to plot the course across the 'sea of sand'.

Wolseley had chosen Rawson wisely for he possessed a maturity and assurance that appealed to Wolseley and Rawson swelled with confidence. When at the start of the night march Captain Edward Hutton asked Rawson how he seemed to know the way to guide the force, Rawson pointed to the sky and said, 'You see those two stars right in front of is, and a third directly below – I am steering by them'.[56] Despite his confidence Rawson had been set a difficult task for it was not until 1884 that the British Army were provided with luminous compasses and his work was made harder for the night sky was covered with intermittent clouds which only provided Rawson with the occasional glimpse of the stars. Even with these handicaps, Rawson achieved all that Wolseley asked of him and much of the success of the assault can be attributed to his navigational skill.

It was not until 3pm on the afternoon before the advance that the troops were collectively informed that they would moving out that night to attack the enemy's stronghold. The commissariat stores were then frantically busy as men collected 200 rounds of ammunition and two days' rations to carry into battle. The men seemed genuinely relieved, even pleased, that at last the waiting was over and that a decisive action was now imminent. Wolseley made a great effort to ride around the camp, brimming with his usual outward display of confidence and offering cheerful words of encouragement and advice to all. To maintain deception the camp's long lines of tents were not struck until after dark, but campfires were kept burning to convince enemy scouts that the British had no plans to attack. At around 11pm the men were formed up in line of the advance at or near 'Ninth Hill' and told to keep silent. No smoking was allowed and loose cartridges, if found, were immediately confiscated and men rebuked. Rifles were unloaded and orders were given that they must remain so on the march. The men must have been reflective and nervous as they waited for the order to advance westward. This finally came at 1.30am in muffled voices which travelled around the various columns and the men sent off.

Plan for the advance was for the left-hand brigade to direct the march as it moved parallel to the railway and 2,000 yards north of it. The headquarters Staff, including Wolseley was behind supported by an escort. To the right and in the centre was the artillery and the right-hand brigade was directed by their divisional commander, Graham. Wolseley's aim was to bring his army to within charging distance, around 300 yards, of the Egyptian position just as dawn emerged. Yet the night was pitch dark, and as the men shuffled across the desert plain a potential disaster almost overtook the march, for the sound of the staff officers' horses was mistaken for enemy units and the centre halted. The two columns on the flanks, 1st and 2nd Divisions did not receive the order to halt and kept on walking. In the darkness the two flanking columns moved ever closer and almost collided into each other. It was at this moment that Wolseley's order to march with unloaded rifles paid off and order was quickly restored as alert officers realized what had happened. Wolseley himself maintained a constant check along the line of march checking on a repeater watch, which had been given to him by Lord Airey, for timing was so important to the success of the attack. Butler, who was by Wolseley's side throughout recalled how the constant striking of the watch seemed to increase Wolseley's inner tension which was apparently palatable.

At 3am Wolseley called a brief halt for the army to ensure the men were positioned correctly and for them to drink and ready themselves. With nerves running high, one Highlander, who had more than water in his canteen, became inebriated and broke out in uncontrollable laughter. He was rapidly overpowered and silenced by his colleagues and removed to the rear to sober up. As the army recommenced its advance the direction of the march went slightly astray from Wolseley's strict plan and the left-hand brigade moved more to the right. Rawson was finding that navigation via the stars was proving problematic for the night sky was constantly obscured by cloud with only the North Star and the Little Bear visible all night. It was thus only possible to take a reading on successive stars which appeared to be directly in front when the North Star was on the right-hand side. As the stars moved across the sky in a north-westerly direction to set, so the British advance veered to the right too. In this slight error Wolseley's luck stayed with him for both he and the various reconnaissance units had missed the position of an Egyptian redoubt with four artillery pieces and if the march had kept on its correct path, then it would have passed close to this redoubt, which was 1,000 yards ahead of the main enemy entrenchments. It seems very likely that the Egyptians in this advanced redoubt would have been alerted to the British attack and that their comrades in the main defences would have thus been forewarned. Fire would have been unleashed from Tel-el-Kebir at a distance of 1,000 yards and the British would have been forced to cross this distance, which was devoid of cover, and it is almost certain that casualties would have been high. The navigational error also had the benefit of shifting the whole advance further to the right and meant that much of the attack would now be against less well-constructed defences. A staff officer wrote after the battle, 'That night the stars in their courses fought against Arabi, not as a figure of speech but literally'. Certainly, the Gods were on Wolseley's side that night.[57]

At 4.50am, as the troops were forming up for the final dressing of the line before the attack, the horizon was lit up in the east. This caused some consternation amongst both the men and the Staff for the initial thought was that the march had fallen behind schedule and that the light was the first rays of dawn, and thus the attack would be going in late and was likely to be detected. However, after a few minutes the light faded and then disappeared, and the desert was returned to darkness. In fact, the light had been that of a comet, which had also been seen over southern Europe. For years afterwards Wolseley was to castigate himself for not knowing that a comet was due that night, such was his attention to detail.

Now the men were in position to attack. Yet the nature of the ground over which the men had passed had perhaps inevitably meant that rather than a uniform front, the units reached the position to launch the attack in the following irregular echelon, with the left thrown forward thus -

**Highland Brigade**

**Artillery**

**2nd Brigade**
**(1st Division)**

**Cavalry**

In the darkness neither the Highland Brigade, led by Alison, or the 2nd Brigade under the command of Graham knew the other's exact position and although the Highlanders were now within the charging distance of 300 yards, Graham's troops were still roughly 900 yards from the enemy's parapet. This would delay the attack on the right and meant that the first minutes of the battle were to belong to the Highlanders.

Just before 5am on the morning of 13 September 1882 the order to attack was given. Bulgers sounded and with cheering from the Highlanders the men rushed towards the earthworks in two long waves for the half-battalion double columns that Hamley had ordered had closed in on each other in the darkness. Hamley had positioned himself between these two columns and he was able to check the advance of the rear companies of the Gordon and Cameron Highlanders and form them into a reserve. At the sound of the bulgers a few isolated shots had rung out from the defences and at a distance of 150 yards out the enemy's pickets had begun a more directed fire at the charging wave of Highlanders and this soon turned into a blaze of fire along the whole Egyptian line. The fire did not slow the attack and with bayonets fixed the first wave of Scotsmen reached the parapets. Here the loose sand and steep slope made it difficult for the assaulting troops to gain a foothold and the Egyptians fired down on their adversaries, claiming several victims. The first men to mount the parapet were Lieutenant Brooks and Private Donald Cameron, both of whom fell dead, riddled with bullets, but gradually more troops reached the summit to jump down inside the defences and engage the enemy with the bayonet.

In this section the Highlanders met strong resistance and although some managed to jump down into the interior of the defences and engaged the enemy in brutal hand-to-hand combat, regiments became mixed together and the sheer numbers of the defenders pushed many of the attackers back, including the brigade commander, Sir Archibald Alison. Those of the brigade still in the interior defences were channelled into a narrow cone or wedge formation as the enemy pressed them from the sides and front. Hamley himself intervened and personally led forward the reserves, which Alison again led over the parapet and despite having his horse shot from under him, Alison and his men gradually began to push the Egyptian infantry back. Alison was to later write of the defenders:

> I must do justice to those much maligned Egyptian soldiers. I never saw men fight more steadily. They were falling back on an inner line of works which we had taken in flank and at every re-entering angle, at every battery and redoubt, they rallied and renewed the fight. Five or six times we had to close on them with the bayonet …[58]

To the left of this position the Highland Light Infantry (HLI) had an even tougher fight on their hands for here the defences were formidable. The ditch was deeper, and the earthworks were the steepest and highest of any point in the outer perimeter. As the men of HLI struggled to gain traction up the sandy slopes, the defenders, who here were Nubian troops, regarded as Arabi's most tenacious and brave men, waited until the attackers had grouped before firing volleys down into them, causing many casualties. The HLI were pushed back, but they rallied and charged again and despite heroic and determined resistance from the Nubian troops, with artillery support, the HLI gradually pushed the defenders back.

On the right the British attack was much more successful. Led by Graham himself the advance was a good 10 minutes after the initial assault from the Highlanders and had to cover over 900 yards of open ground against an enemy who was now fully alerted to the British attack. A Colonel Field left an account of the first moments of the charge by the 2nd Brigade when he wrote,

> It seemed to me that the Egyptian lines were 800 to 1,000 yards distant, and this being the case, we were ordered to lie down and fix bayonets. Four companies were then extended as a firing line, followed by the remaining four as support. We advanced by rushes, lying down to fire. The enemy's bullets were still falling thickly and the entrenchments, and our own firing line still blurred with smoke, when the bugles, to the relief I think, of everybody, sounded the charge. The whole line, every man burning to get at the Egyptians, rushed forward at the double with a continuous shout or roar rather than a cheer. As we approached the misty outline of the parapet at a few yards distance there was a slackening of fire - firing line had at that moment rushed it, followed closely by the supports, and after a minute or two's lay 'with butt and baynit' that part of the works was ours.[59]

The men of the Royal Irish, the Yorks and Lancs, and the Royal Marines, with Graham at the forefront, overwhelmed the first defences, which, unlike the section which the HLI had attacked, were relative weak in their construction. The Egyptians regrouped 60 yards back, but again, as in the left-hand attack, the infantry was supported by artillery and then horse artillery which managed to spur their horses over the captured parapets and lay down a deadly canister fire against any groups of the enemy that tried to make a stand. In a letter to a fellow officer, Lieutenant L. Perry of the Royal Artillery left a vivid account of this action:

> A cheer on our left told us of the assault of the first line of entrenchments, which fell at once; and we then came up to it and found a parapet about 4 feet high with ditches on both sides. The gunners at once set to work to pull this down with pick and shovel, the enemy meanwhile firing heavily from the second line. As soon as I could get my horse over I did, and found myself in the enemy's camp, surrounded with dead and dying of both sides. To those we paid no attention ... in about ten minutes the battery crossed, and we advanced about 500 yards at a sharp trot to the 2nd line, against which we came into action, from rising ground, about 500 yards range. The enemy was now in full retreat and in the upmost confusion, so that after a few rounds the 'cease firing' sounded.[60]

Graham's advance was now supported by the Guards, led by the Duke of Connaught, and the northern Egyptian defences crumbled.

Arabi had been awoken by the first sounds of the British attack and although he had positioned a substantial reserve in the rear, he failed to get them to move forward before the defences at the perimeter collapsed under the strength of the British assault. Although the cavalry reserve made a brief appearance, Wolseley sent the 19th Hussars cantering to meet them and the Egyptians quickly turned their horses to join the general retreat. Arabi himself secured a horse and rode with his second-in-command to Belbeis from where he was able to board a train to Cairo. Once there he hoped to spur the substantial Cairo garrison to resist the British, but Wolseley was determined that he would not give Arabi time to act.

To the south of the Canal General Macpherson's Indian Contingent, supported by a mountain gun battery and the Naval Brigade with their Gatling guns, had advanced steadily, only delayed by the rough terrain over which they were forced to travel. Starting 15 minutes after the first shots from the Highland Brigade on the north side of the canal, the Seaforth Highlanders, attached to Macpherson's command moved forward to be greeted by Egyptian artillery and infantry fire. Whilst Indian infantry marched to outflank the enemy's position the lead company of the Seaforths advanced in rushes, firing controlled volleys at intervals, covering the intervening ground, until the men were called upon to fix bayonets and charge. Within moments the only enemy position to offer any resistance was taken and four artillery pieces captured. Indian infantry also took nearby villages which had been fortified by the Egyptians and for minimal losses the Indian Contingent had cleared the south bank defences in a few minutes. This allowed Macpherson to unleash the Bengal cavalry, in line with Wolseley's pre-planned instructions, to cut off the escape of the fleeing Egyptians who had abandoned their positions in the north and were attempting to escape across the Tel-el-Kebir bridge.

Despite suffering heavy casualties, Alison's Highland Brigade had regrouped and with Hamley sending forward the reserves, the Highlanders finally broke through the stubborn defences of the Nubian troops. Wolseley had earlier instructed Hamley to wait for Graham's troops to support them in any further advance, but Hamley, ignoring these instructions, decided to continue the pursuit and press home his advantage. Soon the Highlanders had taken the Egyptian main camp and moved rapidly onto capture the railway station, with small groups reaching the bridge over the canal.

The forward Egyptian redoubt which Wolseley's assault had fortuitously avoided at the start of the attack, now belatedly began to fire. The only obvious target was the commander and his Staff, whom had to duck as shells whistled close to their heads. A British battery was brought forward to engage the redoubt and its first shots denoted the enemy's magazine, which by doing so ended all Egyptian resistance north of the Canal. Wolseley now rode forward with his Staff over the parapets and through the carnage of the intense fighting inside the defences, passing the bodies of Egyptians and Highlanders alike. The sights were grisly and the pitiful cries of the wounded and dying filled the air. Wolseley arrived at Tel-el-Kebir bridge, at the rear of the Egyptian defences, at the same time as the first of Hamley's Highlanders, who despite their feats and exhaustion managed to cheer the victorious General. Here Wolseley dismounted and lit a celebratory cigar before dictating a telegram to Gladstone informing him of the crushing victory, which the Prime Minister was said to have read with tears in his eyes. In an act of reconciliation to the Duke of Cambridge, he gave the Duke's son the honour of carrying back to the War Office the official despatches reporting the success of the battle. Wolseley let himself indulge in a further five cigars, one after the other, whilst he contemplated his next action, and this rather conspicuous consumption perhaps reflected the stress and strain he had been under. Wolseley then issued his orders for the follow-up operation for he knew he had to keep the Egyptians from reforming and offering any further resistance. To reach Cairo as soon as possible was key to the quick ending of the conflict.

To this end Drury Lowe and his cavalry were ordered onto Cairo, whilst Macpherson followed up his earlier instructions of moving onto Zagazig to capture the crucial railway junction. Led by the 6th Bengal Lancers, the Indian Contingent galloped onto Zagazig where they duly captured locomotives and rolling stock, many of them full of fleeing Egyptians, and secured the vital communications hub. The Indian cavalry then moved along the Sweetwater Canal to Belbeis, where it rendezvoused with Drury Lowe's cavalry division.

Capturing the train station at Belbeis, the British and Indian units discovered that they had missed intercepting Arabi by a mere 15 minutes for he had already boarded a train and was on his way to Cairo. Exhausted by the rigours of the day the cavalry bivouacked at Belbeis for the night. Drury Lowe was hesitant to push onto Cairo without Royal Horse Artillery support, for these units had been slowed by the many narrow bridges they had to negotiate as they crossed irrigation ditches that covered the land. Both Herbert Stewart and Baker Russell urged him to push onto Cairo at first light and to follow Wolseley's orders for haste.

Long before dawn the cavalry units mounted their horses and headed towards Cairo, 39 miles away, across the desert. Despite the heat the cavalry was able to maintain a decent speed and were only slowed by native crowds shouting 'Peace, Peace!' Rather than meeting any Egyptian resistance they only encountered white flags in every village that they passed through. The sun was almost setting when Drury Lowe reached the outskirts of Cairo and stopped outside the Abbassiyeh barracks, home to several thousand Egyptian infantry. Drury Lowe accepted Herbert Stewart's offer to approach the barracks with just fifty lancers to assess the situation. With great bravado and bluff Stewart's presence convinced the garrison commander that any further resistance would be futile and within moments the enemy were surrendering in droves. A similar bluff by Captain Watson of the Royal Engineers also worked as he rode onto the Citadel, home to an additional 5,000 Egyptian troops, and their surrender was similarly agreed. By nightfall over 10,000 of the enemy had handed over their weapons and had been told by the British to simply go home. Arabi awoke on the morning of 15 September to find that he no longer had an army with which to resist and by 11am he surrendered to Drury Lowe with a quiet dignity, which he maintained throughout his subsequent captivity. All that was now required was for Wolseley to enter Cairo as the victor.

The afternoon of 13 September saw Wolseley performing one of the more sombre duties that falls upon a successful commander when visiting the dying Lieutenant Rawson, who had been mortally wounded by shrapnel during the battle. Wolseley knew how much he owed to Rawson for his own success and wrote to his wife, 'He [Rawson] was a fine plucky fellow. When I found him yesterday he was in a large tent, which was so full of wounded, some of whom were dying, that I had difficulty in getting to him. The sight was horrible. Rawson was racked with pain, but managed to mutter "General, did I not lead them straight?"'[61] These words pulled upon Wolseley's emotions, and he was genuinely moved and holding Rawson's hand he replied, 'Yes, I know you were well to the front all the time, old fellow'.[62] Rawson lingered, in great pain, for a further eight days before he passed away.

It was time to count the 'butcher's bill'. The battle had lasted less than an hour and had been a bloody and brutal encounter. Although the final casualty figure was less than Wolseley had initially feared, it was still significant. Egyptian losses were never accurately recorded but they had lost heavily defending the parapets and British canister shot had claimed many victims as they had tried to regroup to offer resistance. The correspondent of *The Standard* estimated between 2,500–3,000 Egyptian dead, with many more wounded although other sources place the figure at around 2,000. The British lost fifty-seven men killed, with nearly 70 per cent of these fatalities coming from the Highland Brigade, which reflected the intensity of their struggles on the first wave of the assault. Similarly, the Highland Brigade endured 43 per cent of the 383 men who were wounded. Despite these losses Tel-el-Kebir had been a great victory of British arms, undertaken by a commander at the height of his powers, unafraid to undertake great risks, including the night march, to secure success. Wolseley was to later write of Tel-el-Kebir, 'I do not believe that at any other point of our military history has the British Infantry distinguished itself more than upon this occasion'.[63]

Writing to his wife the day after the battle, Wolseley clearly unburdened to her his sheer relief at his success, as well as a degree of insecurity as to how he might be viewed at home. He wrote:

> Thank God all has gone well with me: I had a very nervous time of it, for I was trying a new thing, I may say, in our military annals, and its success depended entirely upon the steadiness of our infantry. Troops are seldom steady in the dark, and are so liable to panic that all such operations as that of the night before last have many elements of uncertainty about them which no foresight can entirely provide for … I hope the English people will be pleased: they never can know the difficulties an English commander has to struggle against with an army hastily thrown together without cohesion between its component parts and no organized transport.[64]

Wolseley, along with his Staff and an escort of Scots Guards, left for Zagazig on the afternoon of 14 September, hoping to arrive by train into Cairo within a few hours. However, the line was in a chaotic state, and it was not until 9pm that the train limped into Cairo station. Wolseley required a scapegoat for the continued problems with the railways, which were again causing supply problems. He found one in Hamley who had given responsibility for the hub at Zagazig. The lack of controls on the line even resulted in Wolseley's train running into the back of another, which was carrying Hamley and Alison to

Cairo. Out of spite, Wolseley ordered Hamley to remain at the town of Benha to sort out the railway mess, whilst lesser generals journeyed onwards to Cairo with Wolseley.

Wolseley decided to remain the night at the station, and he entered the city the following morning to take residence in Abdin Palace, former home of Arabi. The spacious and luxurious palace was in complete contrast to the conditions Wolseley had so recently experience, as he explained to his wife in a letter written from the Palace on 15 September, 'What a change in forty-eight hours!! From squalor and misery of the desert, with all its filth and flies, to the cool luxury of this spacious palace. Yesterday living in filth, to-day having iced champagne.'[65] Not all of Wolseley's commanders were billeted in such opulent accommodation for Wolseley told his Staff that neither Hamley nor Willis were to be given help finding billets when they finally arrived in Cairo, whilst Wolseley's favourites, such as Lt. Colonel Hugh McCalmont, stayed in magnificent palaces. Later Willis and Hamley were assigned to farmers' huts which had been formerly used to store vegetables and were consequently filthy and damp. Both men, who were now totally disgruntled to be treated in this rather childish manner by Wolseley, declined their new accommodation and retired to their tents. In the case of Hamley, Wolseley's relationship with him had completely broken down and Wolseley still clearly held a grudge against Willis for his rather panicked command at the first battle of Kassassin. Yet both these men had fought bravely (even if they had been in the shadow of their respective brigade commanders, Alison and Graham) at Tel-el-Kebir and to have been treated so poorly seems rather petty on Wolseley's part. The bitterness between Hamley and Wolseley was to continue into the next decade and the continued rancour reflected poorly on both men.

Once settled in Abdin Palace, and upon hearing that all armed Egyptian resistance across the country was over, Wolseley telegraphed Childers with the news 'The war is over in Egypt; send no more men from England'.[66] On leaving London, Wolseley had confidently predicted to both Cambridge and the Secretary of State for War, that the war would be won by 16 September. He was a day early. Wolseley received a telegram from Gladstone which read 'In the name of Her Majesty and with lively pleasure I propose to you that you should receive a peerage in acknowledgement of your distinguished service'.[67] This was what Wolseley had been working towards and he realized that it would also see an increase in his pension and undoubtedly other financial rewards, However, he knew that even a promise from Gladstone might not be enough to overcome royal opposition.

Childers wrote to Wolseley after Tel-el-Kebir to state that the battle had been 'the most perfect military achievement that England has seen for many a long year. Abroad we have quite regained our military reputation [after battlefield losses in both Zululand and Afghanistan in 1879 and 1880 respectively] ... We owe this to your skill and energy, and to the valour of the Army.'[68] In addition to this praise Wolseley received the additional boost of support from the Duke of Connaught when he wrote to his mother, the Queen,

> Sir Garnet has been most kind to me all the time I have been under his orders, and I don't wish to serve under a pleasanter chief, or one in whom one feels greater confidence. He is the least fussy General I have ever served under, and his orders are short and clear, he never interferes with one and always gives one credit for what one does.[69]

These words seem to have removed the last of Victoria's resistance to Wolseley's peerage.

Wolseley was to enjoy the opulence of his royal residence for a little over a week, for on the afternoon of 25 September Tewfik, the Khedive, made a triumphant return to Cairo and rode through the city with the Duke of Connaught given the place of honour, at the behest of Victoria. Wolseley sat in the carriage with his back to the horses as they passed along lines of cheering troops and civilians before reaching the Ismailia Palace. It was not clear for whom the crowds cheered, the Khedive or Wolseley. The day finished with a thunderous and spectacular firework display and the pinning upon Wolseley's chest of the Sultan's highest award, the Grand Cross of the Osmanieh. Wolseley's mind must have drifted to a consideration of what other accolades he could expect on his return to England.

In his second official despatch after Tel-el-Kebir Wolseley rather deviously decided to over-emphasis the role of the Royal Irish and the Guards Brigade for his own advantage. He was at last learning to play the political game and was working hard to secure a peerage. The situation in Ireland had resulted in huge political upheavals for the Gladstone government. This was partly due to the recent imprisonment of the Irish Independence MP, Charles Stuart Parnell, in the so-called Kilmainham 'treaty' of April 1882 and the turmoil caused by the Phoenix Park murders of 6 May 1882, alongside agrarian agitation over land reforms. So, London, and particularly Gladstone, was delighted to read of Wolseley's positive reports of Irish soldiery, which deflected somewhat from the political crisis at the time. Wolseley also over-stressed the support given by the Guards Brigade, under the command of the Duke of Connaught, to Graham's advance. Wolseley, not knowing of Connaught's letter to his mother, feared resistance from the Queen and the Duke of Cambridge to Gladstone's attempts to secure his peerage. Therefore, by heaping praise on Connaught and Cambridge's son, Fitzgeorge, Wolseley hoped to nullify any royal opposition.

Wolseley's rather sycophantic and dubious approach backfired on him somewhat for the Royal Marines and the York and Lancs, who fought in the front line of Graham's assault, were aggrieved, and felt that their efforts had now been overlooked. This was even more the case with the Highland regiments who had taken the brunt of the brutal hand-to-hand fighting, and the Scottish press were incensed that their troops had not received the praise they were due from Wolseley. In his second despatch after the battle Wolseley mentioned only that the Highlanders had stormed the parapets in a 'dashing manner' and that south of the canal the 'most gallant' Seaforth Highlanders had taken the enemy line in an 'impetuous onslaught'.[70] The Edinburgh *Daily Review* and *The Scotsman* were scathing in their attacks against Wolseley whilst at Fort William a public gathering even passed a resolution protesting at Wolseley's dispatch and condemning the slight done to the Highland regiments. The *Aberdeen Journal* correctly suspected that the praise Wolseley had heaped on the Irish troops was a reflection of political sensitivities and that this 'praise' was needed 'when conciliatory and healing measures are the order of the day'.[71] Once the furore had died down Wolseley did acknowledge that the Highland Brigade had been the first over the Egyptian parapets.

Additionally, the Highland troops felt upset for many of the troops after the battle were assigned burial duty and although this unpleasant job was and is always a necessary feature of the aftermath of battle, many thought that after enduring the most bitter of fighting this task should had been given to other troops. Perhaps Wolseley's antipathy towards Hamley had placed the Highlanders in this unenvious role. The gruesome task of burial went on for four full days and after at least having the benefit of plentiful supplies in Arabi's former camp, the Scotsmen were moved to guard important railway sites with the Black Watch sent to garrison Belbeis and the Gordons sent to Tantah. Due to continued problems transporting supplies the Black Watch suffered for eight days without tents and with only hard biscuits to eat and muddy canal water to drink. Corporal Robertson writing in the *Kinross-shire Advertiser* stated that 'Our luxuries were the mosquitoes and sandflies who did not forget to take it out of our bare legs at night'.[72] The conditions in which these troops were exposed to were insanitary, and dysentery and ophthalmia ripped through the ranks. The Gordons remained at Tantah for 12 days and in that time five officers and 140 men fell so sick they had to be sent down the line for treatment. Both the supply issues and the poor and inadequate medical provision were to be at the heart of Parliamentary examinations at the end of the year and these allowed Wolseley to deflect some of the criticism that may have come his way to the Army Hospital Corp and the Commissariat. As Wolseley enjoyed the opulence of the Abdin Palace, his Highland troops endured the conditions at Belbeis and Tantah and these men might have been less forgiving of Wolseley for their predicament than the British public were.

On the last day of 1882 Arabi and some of his closest associates, who had been found guilty of treason in a trial on 3 December, left Egypt for exile in Ceylon. Coincidently, writing in his diary on this same day, Wolseley's last entry for 1882 reads 'God has been good to me this year ... my constant prayer is that he will not, or rather may not punish me in this world by defeat'.[73] Wolseley was now at the pinnacle of his personal and professional prestige. From here the only way was down, and the next few years would see Wolseley return to the desert where his luck would finally fail him.

## Chapter 5

# Final Field Command

Wolseley left Egypt for England on 21 October 1882, leaving a garrison of 12,000 British troops behind, under the command of Alison, to secure the Khedive's still-fragile position. Wolseley received a tumultuous welcome from an enormous crowd of well-wishers when he arrived at Charing Cross Station a week later. Among the throng were his wife Louisa and Prime Minister Gladstone whose government were still basking in Wolseley's military triumph. The Duke of Cambridge himself had to use his substantial bulk to clear a way through the crowds for Wolseley to get to his carriage and for a brief period in their often-turbulent relationship the two men were at peace and happy to share the success of British arms.

Of greater importance was that Wolseley had at last succeeded in gaining the respect of his monarch. Undoubtedly the favourable letters sent to Victoria by her serving son the Duke of Connaught had transformed her opinion of Wolseley, not just as a general but as a person. There was now no royal opposition to Wolseley being elevated to the peerage and he received the title of Lord Wolseley of Cairo, with a grant of £30,000. He was also promoted to the rank of full general. Furthermore, Wolseley's new royal approval was cemented by an invitation to journey to Balmoral. Once there Wolseley continued his fulsome praise of Connaught and both he and Victoria discovered a mutual dislike of Gladstone's Egyptian policy with both agreeing that the Prime Minster was driven by events, rather than leading them. At a lavish dinner Victoria rose to propose a toast to Wolseley and his stunning success in Egypt. Although a mutual admiration now existed, writing in her diary the Queen clearly showed her fear that Wolseley would return to his old ways when she wrote, 'If only this *really* great General behaves with tact and good taste when he returns, and does not make injudicious speeches'.[1]

For the moment Wolseley's reforming zeal, which had so frequently placed him on a collision course with both the Queen and Cambridge, was put on hold, for Wolseley was badly in need of rest. He and Louisa travelled to Paris for a short holiday and after a further break in the British countryside he returned to his desk of Adjutant-General to find Cambridge, his old adversary, far less confrontational. The great reformer was now to do battle with Gladstone's Egyptian policy, and this was to dominate his mind for the next 18 months.

Wolseley felt that in the aftermath of his battlefield successes in Egypt, British troops should no longer be stationed there, believing their continued presence was solely a political decision. As Adjutant-General he could clearly see that a long-term garrison of several thousand troops would place an intolerably burden on the already overstretched resources of the British Army. He sought and gained the political support of the new Secretary of State for War, Lord Hartington, and together they sought a reduction of the British garrison to 5,000 men. Gladstone too was looking for a way to limit British involvement in Egypt and in October 1882 Lord Dufferin was sent to report to the British Cabinet on ideas for Britain's future policy towards Egypt. Like Wolseley Dufferin favoured a complete withdrawal, but the political and economic situation was the immediate concern for Gladstone, and it was clear that British troops would have to remain for the foreseeable future. In January 1883 Dufferin issued a circular which laid down the position of Gladstone's government: 'Although for the present a British force remains in Egypt for the preservation of public tranquillity, Her Majesty's Government are desirous of withdrawing it as soon as the state of the country and the organization of proper means for the maintenance of the Khedive's authority will admit to it.'[2]

With no timescale set for the withdrawal, both Hartington and Wolseley were disappointed that the situation in Egypt would continue to be a significant drain on Army resources. Wolseley was somewhat pacified by the appointment in December 1882 of his long-standing colleague, Sir Evelyn Wood, to the position of Sirdar, or Commander, of the newly reformed Egyptian Army. Working with a select group of British officers, Wood was tasked with rebuilding the Egyptian Army so that it would provide support and legitimacy to the Khedive, but also allow for the eventual withdraw of British troops. Although great strides were made by Wood and his band of British officers, neither he or Wolseley were under any illusion that the Egyptian Army would be able to resume all its military and policing duties for at least two years or more. Within that time the political and military situation would be radically altered by the rise of an external threat not only to the borders of Egypt itself but also to British authority within the country.

The danger originated in southern Sudan, over which Egypt had nominal control and authority. In the summer of 1881 Mohammed Ahmed Ibn Seyyid Abdullah, a native of the town of Dongola, placed himself at the head of a political and religious movement. He declared himself the 'Chosen One' or Mahdi and claimed he would regenerate Islam and lead a force against all infidels, whether lapsed Muslims or Christian non-believers, to bring them to the true faith. If this had to be done by military conquest, then the self-appointed Mahdi was prepared to lead a force to sweep across the region.

Egyptian rule over the Sudan had been corrupt and ineffective and the Mahdi's words quickly found support amongst the poverty-stricken inhabitants. Soon numerous isolated Egyptian military outposts were capitulating in the face of the Mahdist forces, which with each success continued to grow, both in size and fanaticism.

Gladstone was keen to distance his government from any responsibility to support the Egyptians in their fight in the Sudan, although the Queen and several Members of Parliament felt that Britain had a moral responsibility to assist. Wood made it abundantly clear to Lord Granville that his new Egyptian army was not ready to go into the field and this intelligence was passed onto Gladstone. With the Mahdist threat growing, the Khedive recruited a handful of retired Indian Army officers, commanded by Colonel Hicks, to lead an assorted force of troops and police into the Sudan to confront the Mahdi. Hicks was completely outmanoeuvred by the enemy and was unknowingly surrounded at El Obeid where his ill-trained and under-equipped army was annihilated. The victory spurred the Mahdi to further successes, each of which supplied his growing army with modern Remington rifles and Krupp artillery pieces.

With the deaths of former British officers Gladstone was soon under increasing pressure, both from the press and public, to consider further British military intervention. The Prime Minister naturally turned to the victor of Tel-el-Kebir for his assessment. Wolseley argued that although the Mahdist threat was real and growing, it offered no immediate danger to the borders of Egypt proper and as such the use of British troops against the Mahdi was not yet justified. He favoured an approach which would see the reinforcement of various strategic points, such as Berber, Suakin and Khartoum. This would enable the Egyptians to maintain some political authority over the Sudan, whilst at the same time act as a buffer against a Mahdist incursion into Upper Egypt. Wolseley also advocated those Egyptian forces, under the command of British officers, should be stationed at Assuan in southern Egypt and at Wadi Halfa on the Nile. Wolseley also reluctantly acknowledged that now was not the time to withdraw any further British troops from Egypt. Dufferin approved Wolseley's proposals, as did Hartington, but Sir Evelyn Baring, the British Agent and Consul-General in Cairo, felt that with the destruction of Hicks and his force, the Egyptian government was not strong enough alone to hold onto any position in the Sudan and recommend that all should be abandoned. This was the stance Gladstone had hoped for as he had not wanted to intervene in Egypt in 1882 and certainly had never considered that this might result in further military intervention in Sudan. So once again Wolseley was asked to prepare his thoughts this time on the feasibility of the withdrawal of garrisons in Sudan. He was now very much involved in both the military and political future of the region and this would haunt his thoughts and actions over the next 18 months, providing him with an unwanted legacy.

Wolseley's stance towards the emerging military and political threat in the Sudan was to alter radically when he received news from his long-term friend, Charles Gordon, that he was to resign his commission from the British Army to work in the service of King Leopold of the Belgians, in order to crush the slave trade in the Congo. Wolseley undoubtedly saw an opportunity to not only present Gordon as the answer to how the Egyptian withdrawal from the Sudan could be achieved, but also to utilize his old friend for his own personal advantage and prestige.

Wolseley had very few firm friends throughout his life, but Gordon was certainly one of them. They had served together in the trenches outside of Sebastopol as well as in China, but from there their career paths had diverged with Gordon gaining international fame for leading rag-tag armies to victory against the Taiping rebels, thus saving the country's political cohesion. This earnt him the title of 'Chinese Gordon' and he gained a reputation as an expert at handling irregular forces. He had gone onto serve as Governor-General of the Sudan under the Khedive where he had achieved some success in reducing the slave trade in the region. Gordon was well respected by both Egyptians and Sudanese alike and Wolseley clearly felt Gordon was the man to solve the increasing fraught political and military situation in the Sudan whilst at the same time reinforcing and perhaps enhancing his position in the War Office. There is little doubt that Wolseley held Gordon in high esteem. Indeed, Wolseley described him as a man who 'absolutely ignored self in all he did, and only took in hand what he conceived to be God's work'.[3] Wolseley, never one who could be considered a humble man, wrote that he was 'not worthy to pipe-clay Gordon's belt'.[4] Yet despite his high opinion of Gordon, Wolseley felt no revulsion in now using his friend for his own ends.

In the first weeks of January 1884, Wolseley received a letter from Gordon which informed him of his old friend's decision to resign his commission and accept the position with King Leopold. Gordon had written to Wolseley to seek his assistance in settling his army pension, but Wolseley had other ideas and invited Gordon to London for a meeting at the War Office on 15 January. Fate now intervened in Wolseley's plan, for before their meeting the editor of the *Pall Mall Gazette*, W.T. Stead, obtained an interview with Gordon which caused a sensation. Gordon told Stead that he believed the people of the Sudan deserved to be liberated from Egyptian misgovernment and that in his time as Governor-General the people's lot had significantly improved. Furthermore, Gordon believed that the Mahdist rebellion would not have happened had he not resigned. Gordon also informed Stead that he opposed the Government's policy of evacuation and that he was prepared to return to the region and offer his services. Stead made the most of his 'scoop' and the headline in the *Gazette* the following day was 'Chinese Gordon for the Soudan!' Stead argued that Gordon, as the world's greatest leader of irregular forces, was the ideal man to salvage the mess of the Sudan. What followed within days was a swell of hope and jingoism within other papers and amongst the British public which propelled Gordon towards the Sudan. Even the Queen conveyed to Lord Granville, the Foreign Secretary, that Gordon might be the man for the job.

When Wolseley and Gordon finally met in the War Office, Wolseley's mind was set on a plan. It did not take him long to persuade Gordon to abandon his idea of journeying to the Congo; instead, Wolseley informed him that the Gladstone government were considering asking him to go to the Sudan to evacuate the garrisons there. Gordon expressed his willingness to proceed to Egypt and from there travel to the Suakin coastal region of Sudan to report on the situation and then return. Wolseley knew his friend's temperament well and thought that once in the region Gordon would be driven by his high level of integrity and combined with his strong religious conviction and perceived loyalty to the peoples of the Sudan, and this would overrule any promises he had made to the British government. With such views and personality Wolseley believed that Gordon would not be able to resist widening his involvement and if this was to happen then the likelihood of British military involvement would be high, presenting Wolseley with another opportunity for a battlefield command. Although much of this is conjecture, for the government's negotiations with Gordon, and indeed Gordon's conversations with Wolseley, remained unrecorded, there is enough evidence to support the view that Wolseley exploited Gordon's temperament for his own ends.

For example, as early as 8 February 1884, in a memorandum to the Secretary of State for War, Lord Hartington, Wolseley predicted that Gordon would be unable or unwilling to evacuate Khartoum and that he would, most likely, be besieged there. This would result in a public outcry for his rescue which would necessitate the sending of a relief force.[5] In addition, earlier, on 4 February, Wolseley wrote the following to his wife, 'Please go to my room and look in the second (I think) drawer on left side of my writing-table, and you will find some sheets in my handwriting, describing Gordon's conversation with me when he was here. Please put them in an envelope and send them to me by the bearer.'[6] These words could of course be a simple request, but in light of events they may well have been Wolseley attempting to hide how deep was his involvement in the plan to entice Gordon to Khartoum.

Gordon's mission had earlier been decided upon in a meeting with Lord Hartington in his Whitehall office on 18 January. Other Cabinet members present were Granville, Lord Northbrook, the First Lord of the Admiralty, and Sir Charles Dilke, as well as the Adjutant-General, Wolseley. Surprisingly, given his opposition to further British military intervention in the region, Prime Minister Gladstone was at his country home of Hawarden and did not attend. However, it seems clear that at this moment, and with Wolseley pressing for Gordon's involvement, the Gladstone Ministry viewed Gordon as the man to work miracles in the Sudan. Also, the government was under growing public and Press pressure to be seen to be taking some action; by deciding to despatch Gordon, a national hero, the Government clearly hoped to weather the growing political storm.

No minutes of this meeting were taken, and it was clear that there was significant confusion amongst those present as to what had been decided upon. Granville telegraphed the Queen to tell her that Gordon had been instructed 'to report on the military situation in the Sudan, on measures for the security of Egyptian garrisons and of European population of Khartoum, on best mode of evacuating the interior and of securing safe and good administration of the sea coast [Suakin] by the Egyptian Government, also as to steps to counteract the slave trade'.[7] Indeed both Dilke and Gladstone were certainly left with the impression that Gordon's mission was purely advisory. In contrast Hartington thought Gordon was on a peace mission to evacuate the garrisons and implied that to do so Gordon would require executive powers above that given to him in his advisory role: Gordon himself requested to Granville in the meeting of 18 January that he be given the title of Governor-General of the Sudan. Sir Evelyn Baring, the Consul-General in Cairo, was aware of Gordon's inability to follow orders and on first hearing that Gordon was being considered for some sort of role in the region Baring wrote to Granville stating, 'I would rather have him [Gordon] than anyone else, provided there is a clear understanding with as to what line of policy he is to carry out. Otherwise, not.'[8]

Clarity was decidedly lacking and Baring, despite his earlier words, added to the confusion for on Gordon's arrival at Port Said on 24 January instead of travelling immediately to the Suakin coastal region as planned, the Consul-General summoned Gordon to Cairo where he was informed by Baring that his mission had been radically altered. Baring, with Granville's approval, conferred upon Gordon the title of Governor-General, which Gordon himself had earlier sought. Rather than advising how an evacuation might take place, Gordon was now tasked with not only making this happen but would now be responsible for establishing a native administration to take over from the departing Egyptian officials; this was a huge undertaking. Empowered with an executive position, combined with his own temperament, Gordon was now on a road which would lead to British military intervention in the Sudan and his own date with destiny.

Gordon set out for Khartoum but before he reached the city the political and military situation again violently changed. On 4 February, a force of Egyptian gendarmerie, under the command of an Englishman, Valentine Baker, had been decisively defeated at El Teb, near Suakin by a force led by an ally of the Mahdi, Osman Digna. For both Gordon and the British government, the Mahdist victory clearly demonstrated the poor fighting qualities of the Egyptian troops and that they could not be relied upon to clear the Suakin region from the threat offered by Osman Digna. By his success at El Teb, Osman Digna had cut the fastest route for the evacuation from the Sudan which was across the desert from Berber on the Nile to the Suakin coast, following an ancient caravan route. This was a military situation that could not be tolerated nor could the threat to Suakin that Osman Digna presented.

Baker's defeat caused an outcry in Britain and for once Cambridge and Wolseley worked together to push the Gladstone government to send a punitive expedition to the Suakin. Although intervention in the Suakin was opposed by the Prime Minister and Baring, Wolseley found an ally in the Queen who was becoming more vocal in the expression of her firm opinions as to British policy in the Sudan. Writing to Gladstone after news of Baker's loss, Victoria was very forthright in laying down her views as to the proper course of action:

> The Queen *trusts* Lord Wolseley's plan will be considered *and our whole position remembered* ... we must not let this fine and fruitful country [the Sudan], with its peaceful inhabitants, be left a pray to murder and rapine, and utter confusion. It must be a *disgrace* to the British name, and the country will *not* stand it. A blow must be struck, or we shall never be able to convince the Mohammadans that they have not beaten us.[9]

Before Gladstone's inevitable capitulation in the face of calls from the press, the public and the Queen for British troops to be sent to Suakin, Wolseley had been busy working with the Confidential Mobilisation Committee to produce a scheme for an expeditionary force. His plan, which was quickly agreed at a rather heated Cabinet meeting, would see British troops sent from both Aden and England, along with a contingent from Lieutenant-General Sir Frederick Stephenson's Cairo garrison. Overall command of the force was given to Lieutenant-General Sir Gerald Graham, a long-term friend and comrade of both Wolseley and Gordon. Wolseley ensured that the troops were conveyed quickly to Trinkitat on the Suakin coast, along with ammunition, stores and equipment, field hospitals and medical staff (Wolseley was determined that there would be no repeat of the criticism of medical provision that had come from the 1882 Egyptian campaign) along with three months' rations for 6,000 troops. Such was the organization and speed of implementation that incredibly by 26 February Graham was able to lead his force of nearly 4,000 British troops away from their beachhead at Trinikitat to attack Osman Digna and his warriors.

The story of the next few weeks is a violent one as Graham's forces battled with a fanatical enemy. At the battles of El Teb (29 February 1884) and then at Tamaai (13 March 1884) the British decisively defeated the Mahdists who repeated flung themselves at British squares protected by Martini-Henry fire, bayonets, artillery and machine guns. Yet despite the technological advantages possessed by the British over their foe, both battles were hard fought and bloody. Indeed, at Tamaai the British square was broken and Graham's force suffered over 200 casualties, dead and wounded, although it is estimated that Mahdist losses exceeded 4,000 in this engagement alone. With this defeat Osman Digna, along with his remaining warriors, melted into the surrounding countryside and Graham was able to declare that the Berber-Suakin evacuation route was once again open.

During the few weeks Graham had taken to prevail over Osman Digna and reopen the Berber route, the political situation had once again altered. During Gordon's journey down the Nile to Khartoum, he met with numerous local chiefs to reassure them of the Egyptian commitment of maintaining a presence in the Sudan. He also explained that had been briefed to recruit Sudanese headmen to assume political authority from Egyptian officials, and that he was effectively on a recruitment drive to secure the political support of chiefs in the region. On reaching Berber Gordon even sent a message to the Mahdi offering him the position of Sultan of Kordofan in the hope that this gesture would nullify the Mahdi's military threat. Yet by making this offer Gordon clearly demonstrated how much he had failed to grasp the enormity of the danger to the country that the rise of the Mahdi presented. In Berber, Gordon also met with Hussain Khalifa, a veteran provincial governor of the region and someone whose support was vital if Gordon was to fulfil his brief of recruiting locals as administrators. Gordon made the critical error of taking Hussain fully into his confidence and informed him that in reality the Sudan was to be abandoned by Egypt and that Gordon's main task was to ensure that the garrisons, and specifically Khartoum, were evacuated. The following day Gordon even revealed his hand to other local dignitaries, which caused consternation, for not only had Gordon shown how weak his position was to the Mahdi but the confirmation from Gordon's mouth that the garrisons were to be evacuated served to drive many of the local chiefs along the banks of the Nile towards the Mahdi's cause. All knew if they did not show loyalty to the uprising, they would very likely be overwhelmed as the Mahdi advanced.

Gordon quickly realized that with the breaking of this news all he could now do was to quickly head for Khartoum before the local tribesmen shifted their loyalty to the Mahdi, which would effectively see Khartoum cut off. Gordon had made a huge blunder. His arrival in Khartoum on 18 February 1884 was at first greeted by the inhabitants with jubilation, with many remembering Gordon's previous tenure as Governor-General as a success. Yet in less than a fortnight the mood had dramatically changed as it became clear how perilous the position of the city was. Gordon realized that it would not take long for news of the evacuation to percolate throughout the region and that if British troops were not to be sent the only option was to appoint his successor as Governor-General urgently. Gordon believed that it would require a strong man with a hard reputation to fill his shoes and in his mind, there was only one suitable candidate with sufficient personal charisma to exert authority over those tribes who were wavering over their loyalty to either the Egyptians or the Mahdi. This was an individual named Zubayr Pasha, an important member of a tribe to the north of Khartoum.

Unfortunately, Zubayr Pasha had had a previous life as a slave trader and with this background both Evelyn Baring and the British government considered him an unsuitable candidate. In the first week after his arrival in Khartoum Gordon sent numerous telegrams to Baring urging Zubayr Pasha's appointment, all to no avail. In the meantime, the Mahdi had initially been dismayed by Gordon's arrival in Khartoum but once he realized that no British troops had accompanied the Governor-General the Mahdi instead decided to tighten the noose around Khartoum: soon the telegraph wire was cut. Yet still Gordon remained unduly concerned for he possessed ten armed steamers to maintain communications along the Nile and with these, he estimated he could complete the evacuation of Khartoum in around six months, as long as the tribes along the Nile remained neutral. Furthermore, the news of Graham's victories against Osman Digna's forces in Suakin surely meant that British troops would soon be in Berber ready to support the evacuation.

However, despite the British successes in the Suakin region, the British government was very reluctant to sanction the further deployment of British troops. Indeed, despite Graham's readiness to advance across the desert to Berber, Gladstone's government refused permission and all but a small number of troops remained behind to garrison Suakin, whilst the rest were ordered to Egypt. Not only was this a crushing blow for Gordon, but the Mahdi was able to present the British withdrawal as a victory for they had been forced out the region by the strength and determination of the Mahdist opposition. Whether at this point it would have been feasible for Graham to take a force to Berber across 245 miles of desert is highly unlikely, for the last 100 miles were devoid of water and any force would have been very vulnerable to a surprise attack from Osman Digna's dervish warriors. These facts were highlighted by both Baring and the British commander in Egypt, General Sir Frederick Stephenson, to London and undoubtedly influenced the government's decision to resist Graham's calls to march on Berber: Wolseley too was opposed to the route for similar reasons. When the news reached Gordon on 4 April that help would not be coming from that direction, he wrote in his journal that, 'No human power can deliver us now, we are surrounded'.[10] Graham would always regret that he did not send a small force of cavalry to Berber on his own initiative, without asking for London's approval, for he believed that the presence of British troops in Berber would have deterred the Mahdi from besieging Khartoum.

Even at this stage Gordon could have utilized his steamers to escape via the Nile, but he was convinced British military support would surely come to his aid. In London the dangerous nature of Khartoum's position was certainly not fully realized. Gladstone believed that Gordon was deliberately disobeying Baring's orders to evacuate and that he did not require a rescue mission. Granville refused to accept that an expedition was needed, although Hartington, in response to the Queen's pressing the Cabinet to consider a rescue mission, did state that to launch one at that moment in the heat of the summer was simply not feasible. These words did at least indicate that the Secretary of State for War was contemplating a rescue expedition.

Hartington was also receiving correspondence from Wolseley who behind the scenes was formulating his own plans for an expedition and suggesting more immediate action that could be taken to relieve Gordon's plight. It seems clear that some of this was driven by Wolseley's feeling of guilt, and personal responsibility, for pushing his old friend into such a perilous situation. After all he would have known that Gordon, upon realizing the threat posed by the Mahdi, would never have abandoned the inhabitants of Khartoum to their fate.

With Graham's withdrawal from the Suakin region Wolseley adopted a tougher stance in his correspondence with the Secretary of State for War. He wrote,

> Unless 'something' is now done and done at once … it is tolerably certain that Gordon will soon find himself shut up in Khartoum, unable to do no more than hold his own there as long as his provisions last, even assuming

he is able, with his genius for command to infuse sufficient courage into the miserable troops that no constitute the garrison of that place ...[11]

Wolseley then approached Granville on 22 March with the suggestion that a brigade of Evelyn Wood's Egyptian army be sent to Wadi Halfa, near the Second Cataract on the Nile, and just inside the Sudan. The presence there of a force at least supportive of Gordon's position might, Wolseley hoped, serve to deter the advance of the Mahdi on Khartoum. In addition, Wolseley recommended that a small number of British officers be sent to Berber to again show some level of solidarity with Gordon and make the Mahdi think twice before threatening Khartoum. Yet, much to Wolseley's frustration both of his ideas were rejected by Baring and the military authorities in Cairo. By the end of March, the Mahdist forces had surrounded Khartoum with only the Nile itself offering a means for Gordon to maintain any contact with the outside world.

Wolseley kept badgering both the Cabinet and Baring to sanction some actions in support of Gordon. He again pleaded for a small force of British troops to be sent to Berber, to secure the town and use it as a potential base for the launch of a larger expedition if required. Yet this idea and Wolseley's suggestion that he himself should go to Suakin to command the small garrison there were again rejected. This latter idea, Wolseley thought, would at least demonstrate to the world that the British government were taking the situation in the Sudan seriously, but it also showed how desperate Wolseley was becoming to find anyway to offer support to Gordon.

Wolseley even attempted to use a psychological approach upon Hartington in a letter to his political superior on 13 April when he wrote: ' I presume the government is not prepared to allow General Gordon and his garrison to fall into the hands of the cruel and barbarous enemy now besieging Khartoum ... if you contemplate sending an expedition in the autumn to Gordon's relief, the sooner he is informed the better it will be for him and for our interests.' Finally, Wolseley wrote an accurate warning when he stated to Hartington that 'the English people will force you to do it [the rescue expedition] whether you like it or not'.[12] It seems likely that these words were not meant to be directed towards Hartington but to the wider Cabinet, although Hartington was very much an ally of Wolseley in his attempts to rouse the Cabinet to the need of focusing on the plight of Khartoum, he was a lone voice during these crucial spring months. However, Hartington had instructed Wolseley to produce a detailed plan for a rescue expedition and this Wolseley presented to the Secretary of State War. It was this plan which Wolseley would follow when he was finally given the political instruction to launch the expedition.

Wolseley's memorandum regarding his plans for the expeditionary force was delivered to Hartington on 8 April where it was to cause a few raised eyebrows in both London and Cairo: Wolseley proposed to recreate the Red River Expedition of 1870 with all the non-mounted troops to be transported down the Nile to Khartoum in boats. Wolseley claimed:

> Remembering the great superiority of river over land transport, the ease with which stores of all sorts are carried in boats, the great distance, comparatively speaking, that can be traversed daily in boats, and the vast saving that there would be in expense, I have no hesitation whatever in saying that the river route from Wady Halfa to Khartoum is infinitely preferable to any other.[13]

Despite receiving support from the unlikely source of the Duke of Cambridge, those in authority in Cairo; Graham, Baring, Stephenson and even Wolseley's 'Asante Ring' comrade, Evelyn Wood, were unanimous in their opposition to Wolseley's proposal. All declared it as impracticable not only because of the huge distance involved but also the difficulty in negotiating the five cataracts along this stretch of the Nile. Later, as Wolseley's plans were made more widely known, opposition would also come from Vice-Admiral Lord John Hay who, speaking for the Admiralty, stated that small boats could neither be rowed, poled or hauled along the uncharted reaches of the Nile.

Although these men saw the inherent dangers of the Suakin to Berber route they felt it offered a greater chance of success than Wolseley's plan. Yet this so called 'Battle of the Routes' was brought to an abrupt end with the capture of Berber by the Mahdist forces on 19 May. The Nile route was now the only option open. However, even this was dependent on a political decision which was still not forthcoming.

Wolseley continued to issue further memorandums to Hartington on 13 and 26 April and again on 9 May, with additional details as to both the urgent need for a decision to be made for an expedition as well as more information as to how Wolseley envisaged overcoming the various obstacles. Armed with Wolseley's thoughts and opinions, Hartington himself wrote a memorandum to the Cabinet in which he argued; 'Whether any expedition be ultimately be despatched or not, I think it is clear that if we admit the possibility of having to send an expedition, no time should be lost in making some preparations ...'[14] Hartington's plea was met with silence from his Cabinet colleagues for there were other demands upon them, including a growing political crisis over a widening of the franchise. However, as Wolseley had predicted, the public were becoming increasing aware and concerned over Gordon's plight, with a mass protest meeting held in Hyde Park in May and the opening of public subscription fund to raise money for a relief expedition. Gladstone was even verbally abused in public.

News of Berber's fall to the Mahdi only reached London in June and this spurred on Wolseley to renew his efforts to force a political decision, where he threw all his energies in pressurizing Hartington to make a stand. Yet for all the pressure placed upon him, Hartington was a realist and stated to Wolseley; 'Remember we cannot command things, all the gold in England will not affect the rise and fall of the Nile or the duration of the hot and cold seasons in Egypt'. Yet Hartington conceded that:

> Time is a most important element in the question, and indeed it will be an indelible disgrace if we allow the most generous, patriotic, and gallant of our public servants to die of want or fall into the hands of a cruel enemy because we would not hold out our hands to save him … At any rate I don't wish to share the responsibility of leaving Charles Gordon to his fate, and it is for this reason that I recommend immediate and active preparation for operations that may be forced upon us by and by.[15]

With Gordon's plight growing more severe by the day, Wolseley ramped up his demands and put to Hartington that 6,000–7,000 British troops should now be sent to Wadi Halfa ready to advance towards Khartoum in October. Much was now dependent on the level of the Nile which needed to be high to permit the transit of steamers large enough to move the huge amount of supplies that the expedition would rely upon. Wolseley's latest proposal coincided with a letter from Gordon which had been smuggled out of Khartoum, which asked the size of and the whereabouts of the relief force. Hartington used both to petition the Prime Minister once again, but Gladstone remained inexorable and he replied to Hartington, 'I do not think the evidence as to Gordon's position requires or justifies, in itself, the military preparations for the contingency of a military expedition'.[16]

These words were the final straw for the Secretary of State for War, and he threatened resignation from the government if preparations for a relief expedition were not ordered. In a Cabinet meeting of 25 July a vote was carried in favour of an expedition, nine votes to three, with Gladstone voting against; on 5 August, Parliament granted a Vote of Credit of £300,000 (around £44,000,000 in 2023 values) to enable some preparations to be made for a possible expedition. Both Gladstone and Hartington knew that this ridiculously low credit would be the first of many claims that the expedition would make upon the public purse.

It is clear that at least two crucial months were lost in the spring and early summer of 1884 in which the decision to prepare for an expedition should have been made. Much of this delay can be laid at the door of the Prime Minister and a Cabinet which failed to appreciate the seriousness of Gordon's situation and it was only the threat of resignation by Hartington that prompted a proper debate on the issue within the government. During this period Wolseley was rightly preparing his thoughts and proposals for an expedition and becoming increasingly frustrated by the political inertia. But should he have done more? Certainly, in the light of the threat of Hartington's resignation the Cabinet finally focused on the need to consider an expedition. If Wolseley himself had considered such a step, in April or May of 1884, or made his views more public then surely the ground swell generated would have forced the Gladstone government to either decide upon an expedition sooner, or at least make some preparations. It does now seem that Wolseley can be criticised for not being more vocal during this critical period. In his defence, Wolseley was focused on devising plans and submitting proposals but there is no doubt Gordon's fate was sealed in these months and Wolseley, for whatever criticism he received and faults he made during the actual relief expedition, can also be censured for not taking a greater stand against his political masters in the spring of 1884.

With a decision finally made Wolseley, in characteristic style, set about pulling the logistical side of the expedition together, doing so via the Confidential Mobilisation Committee at the War Office, of which he was President. Orders were placed with over forty firms to construct boats 30ft long with a draught of just 2ft 6in to cope with the ever-decreasing level of the Nile. However, these also had to be lighter enough for men to carry around the cataracts and at the same time durable enough to withstand rapids. Wolseley also sent officers to both naval and civilian boatyards to scour for up to 400 suitable boats which were urgently required to ferry supplies to Dongola. The first 100 boats were built in less than a month and using his experiences from both the Asante and Red River campaigns Wolseley recruited 300 Kroomen from West Africa to man the boats, along with nearly 400 Canadian voyageurs. Unfortunately, since Wolseley's successful Canadian expedition of 1870 the expansion of the railway network had made the voyageurs something of a dying breed, but lumberjacks, renowned for their strength, were recruited in their stead. The purchase of around 1,200 camels was left to Evelyn Wood whose attempts to buy such large numbers pushed up the prices locally. Reluctant to pay the inflated prices, Wood ended up buying inferior beasts. This was combined with the fact that Wood ignored Wolseley's instructions to buy saddles from India and instead acquired lesser-quality ones in Egypt, the inadequacies of which would seriously hamper the expedition causing unnecessary suffering to the animals and reducing their efficiency.

Wolseley had been positioning himself for several weeks to assume overall command of the expedition. He had rightly pointed out to Hartington that the commander of British forces in Egypt, Stephenson, should not be appointed for he considered Wolseley's plan impracticable and could hardly be expected to carry it out with the wholesale effort which would be necessary. The Duke favoured either Generals Earle (then in command of the Alexandria garrison) or Greaves and was subsequently shocked when Hartington proposed Wolseley for the role. Hartington argued that Wolseley would not necessarily take part in the final move towards Khartoum but would be in situ to direct and superintend the preparation and despatch of the force. Apparently, Wolseley's appointment sent Cambridge into a such rage it triggered an attack of gout! His cousin, the Queen, was also critical and bombarded Hartington with a series of telegrams seeking an alternative candidate, claiming that she was 'decidedly opposed to the practice of sending out the Adjutant-General to a distant command'.[17] Yet Hartington stood his ground and although there was also opposition to Wolseley within the Cabinet, from the likes of Dilke and Chamberlain, Gladstone demurred, and Wolseley's command was confirmed.

Wolseley was surprised by his appointment, although whether this was 'feigned surprise' is open to debate for certainly he had been working behind the scenes to reduce the number of suitable candidates. He was personally thrilled and excited to accept the challenge, for he saw the expedition as perhaps the last great opportunity to cement his name in British history. His success was kept secret for as long as possible but when it was announced on the eve of his departure it was met with public jubilation. Wolseley arrived in Cairo on 9 September. En route he had devised a plan to form a Camel Corps of picked men from the Guards and cavalry regiments which would be used in case of urgent necessity. Wolseley envisaged that if needed this Corp would separate from the river column and cross the Bayuda desert from Korti to Metemmeh, thus cutting out the eastward loop of the Nile. Just a few days after arriving in Egypt Wolseley wrote to Cambridge with his idea and again the Duke was thrown into a rage at the thought of his beloved Guards upon camels. Despite this he was forced to coincide, and Wolseley was able to write to Hartington that 'These Camel Corps will really be worth any Brigade of troops I could collect here. In fact, they will be, in reality, the finest troops in the world.'[18] Events would later demonstrate that they would have to be, so as to overcome the enormous threat presented by the Mahdists.

Whilst the men of the Camel Corps learnt to handle the unpredictable nature of their new mounts, Wolseley worked with his Staff to calculate the stores and provisions that would soon be sent south. Once again men of the infamous 'Ring' were to feature prominently in Wolseley's appointment, but these were no longer the young men who had displayed such energy and zeal in the Red River or Asante campaigns, but now senior officers some of whom had perhaps rather over-inflated views of their own abilities and a liking for personal comfort. Major-General Redvers Buller became Wolseley's Chief of Staff whilst Evelyn Wood stood down from his role of Sirdar of the Egyptian Army to command the lines of communication. Other notable figures were William Butler who was to play an important role in the movement of vessels through the cataracts and Henry Brackenbury who was to be second in command to Major-General Earle, the commander of the river column, whose appointment Wolseley had to rather ungraciously accept, due to Earle's seniority. In reflecting on the performance of his once dependable team, Wolseley wrote to Louisa,

> I have always gone on the principle of getting hold of all the really able men I can find, but the moment they feel they have an assured footing and can do really good Staff service, they torture themselves with jealousy one of the other … it is often very difficult to keep them in their places … they soon realise their own worth, and are inclined to serve you only on their own terms.[19]

These characteristics were to be prominent through the relief expedition and Wolseley can be criticised for not taking sterner action, including replacement, against some of his now less-able 'lieutenants', whose failings caused delays and frustration in the journey down the Nile.

The draw of the expedition meant that Wolseley spent a great deal of time in his first weeks in Egypt dealing with requests for employment from thrill seekers, opportunists or the simply bored. Most he was able to fend most off, but one such person who he was keen to welcome was Colonel Fred Burnaby, who was a true Victorian adventurer and eccentric, one who had a natural disregard for authority and as such was intensely disliked by the likes of Cambridge. Wolseley, however, saw great appeal in Burnaby's personality and bravery, assigning him to the Camel Corps, along with the likes of Count Gleichen.

Gradually the forces began to arrive. A total of 11,000 British troops from Britain, Gibraltar, Malta and Bombay, along with a proportion of the British garrisons in Cairo and Alexandria were required to man the long line of communication down to the Nile, as well as hold strategic points such as Dongola and Korti. Wolseley envisaged that only the Camel Corps, 400 Mounted Infantry and a selection of troops drawn from various regiments, which included the Royal Sussex and the Gordon Highlanders, as well as the Naval Brigade, would actually march to Khartoum. This would be around a quarter of his total force, which demonstrated how much the expedition was driven by logistics and the simple requirement to use troops to transport the very stores that they needed.

It was essential that supplies were accumulated at Wadi Halfa before any further advance could be considered. Within weeks this sleepy little town was transformed into lines upon line of bell tents for both troops and their stores. The movement of men and the food they required was an enormous undertaking as for example over 1,600,000 tons of bully beef were needed to feed the troops alone and could only be done by utilizing steamers on this stretch of the Nile. Wolseley had entrusted Buller with the task of negotiating the hire contracts with the steamer companies, which included Thomas Cook, yet Buller failed to adequately examine the paperwork and at a critical moment the steamers were halted through lack of coal for their boilers. Wolseley had to intercede, and he galloped back from Dongola on his camel, a personal gift from the Khedive, to rectify the contractual mess, but ten critical days were lost before the accumulation of supplies recommenced. Wolseley was furious with Buller and did sanction his Chief of Staff, yet this was not to be the last time he would be let down by his once-able 'lieutenants'. One result of this incident was that Wolseley took on a far greater 'hands on' role during the expedition, becoming reluctant to delegate to his Staff and ending up 'bogged down' in minor details, where he perhaps failed to see the greater threats to the success of the expedition. One journalist stated in relation to the handling to of the whalers at the Second Cataract: 'One is impressed by the strong element of improvisation in the transport arrangements, and the number of decisions with respect to them that were made by the Commander-in-Chief.'[20] In addition, the old 'Asante hands' were bickering amongst themselves (this was particularly true of Buller and Wood) for power and prestige and this did not lead to a healthy or positive environment just at a time when all would need to work together to overcome the numerous hurdles that the expedition faced.

This unnecessary delay was just one of many that plagued the expedition. As predicted by Vice-Admiral Lord Hay and the Admiralty, traversing the Cataracts south of Wadi Halfa was much more difficult than Wolseley had envisaged. Indeed, one of the precious steamers was wrecked during its transit of the Second Cataract. Problems became apparent in the first days. As so many boats had been ordered from different shipyards the fixtures and other equipment were not interchangeable and much of the fittings had become separated in transit to Egypt. Thus, much time was lost as the crews tried to sort out this resulting confusion. Further delays ensured in transporting the boats on the Egyptian railways and it was not until the end of September that the first steamers left for Assuan carrying the boats. At Wadi Halfa more days were lost for native craft ahead of the expeditionary force were given priority through the Second Cataract. All this meant that the river column was behind schedule even before it had started.

On 17 November, Wolseley received his first direct communication from the besieged Gordon, dated 4 November. In many ways it was reassuring to hear from his old friend but his news that food was running low and that desertion to the Mahdist cause was being increasing common was worrying. Yet, of the most concern was that Gordon stated he could 'hold out for forty days with ease; after that it will be difficult'.[21] Taking in account the ten days it had taken for Gordon's note to arrive Wolseley realized that Gordon would be under serious threat from the middle of December and consequently he had less time to reach Khartoum than he first thought. Wolseley now aimed to concentrate his force at Korti and from there use the Desert Column, consisting primarily of the Camel Corps, to strike out across the Bayuda Desert to Metemmeh. There they were to rendezvous with steamers sent from Khartoum and proceed to the city. Yet before this could be considered Wolseley had to make the passage to Korti and progress continued to be slow and very hard work.

To move the 11,000 British troops, 7,000 Egyptian soldiers, nearly 40,000 tons of supplies and 30,000 tons of cereals, required a fleet of 700 small boats, 800 whalers, 27 steamers and around 5,000 locals to help portage supplies through the Cataracts. In the haste to move supplies the boats had been severely overloaded and when this was pointed out by Butler it was initially dismissed. When loads were later halved on Butler's pressing, the daily distances significantly increased. Yet Wolseley was critical of Butler's dogmatic stance and described Butler in his campaign journal as one who 'can neither work in an ordinary groove, nor work in harmony with the talents of other men in a team'.[22] Unfortunately, these words could have been directed to other members of Wolseley's Staff for in the same entry of 30 November Wolseley wrote: 'All my old companions, men who I have brought on … are now reaching that age & standing in the service when it is difficult to place them in a small Army in the field, and when there, each and all are so jealous one of the other, that the team is a difficult one to drive.'[23] Writing in the same journal on 25 November Wolseley clearly showed signs of concern for the success of the expedition, as well as his disdain for the Prime Minister when he wrote,

> It is the hot weather coming on which terrifies me: had this wretched Mr. Gladstone only had the grasp of a Statesman he would have begun

> this business two or three months earlier and we might now have had in that case ample supplies here by this date for all the Force. May God grant me success; without his aid I can do nothing.[24]

The pedestrian transit of the Cataracts added to delays. Of the five that had to be overcome the Second, just below Wadi Halfa, was the most formidable. Nine miles long, here the river narrowed making it run wildly and forming deadly whirlpools. The worse section was a deep gorge known as Bab-el-Kebir, or the 'Big Gate', where the waters churned violently. Yet, despite naval experts pronouncing it impassable, with the help of 4,000 natives as well as 1,500 troops, the steamers were hauled through. Even the whalers made the descent. Of the 549 whalers, 166 navigated the 'Big Gate', with the rest unloaded and portaged around the obstacle. Although only three whalers were smashed by the waters, movement through this Second and subsequent cataracts was slow and exhausting work. The daily routine as troops and supplies headed for Korti was unceasing. All rose at dawn and men placed their hardened, blistered hands upon oars and poles as they worked their way around rapids and sandbanks and lugged whalers and stores over greater obstacles. It was unceasing labour under a fierce sun. Uniforms soon turned to rags and bodies became infected with boils and infested with lice, and many were forced or choose to row either naked or with minimal covering. In addition it was the first time they some had ever been in a boat; the fear of drowning terrified many. Yet despite the herculean efforts of the men, it was never enough for speed was everything.

Wolseley recognized the hardship and difficulties his troops faced in a Special Order of 30 November, which was read to every man as they passed through the Third Cataract. Wolseley wrote,

> The labour of working up this river is immense. To bear it uncomplainingly demands the highest soldierlike qualities – that contempt for danger and that determination to overcome difficulties ... The physical obstacles that impede our rapid progress are considerable, but who cares for them when it is remembered that General Gordon and his garrison are in danger? Under God, their safety is now in your hands, and, come what may, we must save them.[25]

To reinforce the need for urgency Wolseley offered £100, out of his own pocket, for the best transit time of a battalion from Sarras, below the Second Cataract, to Korti. The winnings went to the recently arrived Royal Irish Regiment who covered the distance in 37 days, whilst the Duke of Cornwall's

Light Infantry won the 'wooden spoon' for taking the greatest time, 49 days. The Queen criticized Wolseley for introducing a financial reward to troops for only doing their duty. Wolseley was stung by the Queen's words which clearly showed how little appreciation Victoria had for the urgency of the mission.

Wolseley arrived in Korti on 16 December and hoped that all the efforts of the men would mean that the necessary supplies and troops of the Desert Column would be at Korti around Christmas Day. Indeed, slowly, everything came together at Korti; arms, stores and troops; the men were even able to enjoy date pudding on Christmas Day and an improvised variety show. On 27 December Wolseley was able to announce his plans for the force to his senior commanders, Wood, Earle, Buller and Stewart. The force now concentrated at Korti would be divided to form a River Column, under the command of Earle, and a Desert Column, led by Herbert Stewart. Earle's force was to continue its journey along the Nile, capture Berber and rendezvous with the Desert Column at Shendi, south of Metemmeh. Wolseley envisaged that Stewart's mobile command of principally the Camel Corps, would cross the Bayuda Desert to reach the Nile at Metemmeh where it would meet steamers sent from Khartoum; Stewart would then utilize the steamers to send some of his troops to liberate Gordon. Given the pressure of time Wolseley's plan was the only realistic one open to him and one that he had foreseen when he had first conceived the idea of the Camel Corps. Yet his plan had assumed that a Desert Column would be unopposed, nor had it considered that it would be difficult to source camels. Wolseley had also not foreseen the misery that overwork and poor-quality Egyptian saddles would inflict on those beasts he did have.

Both Wood and Buller can be criticised for poor decision making surrounding the purchasing of camels and their saddles in the first few weeks of the campaign. However, Wolseley too can be considered at fault for not taking a greater interest in the procurement of these beasts which were so vital to the success of the mission. Instead, Wolseley seemed to have been reliant upon false promises from local chiefs that fresh camels would be supplied. For example, the Mudir of Dongola promised camels as did the chief of the Kabbish tribe who assured Wolseley that camels would be waiting at Korti. Rather than relying on dubious promises, Wolseley should have better understood the growing influence of the Mahdi over the local tribal leaders. Instead of trying to placate those adverse to the British in their lands, or opposed to the expedition, he should have secured camels by force, even at the risk of antagonising tribal leaders.

With no fresh camels waiting at Korti, the fate of the Desert Column was already decided. To overcome the shortage of camels Wolseley and Stewart were forced to adopt a plan which would see the establishment of a half-way post at the Jakdul wells, 100 miles to the south. Here stores would be left and guarded whilst the camels returned to Korti to bring up the remainder of the supplies. Once sufficient stores had been accumulated the bulk of the force would then head-out across the desert to reach Metemmeh. The initial advance of the Desert Column began on 30 December and as Wolseley recorded in his diary; 'It is the beginning of the first scene in the last act of this Khartoum drama. May God bless this expedition, and grant that it be in every aspect a complete success.'[26] Yet in the three days that it took Stewart's force to reach Jakdul the camels were exhausted, and it had already become clear much of the equipment designed for the expedition was defective, including the water bags which lost precious water through leaks and evaporation. Supplies were quickly deposited, and the bulk of the force returned with its unloaded camels to Korti for 5 January. After just three days' rest the reluctant camels were again reloaded for their return to Jakdul.

Wolseley had always intended to join Stewart on this last leg to Metemmeh, but with the telegraph only reaching as far as Korti, Hartington insisted that Wolseley remain there where he could receive reports from the two advancing columns, issue any necessary instructions and keep London informed of progress. For Wolseley, enduring the wait without participating in either advancing column was simply a torment. He confided in Buller that 'This is the first time in my life that I have been chained to the rear in a campaign and I hope it may be the last. To lead a storming party a day would be child's play to the anxieties of this position.'[27] Wolseley had every right to be anxious, for on 31 December he received a final communication from Gordon, smuggled out of Khartoum, which told him not only on the city's perilous position but also advised Wolseley to ensure that his rear lines of communications be secured by the capture of Berber. This information was passed onto Earle and Wolseley realized that the need for extra caution would undoubtedly slow the River Column, therefore Gordon's fate rested completely on the successful advance of the Desert Column. However, the ferrying of supplies to the Jakdul Wells and the resultant slowness of the advance had alerted enemy spies to the British intentions and the Mahdi had despatched a force 14,000–15,000 strong to oppose the 1,400 men of Stewart's command.

The enemy let the desert take its toil upon the British; the 43 miles between Jakdul and the next available water at Abu Klea were torturous under an unforgiving sun. By the evening of 16 January, with water running dangerous low, the column had reached Abu Klea only to discover the enemy occupying the wells and waiting for their prey. The British had to secure water to survive; the next morning Stewart advanced his men in a square formation which was soon enveloped by the charge of fanatical warriors. The subsequent battle was one of the bloodiest of Victoria's reign. In the space of just 10 minutes 1,100 warriors of the 5,000 engaged were killed whilst over seventy British soldiers, including the much-loved Burnaby, died and nearly a hundred were wounded when the square was broken. Stewart's disciplined force regained their formation and secured the wells. The night was spent fortifying Abu Klea with a brush zariba, in which the wounded were placed, and a force left to protect them, whilst those fit enough were pushed forward the following day towards Metemmeh.

After another frustrating and exhausting day Stewart's force awoke on the morning of 19 January to see the sun glistening on the Nile and the smoke from Gordon's steamers rising into the air. Yet the men also saw thousands of Mahdist warriors emerging from Metemmeh hell-bent on stopping the British reaching the river. There would have to be another bloody battle, but before Stewart could begin the advance the Mahdists showered the column with Remington bullets, many of which claimed British victims, one of whom was Stewart himself, who suffered a mortal wound to his groin. Command now fell upon Sir Charles Wilson, an intelligence officer who had never led men in battle. He formed his men into an advancing firing line and the accuracy and killing-power of the Martini-Henry rifle ensured that no warriors were able to engage in hand-to-hand combat with the British, the enemy evaporating in the face of such determined fire. With the light now beginning to fade Wilson was able to finally make contact with those onboard Gordon's steamers.

Wilson's detractors, which was to include Wolseley himself, blamed him for now wasting three crucial days at Metemmeh whilst he secured his position and made reconnaissance up and down the river to gauge the threat from the enemy to his own force. It was not until 24 January that Wilson set out with a detachment of the Royal Sussex on-board two steamers for Khartoum. The defeats at Abu Klea and Abu Kru had demoralized many of the warriors surrounding Khartoum and all but one of the Mahdi's advisors had called for a retreat. Yet Wilson's delay had encouraged the Mahdi to make an assault upon Khartoum and on the morning of 26 January the city finally fell in a bloody assault which saw the massacre of its remaining inhabitants and defenders, including Gordon. Wilson arrived on 28 January, two days late and for the first time in his military career Wolseley was now to suffer the ignominy of failure.

News reached Korti on 21 January of the Battle of Abu Klea and Wolseley was impressed by Stewart's handling of the troops and the discipline of the men under the most difficult and dangerous of circumstances. It was another week before details of the victory of Abu Kru reached Wolseley and with it the news of Stewart's wound. Instinctively Wolseley knew that his prodigy would die although in a telegram to the Queen on 29 January Wolseley informed Her Majesty that although Stewart's wound was serious, he was doing well. Similarly on the same day Wolseley wrote to Hartington stating that the 'Notes from medical report received ... General Stewart progressing most favourably; wonderfully free from inflammatory symptoms and suffering comparatively little pain ... Every hope of rapid recovery.'[28] The strain of both waiting for news from Wilson and his concern for Stewart had led Wolseley to abandon his attempts to give up smoking which he had started a month before; he now returned to his cigars and in a letter to his wife of 27 January Wolseley wrote; 'I don't show it, for I laugh and talk as usual, but my very heart is being consumed with anxiety about Stewart's column'.[29]

Finally on 4 February Lord Cochrane arrived in Korti with the shocking news that Khartoum had fallen. Wolseley's first act was to again write to Louisa so as to unburden himself to his wife. He wrote:

> Oh my dear child I am in despair – News just in that Khartoum was taken by treachery on 26th January. My steamers reached Khartoum on 28th just in time to see it occupied by the enemy ... Poor Gordon! For his sake I sincerely hope he is dead ... I should think this blow will kill poor Gladstone. He alone is to blame. Had he been a statesman, this misfortune could never have fallen upon us: but he neither could nor would realise the necessity for making preparations for the relief of Khartoum.[30]

Although there was clearly some truth in these last words, fault for Gordon's death did not rest solely on the Prime Minister's shoulders.

Fortunately for Wolseley, when the news of Gordon's fate reached London the public outcry and outrage was initially directed at politicians rather than military men. This gave Wolseley an opportunity to prepare his defence and crucially find a scapegoat for the failure of the expedition. Although Wolseley was always scathing in private about Gladstone's reluctance which had caused such delay in authorizing the expedition, in effect placing it in a position in which success was unlikely, he turned his wrath in public onto Sir Charles Wilson. Wolseley was convinced that the critical days lost at Metemmeh, due to Wilson's indecision, before the steamers left for Khartoum had cost Gordon his life. Wolseley told his wife that he could not bear to have Wilson in his sight and inferred that the lack of damage to the steamer *Bordein* suggested that Wilson had not pushed on to Khartoum as far as he might. This was a particularly cheap slur on Wilson's courage and Wolseley made further implied accusations when he sent Wilson's official report on his actions at Metemmeh to Hartington with the comment that he did not propose to add any remarks of his own and that 'the reasons given by Sir Charles Wilson must speak for themselves'.[31] Hartington referred the matter to Cambridge, who certainly would not support Wolseley in his stance against Wilson. Although Wilson felt that he had to publish a book to justify his command decisions and tell of his role in the campaign there was not the appetite in either the War Office or Parliament to blame him. On his return from Egypt, Wolseley would turn to other failings to deflect criticism of his command. Indeed, this became something of a crusade once he was behind his War Office desk.

To Wolseley's astonishment the Government's initial reaction to the death of Gordon was to instruct him to prepare for a renewed campaign against the Mahdi. Wolseley was given *carte blanche* to carry out further operations as he saw fit but writing to Hartington, he explained that to attack the Mahdi in the heat of the summer would be madness and that he would recommence operations in the autumn. Meanwhile his short-term goals were to capture and secure Berber and Metemmeh. Yet, within the space of two weeks Wolseley had to scale back even these limited objectives. Buller was despatched to the Jakdul wells and from there onto Abu Klea and the Nile. His assessment of the fighting strength and resilience of the remaining men of the Desert Column was a sobering one for it was abundantly clear to Buller that the troops were spent as an offensive fighting force. In addition, with the capture of Khartoum the Mahdi had become emboldened and Buller was forced to retreat to Korti with up to 50,000 warriors shadowing their every move and snipers regularly claiming victims in the dwindling numbers.

The River Column were able to renew their offensive, but the falling level of the Nile and supply problems impeded the advance on Berber. On 10 February the Column was opposed by a force of 9,000 Mahdists at a place named Kirbekan. Here Earle conducted an old-fashioned, but highly effective strategy of luring in the enemy to his centre, whilst men of the Black Watch and South Staffs flanked the Mahdist position and completely routed them. For around sixty casualties the British killed nearly 2,000 warriors, although the cost in terms of senior British officers was high, with Colonels Coveny and Eyre killed in battle and General Earle dying during the mopping-up operations. Command fell to Brackenbury who continued the advance only to be summoned back by Wolseley in light of the retreat of the Desert Column. Both Columns were back in Korti by the middle of March.

It is clear from his campaign journal that Wolseley had given up on any hopes of a further offensive in the short term well before the return of the columns to Korti. Writing in his journal on 17 February Wolseley unburdened his anguished mind;

> How one month has dissipated all my high hopes! … I find myself obliged to retreat! What a horrible word! And to retreat before a rabble such as that the Mahdi commands! It is a heavy blow to sustain, a heavy punishment to have inflicted upon me – and yet I know it is all for the best. God has something better in store either for England or for me … God's will be done, but it breaks my heart.[32]

Two days later Wolseley received the news he had feared that his friend and colleague Herbert Stewart had finally succumbed to his wound. Again, in his campaign journal Wolseley opened his heart when he wrote;

> I feel as if I had lost my right arm … I cannot hope to see his like again. He was out and out the best man I had about me … It is at moments like this that a loathing comes over me for war, that science and art in the study and practice of which I have spent my whole life and to which I have devoted all my energies and brain power God has gifted me.[33]

The men of the failed expedition moved from Korti to summer quarters in Dongola where the biggest threat was boredom. Here, they waited for the next command from Wolseley or the ever-changing minds of politicians. Wolseley left his beloved troops here and journeyed to Cairo under orders from Hartington for he was needed to direct possible operations in the Suakin region. Although reluctant to leave Dongola once housed in an Egyptian palace, and with his wife and daughter once more with him, Wolseley realized how much strain his body and mind had endured, and he relaxed for the first time for many months. This cordial environment was shattered by the so-called Pendjeh crisis in Afghanistan in which Russian forces crossed the border and seized the village of Pendjeh as a bargaining tool whilst an Anglo-Russian Commission was seeking a resolution for the disputed region of Afghanistan. Gladstone was incensed by the Russian action and called out the reserves for a full mobilization of the British Army. Naturally, the troops in the Sudan would be needed and despite Wolseley's protestations that the Sudan could not be abandoned, Gladstone got his way and on 11 May a complete evacuation of the Sudan was ordered. Wolseley was furious and even considered resignation, but he remained in Egypt to oversee the withdraw of the majority of British forces and it was here that he had the satisfaction of hearing of the fall of the Gladstone administration. He managed to persuade the new Conservative government, led by Lord Salisbury, to retain some troops at Wadi Halfa and Dongola and it was these men, along with soldiers of the Egyptian army, that defeated the final threat of the Mahdist army at the battle of Ginnis on 30 December.

The Gordon Relief Expedition had failed; with it Wolseley's incredible run of success as a field commander had come to a sorrowful end. Many writers, such as Henry Keown-Boyd, Michael Asher and Adrian Preston, have argued that Wolseley never really grasped the many and major problems facing the expedition from the start. Certainly, the master of logistics in the Red River and Asante failed to get control of this crucial aspect of warfare during his last field command. Indeed, it could be argued, that by bringing voyageurs from Canada and still relying heavily on the men of his 'Asante Ring' Wolseley was living in the past and he clearly felt all would be well providing he had his once-reliable team around him. Yet Wolseley realized early in the expedition that these men had grown self-serving in their older age and somewhat complacent, but for all his moaning to his wife and others he neither replaced them nor did he take personal control of problems when they became apparent (such as the lack of camels), as he had done in earlier years. The ruthlessness Wolseley demonstrated in securing the necessary porters during the Asante expedition had gone, just when it was most needed.

There were many reasons for the failure of the campaign, with no one element or person solely to blame. Certainly, the hesitation displayed by the Gladstone government to authorize operations placed Wolseley in an acutely difficult position with time always against his success. However, the once reliable campaigner failed to stamp his authority on both command and logistics; in a situation in which he was always going to struggle to save Gordon, this failure condemned his old friend to his fate.

## Chapter 6

# Success and Frustration

With the fall of the Gladstone government Wolseley would now be reporting to a new Secretary of State for War. He had grown to like and respect Hartington and was genuinely disappointed to see him leave. At the end of June 1885, in his official departing letter to Wolseley, Hartington wrote that he had just missed success and this should not be attributed to 'any fault either of design or execution on your own part …'[1] Indeed, it appears that the country, and certainly its politicians, had grown weary of the furore that had surrounded the expedition and the need for blame, or a scapegoat, for the expedition's failure was not sought. On 12 August the new Conservative Prime Minister, Lord Salisbury, rose in Parliament to offer his thanks to Wolseley and all those who had taken part in the expedition. In the subsequent debate no criticism of either Wolseley or Wilson was voiced and the high cost of the operation (reportedly in the region of £3,000,000, close to £500,000,000 at 2023 levels) was not even touched upon.

This did not stop Wolseley's attempts to deflect from the expedition's failure. Whilst still in Egypt Wolseley had written to Hartington to highlight that, in his opinion, troops had been let down by the performance of their senior officers and he even claimed that some lieutenant-colonels were entirely unfit for their position. This letter was a continuation of Wolseley's crusade for promotion via merit rather than seniority, but its timing was poor for with Hartington's imminent departure, Wolseley received no response and even an anonymous magazine article, written by Wolseley under the name of 'Centurion', received scant attention. However, his campaign against faulty equipment, specifically the claims that bayonets bent and Martini-Henry rifles had jammed in the ferocious fighting at Abu Klea, did receive more notice. A special Parliamentary committee on small arms took evidence from many of the survivors and minor recommendations were made, but the service life of much of the weapons taken on the expedition was coming to an end and the controversy surrounding faulty equipment soon faded. However, Wolseley could claim a small success as the Government agreed that the testing of munitions would, in future, be in the hands of the military rather than the manufacturers.

In 1886 the Intelligence Branch produced a confidential memorandum on the Nile Expedition which was a compilation of reports from the senior officers who had taken part. It is of interest for what it does not say rather than what it does. Buller defended the contract he oversaw with Thomas Cook, which had resulted in delays to the transit down the Nile, and made recommendations for future contracts of a similar nature. However, Wolseley only made two paragraphs of comment in the report, which were under a section entitled, 'General Observations'. He thanked General Grenfell for collecting the various musings from those involved in the Expedition and said this had been 'so well arranged and so admirably reported on that he [Grenfell] has practically left nothing for me to say'.[2] This is an extraordinary statement from Wolseley, whose only observation was on the difficulty in purchasing native vessels to transport men and supplies, and that without the whalers the expedition could never have left Halfa. No mention of the issues surrounding the camels or other logistical problems surrounding the expedition were made and it seems apparent that Wolseley did not want such matters discussed further. The report was not circulated outside of the War Office.

Whilst Wolseley was able to nullify any direct criticism of his own performance during the Gordon Relief Expedition, its failure had removed some of the lustre which had previously surrounded him. Certainly, his cloak of invincibility had been lost and Wolseley was never viewed with the same degree of authority ever again, whether at the War Office or by politicians. Before the Nile Expedition, Wolseley was seen by many as a man not to be trifled with, whose grasp of detail and great experience could bemuse and overwhelm both friend and foe. But failure meant that where before individuals might tremble to receive a memorandum from Wolseley, now these could be dismissed or at least passed over. Even Wolseley believed that he had passed the pinnacle of his career, yet he was not one to simply fade away and his reforming zeal remained as strong as ever, as did the disagreements with the Duke of Cambridge.

In the five years Wolseley remained in the post of Adjutant-General, Britain experienced significant political turmoil, with three changes of government in this short period. As a result, Wolseley served under three Secretaries of State: the Conservatives William Henry Smith and Edward Stanhope and the Liberal Henry Campbell-Bannerman. In addition, Lord Salisbury, who was Prime Minster of the two Conservative governments in these years, had a strong personal dislike of Wolseley which saw him more inclined to ignore than accept the Adjutant-General's reforms.

Despite the difficult political position Wolseley found himself in, he could still not resist airing his views on defence issues in public, which placed him in conflict with his political masters. This was clearly seen in the debate over the preparedness of Britain's defences to thwart an invasion of home soil, with the French being the most likely threat. The journalist W.T. Stead had highlighted the poor state and strength of the Royal Navy as compared to that of the French and Wolseley had taken the opportunity to fuel the conversation further by similarly pointing out deficiencies in Britain's land defences and the inadequate size of home forces. Wolseley even publicly supported the Parliamentary candidacy of his old colleague from the Sudan, Lord Charles Beresford, who had resigned his naval commission to stand for Parliament to campaign for a stronger navy. This was not the action expected of an Adjutant-General and for this he received a reprimand from Stanhope, although in private Cambridge supported Wolseley's stance. Salisbury went further and spoke of Wolseley abusing his power to stir unrest and Wolseley felt he had to defend himself in his maiden speech in the House of Lords on 14 May 1888. He argued that publicity was vital to gain the support of the public for the essential and considerable expenditure that was required.

The debate surrounding home defence rumbled on until 1889. Brackenbury in the Intelligence Department largely supported Wolseley's claims of the possible invasion threat from France, whilst Colonel Ardagh argued in a memorandum to Stanhope on home defence that a ring of fixed defences around London should be built, which was very similar to Wolseley's suggestions. Wolseley's public entry into the argument certainly claimed some successes. Funds were secured to extend and improve existing defences, such as at Tilbury Fort, and sixty 'Stanhope storehouses' were built from Aldershot south to the coast. These would house both soldiers and munitions in time of crisis, as well as ease the mobilization of troops to either meet an invading force or to be sent to ports for despatch to areas of imperial concern. However, the biggest winner in the defence argument was the Royal Navy who under the 1889 Naval Defence Act secured significant funds for new ships.

In answer to Wolseley's musing about home defence and the role of the Army, Stanhope responded at the end of 1888 with a memorandum which set out the function of the Army with Stanhope largely agreeing with Wolseley's propositions. Thus, the Army was seen as supporting the civil authorities in Britain, as having garrison duties in fortified defences and coaling stations around the globe and at home, as well as providing troops for India. Finally, to have sufficient men and resources for mobilisation, in times of crisis, of two Army Corps for both Home and Overseas service. With concern of a potential invasion threat Wolseley had argued for the mobilization of three Home Army Corps, but the government was not prepared to increase the size of the Army. Stanhope's memorandum clearly positioned the British

Army's role as for home and imperial defence. Indeed, in the introduction to the memorandum Stanhope wrote, 'The probability of the employment of an Army Corps in the field in any European war is sufficiently improbable to make it the primary duty of the military authorities to organize our forces efficiently for the defence of this country'.[3] Wolseley had clearly influenced the Secretary of State, although writing to his wife, he was disdainful of Stanhope; 'I am sick of him[Stanhope] … He is nothing more than a little party politician dressed up as a statesman.'[4]

In other 'battles' Wolseley pushed for and oversaw the successful introduction of both the Lee-Metford magazine rifle and the Maxim machine gun, as well as improvements in artillery and shells. Yet he was unsuccessful in his efforts to significantly increase soldier's pay and the size of the Army, which he continually argued was too small to meet the needs of home defence as well as its imperial commitments. Instead, Wolseley worked effectively with Sir Evelyn Wood in the Eastern Command as well as at Aldershot to improve training, drill and musketry across the army. Despite setbacks in his attempts to modernize the Army he was able to write to the Duchess of Edinburgh in 1887 with sense of satisfaction, that

> I am glad to say that … we have never in our history been so ready for war as now … after ten years of struggling against every species of opposition, I leave everything ready for the rapid mobilisation of two Army Corps – about 65,000 men, or twice the force we landed in the Crimea … we can land this little army in a very perfect condition.[5]

The year 1889 saw Wolseley surrounded in controversy when on three occasions he caused embarrassment to the government with his writing and public speeches. For an article in the *Fortnightly Review*, Wolseley received a rebuke from both Cambridge and Stanhope with the latter conveying the view that 'it is undesirable for officers on Full Pay of the Army expressing their opinions by any other way than by legitimate channels of communication to the Commander-in-Chief'.[6] In May Wolseley reportedly made a speech at the Oxford Union, which carried a thinly disguised attack on the Liberal Opposition and in October he embarrassed the government further by not denying rumours that he had agreed to travel to America to unveil a statue of the former Confederate general, Robert E. Lee. Clearly, when it came to the public political arena, one in which he should not have been involved, Wolseley was his own worst enemy.

However, in 1890, when Wolseley stepped down as Adjutant General he received letters of praise from both Stanhope and, surprisingly, from

Cambridge. Despite their frequent disagreements the Duke had the grace to acknowledge that Wolseley had always fought for the Army to be strengthened and improved. Cambridge wrote,

> I must tell you how much I have at all times appreciated the assistance I have derived from you as Adjutant General ... The changes that have so constantly taken place ... have rendered the duties of your office especially arduous, and I have always admired the characteristic vigour and energy you have thrown into them.[7]

With no thoughts of retirement Wolseley was keen to find a new position that would keep him close to Whitehall. He refused an offer of the Governor-Generalship of Victoria, Australia and when Stanhope tried to entice him to India as Commander-in-Chief, Wolseley declined the post which he had coveted for so long. With relations improved with Russia, he told Stanhope that if 'profound peace reigns in India to go there would be to me professional suicide'.[8] However, Wolseley did accept the Government's next offer of Commander-in-Chief, Ireland and he journeyed there in late 1890 to take on the role. Wolseley was proud of his Anglo-Irish Protestant roots and he certainly had sympathy with those opposing Home Rule. Indeed, he privately confided to his old friend and colleague Frederick Maurice that he would gladly lead Ulsterman in their fight against Gladstone's policy and informed another confidant that he would be unable to serve in Ireland if a civil war broke out. Therefore, it is surprising that Wolseley was offered the position and the appointment perhaps reflects the need to find a suitably senior role away from the War Office. Wolseley still had ambitions to replace Cambridge when he finally retired from his long-held role as Commander-in-Chief of the British Army. But the Duke's retirement did not appear imminent, so by accepting the position in Ireland Wolseley felt that he was in a good place to maintain some influence in Whitehall and could react if an opportunity to succeed Cambridge presented itself.

Britain had up to 30,000 soldiers stationed in Ireland, split between two commands at the Curragh, near Dublin and in Cork. With decades of agrarian disturbances and violent opposition to Gladstone's attempts to establish Home Rule, many of these troops were scattered around the country in small garrisons ready to quell any further agitation. But with the defeat of the First Home Rule Bill, conflict had significantly lessened, and Wolseley's arrival coincided with a period of relative calm. It was only when Gladstone attempted to introduce a Second Home Rule Bill in 1893 did disturbances surface in Belfast. Wolseley journeyed north and by April 1893 he was able to confirm that law and order had been restored. With the Bill being rejection once more by the Lords, an uneasy calm was restored.

With Ireland relatively peaceful throughout Wolseley's tenure, the Commander-in-Chief struggled with boredom. Wolseley undertook numerous tours of the countryside to visit the scattered garrisons; as much to escape society and entertaining in Dublin, which he found dull, as to check on military readiness. When Cambridge reprimanded him for not writing regular military reports on Irish affairs, Wolseley replied 'I have little military work to do and still less to write about'.[9] Although he was able to improve training, and held regular manoeuvres, it is clear military matters did not fill his days. Wolseley was able to begin a two-volume biography of the Duke of Marlborough and a shorter sketch on Napoleon during his five years in Ireland. Wolseley made frequent visits back to the War Office to sit on the recently established Promotion Board, which was one of his pet projects that he had been able to introduce despite hostility from Cambridge. During these trips he learnt that moves were afoot to finally persuade the Duke to retire and Wolseley waited impatiently for the expected summons to succeed into the role of Commander-in-Chief.

When a disgruntled Duke was finally persuaded to retire in the spring of 1895, the expected succession of Wolseley was mired in political controversy. In June the new Secretary of State for War, Campbell-Bannerman, announced that Cambridge was finally standing down, but his successor was not immediately named. The Liberal Prime Minister, Lord Roseberry, angered by Wolseley's public opposition to Home Rule, decided to recommend the then Adjutant-General, Sir Redvers Buller, for the position. Wolseley heard of Buller's appointment whilst on holiday and was incredulous that his old colleague had usurped him. Writing to Colonel Childers Wolseley stated, 'It is a horrible finish to my career, to be superseded by one of my own lieutenants [Buller], whom I may say I created a General officer'.[10]

However, Wolseley was fortunate, for the Roseberry government was forced to resign after losing a vote of censure. The Conservatives returned to power under Lord Salisbury, who was no friend of Wolseley. Three months of jostling and intrigue amongst the likely candidates; Wolseley, Lord Roberts, the Queen's son, the Duke of Connaught, and Buller, now commenced, with even Cambridge making the case for his own return. On hearing of Connaught's candidacy, Wolseley, to his credit, volunteered to remove himself from consideration, but the government having managed to remove one royal personage were not going to have another one fostered upon them. In August Wolseley's appointment was confirmed by the Secretary of State, Lord Lansdowne. Roberts was given Ireland and Buller remained as Adjutant-

General and worked successfully alongside Wolseley. Although there was no open animosity between the two, Wolseley would never trust Buller as he had before. Wolseley even named one of his own horses, which had an unreliable disposition, 'Sir Redvers', so it is clear what Wolseley really thought of his once loyal comrade. The Queen, disappointed that her son had failed to win the contest, telegraphed Lansdowne stating, 'I sanction Wolseley's appointment, but I do not think it is a good one', and following this, she advised Lansdowne to 'impress upon Lord Wolseley the absolute necessity of not having anything to do with the Press'.[11]

Having been promoted to the rank of Field Marshal the year before, Wolseley had finally achieved the ultimate prize. Britain's most accomplished soldier of Victoria's reign was seen by many as deserving of his new role, but, as he would soon discover, it was one that had significantly altered. In 1890 Lord Hartington had chaired a commission which had recommended that once the Duke had retired as Commander-in-Chief, the War Office should introduce a Chief of Staff position. The commission felt that the centralising of power under a Commander-in-Chief weakened the roles and sense of responsibility across other military department heads and produced inefficiencies. At the time both Cambridge and Wolseley voiced their opposition, fearing rightly, that it would result in an extension of civilian powers, specifically those of the Secretary of State, at the expense of the military. Campbell-Bannerman ultimately rejected Hartington's recommendation and stated that the position of Commander-in-Chief would be retained but with substantially reduced powers. With the fall of the Liberal government, it fell to the Conservatives, specifically Lansdowne, to make their own proposals.

Wolseley had served under several Secretaries of State for War, both Conservative and Liberals. Some, such as Cardwell, Childers, and Hartington, he had personally liked and had worked with them to introduce several reforms, often battling against the inertia of Cambridge. Others, such as Stanhope, he had disdained or through force of personality and reputation had been able to manipulate to a degree. Now Wolseley was faced with Lansdowne, a most determined and driven individual who was intellectually superior to other Secretaries he had worked with, and Wolseley had to face this challenge at a point when his own mental capacities were beginning to fail him.

Lansdowne removed the concentration of power from the hands of the Commander-in-Chief and five senior offices were introduced. The Commander-in-Chief remained now as a chief adviser to the Secretary but with general command of all forces. The Adjutant-General was responsible for recruitment, training, education, and discipline; the Quartermaster-General focused on supplying food, forage, fuel, transport, pay and quartering whilst the Inspector-General of Fortifications ensured the barracks, lands and store-buildings were maintained. Finally, the Inspector-General of Ordnance had the task of the efficient and safe holding of military stores. Although Wolseley was to supervise the other four offices, all five were directly responsible to the Secretary of State. These changes came into effect by an Order of Council of 21 November 1895.

Almost immediately Wolseley realized that as Commander-in-Chief he had responsibility without real control or dignity. He had accepted the post on the understanding that there would 'be no material alterations in the position',[12] but within a day of taking the position Lansdowne announced the new structure. Wolseley privately complained that he was now merely 'the fifth wheel on the coach'[13] and 'vice-chairman of a debating society'.[14] After years of wishing for the position of highest military authority he now felt undermined. Wolseley knew that the public would see the Commander-in-Chief as responsible for the efficiency of the Army and that they would not understand that the Army was now be effectively overseen by an Army Board.

Wolseley's reaction to being placed in such a position was, predictably, to fight against it. He was adamant that the four heads of department should not have direct access to the Secretary of State, nor did he feel that he could provide supervision if he did not know what his heads of department were doing. In addition, with senior men as heads of their departments; at the pinnacle of their careers, there was a real danger that they would make decisions at the expense of the efficiency of the Army as a whole. Most importantly, Wolseley believed politicians only thought of peace and expenditure, and quite forgot the need to prepare for war. He felt he was now a commentator rather than a leader. Although he tried to amend his role, making several reasonable suggestions, Lansdowne was not to be moved for he had achieved his goal of placing firm political control upon all departments within the Army.

Although Wolseley could feel disgruntled, he did not help his cause, for rather than trying to adapt and work with the new structure he tried to circumvent it. For example, in his autobiography, Sir Evelyn Wood, who replaced Buller as Adjutant-General in 1897, wrote that Wolseley ordered him to address any matters he wished to discuss with the Secretary of State through him first and that effectively Wolseley undermined Wood's own independence. Any correspondence that Lansdowne had with Wood was intercepted by Wolseley first. Such actions clearly contravened the spirit of the new structure, and it is hardly surprising that relations, both working and personal, between Lansdowne and Wolseley deteriorated.

The atmosphere in the War Office at this time was described by an officer of the Royal Engineers named Edmunds who was appointed to the Intelligence

Branch in 1898. In an unpublished autobiography, Edmunds wrote of the perpetual rivalries for precedence as departments and their heads battled for supremacy. Edmunds also recalled how lax the work ethic was at this time with the day starting at 11am, for Wolseley expected everyone to ride in St. James Park before starting work. Edmunds also claimed that if an officer wanted to go on leave, he wrote a message, such as 'away until the 12th'[15] and fixed it to his desk and then departed, leaving his office door open to signify his absence. It is almost beyond belief that the victor of Tel-el-Kebir would tolerate such laxness and indicates that Wolseley had lost much of his drive.

The man who had once been 'Our Only General' had lost the appeal and ability to rouse public sentiment and Wolseley was no match for Lansdowne's intellect or resolve. This was particularly true after bouts of illness affected Wolseley. First, he suffered from a bad case of influenza which sapped his strength and in 1897 he appeared to have suffered a mild stroke which triggered a decline in his memory that became progressively more noticeable. Wolseley would engage in fierce arguments with colleagues in which he would dispute all knowledge of a memorandum he had written only days before and Lord Hamilton, then Secretary of State for India, recalled a conversation in which Wolseley denied knowing Beauchamp Duff, who was then his assistant private secretary. Leo Amery was the first of many commentators to point-out that Wolseley's appointment had come 10 years too late for him to really use the position of Commander-in-Chief to make the necessary reforms he had so earlier been evangelical about.

Lansdowne and Wolseley were, however, able to work together to secure a large tract of land upon Salisbury Plain for large-scale Army manoeuvres and the first such exercise took place in 1898. Two years before Wolseley had overseen the publication of *The Infantry Drill Book* and had been at the heart of the discussion of both defensive and offensive formations in the changing battlefield of modern artillery, bolt-action magazine rifles and machine guns. The *Book* affirmed Wolseley's belief that troops needed to advance in extended order of a minimum of one and a half yards per man, but it was left to the discretion of local officers as and when to extend formations. However, individual colonels had considerable independence when it came to the training of their battalions, and it seems clear that many preferred to focus on formations more suitable for the parade ground. Leo Amery claimed in his seven-volume *Times History of the War in South Africa* that even at the Aldershot manoeuvres, densely-packed attacking lines, with an average of three men per yard, were common. One junior officer noted that battalion assault training in July 1899 consisted of the attacking line being in tight bunches of twenty men each who advanced to within 200 yards of the enemy before breaking formation. The officer recorded, 'I could not believe it was serious practice for modern warfare. We should all have been wiped out.'[16] Unfortunately, similar formations were seen just a few months later as British regulars advanced towards unseen Boer troops, armed with modern rifles and artillery. The disastrous and deadly results were inevitable. Wolseley should surely have stamped his remaining authority upon all colonels of battalions to ensure that the best formations were taught and applied in the face of rapidly changing battlefield technology. That he did not is an indication that he had lost some of his grasp of where his beloved Army needed to be in his preoccupation with the loss of his own authority.

The impending risk of war with the Boers of South Africa dominated Wolseley's thinking in the years 1897–9 and he wrote repeatedly to Lansdowne of the need to address both troop levels and their disposition. Unfortunately, relations between the two men had deteriorated to such an extent that Lansdowne was now more inclined to scorn Wolseley than listen to him. Wolseley's diary of 12 April 1897 records, 'Am still pressing the Government to largely augment the force at the Cape. Lansdowne is, and always has been opposed to it.'[17] The following day's entry states that Wolseley had proposed strengthening the position in Natal by sending two batteries of field artillery, as well as an extra battalion, but once again Lansdowne blocked the move. By the summer of 1899 war was looking increasingly likely and writing to Lansdowne on 24 August Wolseley's exasperation was clear;

> At this moment we are *not* locally prepared for war in South Africa, so that if it comes upon us under present circumstances we shall surrender the initiative to Kruger, and in no recent case that I can think of would that loss of initiative be more likely to seriously injure our national prestige or be more hurtful to the party in office, if I may venture upon such a political comment.[18]

Wolseley must share some blame for the government's inertia, for the assessments of the Boer threat compiled by the Intelligence Department were held by Wolseley and not passed onto Lansdowne.

Despite Wolseley's warnings, Britain and the Boers 'marched to war'. Kruger's ultimatum to withdraw British troops from South Africa, as well as turnaround the 10,000 reinforcements Wolseley had rather belatedly managed to get the government to agree upon in September was received in London on 10 October 1899. The Commander-in-Chief rose to the challenge of mobilization with a vigour he had not displayed for some time. Utilizing many of the 'Stanhope storehouses' to dispatch troops to south coast ports, ready for transit to the Cape, Wolseley was able to efficiently send a full Army Corps of 47,000 men, under the command of Buller to South Africa. Wolseley confidently predicted that these men were '... the very ablest soldiers ...thoroughly equipped for war'.[19]

Wolseley's optimism was, however, not justified for before Buller had reached the Cape British forces had been defeated at the Battle of Talena Heights (20 October 1899). The British commander, Sir George White, had foolishly decided to consolidate his remaining forces at Ladysmith where they were encircled and besieged by the enemy. On arriving at the Cape, Buller had to alter his strategy to relieve Ladysmith. This would take three months and resulted in several significant British defeats. These loses demonstrated huge tactical weaknesses in the British force, both amongst senior commanders as well as junior officers as they led their men in futile frontal attacks. Buller was replaced by Wolseley's great rival, Lord Roberts. Although the two were the same age, the deterioration in Wolseley's memory, and poor relations with Lansdowne, meant that he was never seriously considered as a replacement for Buller. The Commander-in-Chief was not even consulted on Roberts's appointment, and this illustrates how much Wolseley's influence had waned.

Wolseley spent the last months before his retirement in November 1900 behind his desk at the War Office, offering what support he could to both Buller and Roberts and, working with Evelyn Wood, he ensured the welfare of troops in South Africa was not ignored. Yet he was now an isolated figure and his departure, and replacement by Roberts, was met with little fanfare. There was no official expression of thanks for his 50 years of service and indeed mutterings had already started that his lack of preparedness had led to the early British defeats. Once again, Wolseley did not help himself for rather than making a dignified exit, he protested publicly about civilian interference in the administration of the army, which forced the government to defend itself and it constituted a committee of inquiry to examine the administration of the Army. This committee presented its report in May 1901, and it vindicated many of the grievances that Wolseley and other senior officers had voiced. It also recommended further reforms that enhanced the role of the intelligence branch and saw greater coordination across departments. In his last parting gesture, Wolseley had insured that his relationship with Lansdowne had irretrievably broken down and this was to cost Wolseley's reputation dear.

With politicians, and in particular Lansdowne, in need of a scapegoat for the early battlefield calamities of the war, mutterings continued against Wolseley's performance as Commander-in-Chief. Wolseley felt that he needed to defend himself in a debate on Army matters in the Lords on 4 March 1901. He gave a speech in which, making no personal attacks, he condemned the administrative system at the War Office, which he blamed for the disastrous setbacks and implied that if he had been given a free hand then the War would have taken a much more satisfactory course. Although a rather disillusionary and self-seeking speech, it was initially respectfully received. Then, however, Lansdowne rose to his feet and responded to Wolseley's claims with a personal attack against the former Commander-in-Chief and gave three specific examples in which Wolseley had failed to alert or prepare either the government or the Army to the threat posed by the Boers. Both the Duke of Devonshire and the Prime Minister, Lord Salisbury, tried to deflect Lansdowne's personal rebukes, but it was clear for all to see that it was implied in Lansdowne's words that Wolseley had failed to perform his duty.

Naturally, Wolseley was stung by such an attack. On 15 March Wolseley returned to the Lords to move that all papers surrounding the allegations that Lansdowne had earlier made against him should be made available so that he may defend himself. The Government made the question a party matter and refused to produce the necessary papers, minutes etc, on the grounds of National security. Only thirty-eight peers supported Wolseley in the vote and the Government easily won with a large majority. Roberts fled the chamber having supported the Government. Wolseley wrote to this wife; 'I am disgusted to death with the treatment I received from that poor little contemptible creature Lansdowne ... If I were ten years younger I would move heaven and earth to have it out with him, but now it is too late.'[20] This was Wolseley's final appearance in the Lords, and he never made public reference to what he later described as the most unpleasant incident in his life. Scorned by politicians and now a figure of the past, Wolseley largely left public life. The Government allowed him to abandon all the ceremonial duties linked to his many honorary offices. It was a humiliating end for the once-great warrior.

# Conclusion

After such a long and demanding career, Wolseley's last 12 years were an anti-climax and a time of decline. He and his wife spent their time between a 'grace and favour' apartment at Hampton Court and their winter residence at Menton, on the French Riviera. On the urging of friends, Wolseley wrote two volumes of autobiography, the second of which concluded with the Asante Expedition. Both works were remarkable only for their dull prose, rather than any great revelations. Mediocre sales and a failing memory meant Wolseley never completed his memoirs. He was occasionally visited by old comrades, but these visits could be painful. On one occasion William Butler, who had served Wolseley from the Red River to the Nile, was not even recognized by his old commanding officer and Butler was hugely upset by the visit. Of particular sadness was that in Wolseley's final years, he and his wife became estranged from their only child, Frances. It is not totally clear why the split occurred; it may have been because of Frances' sexuality, her independent character, or her choice of career as a writer and gardener, but at the time of Wolseley's death, father and daughter had not seen each other or corresponded for some time. The family rift continued between mother and daughter until Louisa's death in 1920, when Frances discovered that she had been largely left out of her mother's Will. Frances was heiress to the viscountcy, under special remainder, but it became extinct upon her death.

Wolseley died in his villa in Menton on 26 March 1913, from complications arising from a chill. During his eventful career Wolseley had always dreaded dying in his bed, but that was his final fate. Upon his passing, Britain seemed to wake up to what it had lost, and Wolseley's funeral was full of pomp and honour. Hundreds of troops, from regiments that had served under Wolseley's various commands lined the funeral route and, on 31 March 1913, Wolseley was laid to rest in the crypt of St. Paul's Cathedral, near another former Commander-in-Chief, the Duke of Wellington; the man who had given Wolseley his first opportunity in the British Army.

So, what of the man and his legacy. Well, Wolseley was, in the opinion of many of his contemporaries, as well as historians, a difficult, cantankerous, arrogant, impatient and vain man. He was frequently contemptuous of both colleagues, politicians and even friends who failed to meet his own high personal standards or show a strong work ethic. Even for the low standards of his day, he was very racist. Yet, he was undoubtedly brave, driven, intelligent and a man of great foresight and vision, who could quickly grasp a situation, whether that was on the battlefield or in the planning of a campaign. His organizational and logistics skills were outstanding; this was perhaps his greatest gift to the Victorian Army and exemplified in his *Soldier's Pocket Book*.

Wolseley was also a generally lucky soldier, and this can be considered the most important factor in his rise. He survived enormous dangers fighting in Burma, India, and China, when many of his young comrades did not and were lost to history. He had the fortune to come under the patronage of Hope Grant who quickly recognized his talents and propelled him to become the youngest colonel in the British Army. Upon reaching that rank, his career never looked back, and he quickly became the 'go-to' man to resolve the latest imperial crisis. Such a phenomenal rise created jealousy and with Wolseley's drive to reform many, particularly at the War Office and Whitehall, became his enemies. Wolseley had few diplomatic skills and his impatience led him to public utterances and words in the Press which, on occasions, hindered his own career and his desire for reform. It is interesting to wonder how much more might have been achieved around reform if Wolseley had been less confrontational.

Yet, Wolseley, either on his own initiative or working with the likes of Cardwell, Hartington and Wood, did achieve important reforms within the British Army, often in the face of significant opposition from politicians, the Duke of Cambridge and Victoria. The ending of the purchase system and the introduction of promotion by merit rather than seniority, significantly improved the professionalism of officers, as did Wolseley's support of graduates of the Staff College. One of his greatest legacies was, arguably, the development of the 'Asante Ring' of outstanding officers who, under Wolseley's patronage, were able to break away from the old system of advancement and offer a new dynamism of leadership to the British Army, just when it needed it most. Of course, the counter-argument is that the existence of 'the Ring' deterred the promotion of others, but this hard-core of officers went onto senior positions and were able to raise standards further.

On campaign Wolseley was undoubtedly a master of logistics and when he was tested in battles, such as Amoaful or Tel-el-Kebir, he displayed great tactical astuteness to produce major victories. Clearly Wolseley's last field command, the Gordon Relief Expedition, was a failure and there were several factors for this, some of which were out of Wolseley's hands. However, the once master of logistics was either overwhelmed by or failed to grasp the enormity of the challenge. He was also less successful when given pseudo-political roles such as in Cyprus, Natal and at the conclusion of the Anglo-Zulu war. It seems his impatience and desire to move onto the next task resulted in rushed and incomplete decision-making which later generated political difficulties.

After years of hard work, endeavour and scheming, Wolseley, in 1895, finally succeeded to the position he had coveted for so long; that of Commander-in-Chief. For the great reformer this was finally his chance to further reform the British Army. Historians, such as Joseph Lehmann and more recently Halik Kochanski, have painted a picture of partial success and indeed Wolseley did make some important changes. These included the purchase of lands for large-scale manoeuvres and training and the establishment of a mobilisation scheme, whereby a substantial expeditionary force of one or two Army Corps could be despatched quickly and efficiently. Finally, despite what Lansdowne and others implied, Wolseley did possess the foresight to realize the dangers the Boers presented and, with his now-reduced powers, did his best to increase troop levels in South Africa before the outbreak of war and raise political awareness of the threat.

Others, such as Edward Spiers, are more damming in their assessment of Wolseley's tenure. Undoubtedly both Wolseley's mental and physical deterioration limited his ability during this crucial five years, but too much of the energies he still possessed were wasted in his pre-occupation with his loss of authority and attempts to undermine rather than work with and in the new structure. Lansdowne, like Wolseley, was a driven, determined, and confrontational individual, but Wolseley should have tried harder to work within the new systems and with the Secretary of State, rather than to fight with his back up against a proverbial wall.

Some historians see Wolseley as the father of the modern British Army, or at least the individual who paved the way for the professional army that made-up the Expeditionary Force that was sent to France in 1914. Indeed, a former Secretary of State for War, St. John Broderick, wrote to Evelyn Wood in 1918 and stated: 'When history is written I feel that the Army of Mons [the Expeditionary Force] will be ascribed to Lord Wolseley, yourself and his other comrades, who first broke down the old gang'.[1] I believe that this is over-emphasizing the longevity of Wolseley's legacy. He possessed the foresight to recognize that modern weaponry had transformed the Victorian battlefield and had the determination to ensure that the British Army possessed the most modern rifles and machine guns. Yet, at the crucial moment in his tenure as Commander-in-Chief he failed to transform the training of offensive operations, although he had specified the formations that should be followed in the *Infantry Drill Book*. This failure was to cost the lives of many troops in the opening weeks of the Boer War and must be laid firmly at Wolseley's feet.

Wolseley was a Victorian general. The finest, most successful of the Queen's long reign. His personal valour and determination to succeed, whether on campaign or from behind a desk, are a huge credit to him and a fine legacy. However, to take that legacy beyond the Victorian era is an error. Wolseley, like many great individuals, and I do believe in his field he was great, was a person for the moment and to place him anywhere else is a mistake. He was rightly laid to rest next to Wellington; two truly GREAT nineteenth-century generals side-by-side.

# Notes

**Introduction**

1. W. Wright, *A Tidy Little War: The British Invasion of Egypt 1882* (The History Press, Stroud, 2009), p. 124.
2. C. Robinson, *Celebrities of the Army* (Newnes, London, 1900), p. 7.

**Chapter 1: Death or Glory**

1. E. Holt, 'Garnet Wolseley Soldier of Empire', *History Today*, October 1958, p. 706.
2. J. Keegan and A. Wheatcroft (eds.), *Who's Who in Military History* (Routledge, Abingdon, 1995), p. 322.
3. G. Wolseley, *The Story of a Soldier's Life*, Vol. 1 (Archibald Constable, London, 1903), p. 7.
4. Ibid., p. 10.
5. Ibid., p. 52.
6. Ibid., p. 70.
7. E. Wood, *Winnowed Memories* (Cassell, London, 1917), p. 315.
8. C. R. Low, *A Memoir of Lieutenant-General Sir Garnet J. Wolseley*, Vol. 1 (Richard Bentley, London, 1878), p. 99.
9. S. Manning, *Soldiers of the Queen* (Spellmount, Stroud, 2009), p. 86.
10. J. Lehmann, *The Model Major-General – A Biography of Field-Marshal Lord Wolseley* (Houghton Mifflin, Boston, 1964), p. 48.
11. Wolseley, *The Story of a Soldier's Life*, Vol. 1, p. 272.
12. Lehmann, p. 66.
13. Wolseley, *The Story of a Soldier's Life*, Vol. 1, p. 342.
14. H. Kochanski, *Sir Garnet Wolseley – Victorian Hero* (The Hambledon Press, London, 1999), p. 24.
15. Ibid., p. 26.
16. Low, Vol. 1, p. 194.
17. P. C. Smith, *Victoria's Victories* (Spellmount, Tunbridge Wells, 1987), p. 75.
18. Lehmann, p. 93.
19. G. Wolseley, *Narrative of the War with China in 1860* (Longman Green, London, 1862), p. 137.
20. G. Wolseley, *The Story of a Soldier's Life*, Vol. 2 (Archibald Constable, London, 1903), p. 53.
21. Lehmann, p. 110.

**Chapter 2: Independent Command**

1. Wolseley, *The Story of a Soldier's Life*, Vol. 2, p. 116.
2. Kochanski, *Sir Garnet Wolseley*, p. 33.
3. Ibid.
4. Lehmann, p. 121.

5. Wolseley, *The Story of a Soldier's Life*, Vol. 2, p. 135.
6. Kochanski, *Sir Garnet Wolseley*, p. 39.
7. Low, Vol. 1, p. 275.
8. Wolseley, *The Story of a Soldier's Life*, Vol. 2, pp. 154–5.
9. Lehmann, p. 128.
10. Ibid., p. 135.
11. G. Stanley, *Toil and Trouble – Military Expeditions to Red River* (Dundurn Press, Toronto, 1989), p. 65.
12. P. McNicholls, *Journey through the Wilderness – Garnet Wolseley's Canadian Red River Expedition of 1870* (Helion, Warwick, 2019), p. 59.
13. Ibid., p. 60.
14. Ibid., p. 59.
15. G. Arthur (ed.), *The Letters of Lord and Lady Wolseley, 1870–1911* (William Heinemann, London, 1922), p. 2.
16. McNicholls, p. 62.
17. Lindsay to WO, PPP568, Correspondence and Journal, No. 8, 27 May, 1870.
18. Wolseley, *The Story of a Soldier's Life*, Vol. 2, p. 179.
19. McNicholls, p. 62.
20. The Buller Papers DHC 2065M add2/SS1 Wolseley's Standing Orders for the Red River Expeditionary Force.
21. Wolseley, 'Narrative of the Red River Expedition', *Blackwood's Magazine*, Vol. 109, February 1871, p. 53.
22. Wolseley, *The Story of a Soldier's Life*, Vol. 2, p. 187.
23. Lehmann, p. 143.
24. Stanley, p. 112.
25. Ibid., p. 115.
26. Lehmann, p. 145.
27. Ibid., p. 146.
28. The Buller Papers, DHC, 2065 Madd2/SS3 Letter from Captain R.H. Buller to his sister Miss Henrietta Buller sent from Fort Garry 24 August 1870.
29. Wolseley, 'Narrative of the Red River Expedition', pp. 53–4.
30. McNicholls, p. 129.
31. The Buller Papers, DHC, 2065 Madd2/SS3 Letter from Captain R.H. Buller to his sister Miss Henrietta Buller sent from Fort Garry 24 August 1870.
32. McNicholls, p. 131.
33. Ibid.
34. Ibid., p. 138.
35. Stanley, p. 156.
36. The Buller Papers, DHC, 2065 Madd2/SS3 Letter from Captain R.H. Buller to his sister Miss Henrietta Buller sent from Fort Garry 24 August 1870.
37. Low, Vol. 2, p. 77.

**Chapter 3: The White Man's Grave**

1. Wolseley, *The Story of a Soldier's Life*, Vol. 2 , p. 226.
2. Lehmann, p. 158.
3. Ibid.
4. Wolseley, *The Story of a Soldier's Life*, Vol. 2, pp. 251 & 253.
5. G. Wolseley, 'Our Autumn Manoeuvres', *Blackwood's Magazine*, Vol. 112, November 1872, pp. 627–44.

6. Wolseley, *The Story of a Soldier's Life*, Vol. 2, pp. 247–8.
7. W. D. McIntyre, 'British Policy in West Africa: The Ashanti Expedition of 1873–4', *The Historical Journal*, Vol. 5, No. 1 (1962), p. 32.
8. B. Vandervort, *Wars of Imperial Conquest in Africa 1830–1914* (UCL, London, 1998), p. 89.
9. Arthur (ed.), p. 10.
10. H. Brackenbury, *The Ashanti War – A Narrative – Prepared from the Official Documents* (William Blackwood, Edinburgh, 1874), Vol. 1, pp. 157–8.
11. B. Bond (ed.), *Victorian Military Campaigns* (Tom Donovan, London, 1994), p. 180.
12. L. Maxwell, *The Ashanti Ring – Sir Garnet Wolseley's Campaigns, 1870–1882* (Leo Cooper, London, 1985), p. 28.
13. TNA WO 147/3 Entry 2 January 1874.
14. W. W. Claridge, *A History of the Gold Coast and Ashanti*, 2 vols (John Murray, London, 1915), Vol. 2, pp. 92–3.
15. Lehmann, p. 186.
16. A. Lloyd, *The Drums of Kumasi – The Story of the Ashanti Wars* (Panther, London, 1965), p. 102.
17. Wolseley Journal, 10 December 1873, TNA, WO 147/3.
18. Arthur (ed.), p. 17.
19. R. Brooks, *The Long Arm of Empire – Naval Brigades from the Crimea to the Boxer Rebellion* (Constable, London, 1999), p. 125.
20. TNA WO 147/3 Entry 31 January 1874.
21. TNA WO 147/3 Entry 4 February 1874.
22. Ibid.
23. Lehmann, p. 197.
24. TNA WO 147/3 Entry 4 February 1874.
25. J. H .Thomas, *A Full and Authentic Diary of the Ashanti Expedition* (Pembroke, 1875), p. 19.
26. Lehmann, p. 203.
27. Wolseley, *The Story of a Soldier's Life*, Vol. 2, p. 370.
28. TNA WO 147/3 Entry 4 March 1874.

**Chapter 4: Our Only General**

1. Lehmann, p. 204.
2. Cost of Principal British Wars 1857–1899 – compiled by the War Office, NAM 8008–70.
3. F.W. Butler, *The Life of Sir George Pomeroy-Colley* (John Murray, London, 1899), p. 121.
4. Lehmann, p. 208.
5. Kochanski, *Sir Garnet Wolseley*, p. 94.
6. Wolseley to Cambridge, 26 February 1879, RA.
7. Lehmann, p. 242.
8. F. Maurice, *The Life of Lord Wolseley* (Heinemann, London, 1924), p. 115.
9. Ibid., p. 116.
10. W. Wright, *A British Lion in Zululand – Sir Garnet Wolseley in South Africa* (Amberley Stroud, 2017), p. 100.
11. A. Preston (ed.), *The South African Journal of Sir Garnet Wolseley* (A.A. Balkema, Cape Town, 1973), p. 55.

12. Ibid., p. 56.
13. Ibid., p. 61.
14. S. David, *Zulu – The Heroism and Tragedy of the Zulu War* (Viking, London, 2004), p. 366.
15. A. Greaves, *Crossing the Buffalo – The Zulu War of 1879* (Weidenfeld & Nicolson, London, 2005), p. 328.
16. Maurice, p. 123.
17. TNA WO 147/7 – Wolseley Private Journal kept whilst on campaign – 28/11/1879.
18. Wright, *A British Lion in Zululand*, p. 284.
19. TNA WO 147/7 – Wolseley Private Journal kept whilst on campaign – 28/11/1879.
20. Ibid.
21. Maurice, p. 126.
22. Wright, *A British Lion in Zululand*, p. 309.
23. Kochanski, *Sir Garnet Wolseley*, p. 105.
24. Arthur (ed.), p. 46.
25. Wright, *A British Lion in Zululand*, p. 324.
26. Lehmann, p. 281.
27. For a detailed examination of Evelyn Wood's involvement in the peace negotiations see S. Manning, *Evelyn Wood VC, Pillar of Empire* (Pen & Sword, Barnsley, 2007).
28. Kochanski, *Sir Garnet Wolseley*, p. 110.
29. Ibid., p. 111.
30. Lehmann, p. 282.
31. HC Deb 31 May 1880 vol 252c767
32. Lehmann, p. 286.
33. G. Wolseley, 'Long and Short Service', *Nineteenth Century*, XX (1881), p. 559.
34. For a fuller understanding of the evolution of weaponry on the Victorian battlefield see S. Manning, *From Bayonet to Barrage* (Pen & Sword, Barnsley, 2020).
35. Lehmann, p. 284.
36. Ibid., pp. 294–5.
37. W. Blunt, *The Secret History of the English Occupation of Egypt* (A.A. Knopf, New York, 1922), p. 227.
38. Lehmann, p. 301.
39. P. Mansfield, *The British in Egypt* (Holt, Rinehart & Winston, New York, 1972), p. 47.
40. Lehmann, p. 303.
41. Wright, *A Tidy Little War*, p. 185.
42. Arthur (ed.), p. 74.
43. Wright, *A Tidy Little War*, pp. 189–90.
44. Ibid., p. 177.
45. Ibid., p. 206.
46. Ibid.
47. D. Featherstone, *Tel-el-Kebir* (Osprey, Oxford, 1993), p. 55.
48. E. Spiers, *The Late Victorian Army 1868–1902* (Manchester University Press, 1992), p. 284.
49. Maurice, p. 153.
50. E. Spiers, *The Scottish Soldier and Empire* (Edinburgh University Press, 2006), p. 70.
51. Arthur (ed.), p. 75.
52. Lehmann, p. 321.
53. Arthur (ed.), p. 77.

54. Wright, *A Tidy Little War*, p. 283.
55. Lehmann, p. 322.
56. Wright, *A Tidy Little War*, p. 234.
57. G. Tylden, 'Tel-El-Kebir, 13th September, 1882', *Journal of the Society of Army Research*, Vol. 31, No. 126, 1953, p. 57.
58. Featherstone, *Tel-el-Kebir* pp. 82–3.
59. Smith, *Victoria's Victories* (Spellmount, Tunbridge Wells, 1987), pp. 162–3.
60. Lt. Perry, letter to 'my dear Synge', 16 September 1882, Ref: RAM, MD 22.
61. Arthur (ed.), p. 79.
62. W. Wright, *A Tidy Little War*, p. 262.
63. Mansfield, p. 49.
64. Arthur (ed.), pp. 78–9.
65. Ibid., p. 79.
66. Lehmann, p. 334.
67. Arthur (ed.), p. 80.
68. Wright, *A Tidy Little War*, p. 266.
69. Ibid.
70. Spiers, *The Scottish Soldier and Empire*, p. 74.
71. Ibid., p. 76.
72. 'A 42D Man at Tel-el-Kebir', *Kinross-shire Advertiser*, 28 October 1882.
73. W. Wright, *A Tidy Little War*, p. 278.

**Chapter 5: Final Field Command**

1. Lehmann, p. 337.
2. Kochanski, *Sir Garnet Wolseley*, p. 148.
3. Ibid., p. 152.
4. Lehmann, p. 341.
5. M. Asher, *Khartoum The Ultimate Imperial Adventure* (Viking, London, 2005), p. 94.
6. Arthur (ed.), p. 115.
7. Kochanski, *Sir Garnet Wolseley*, p. 153.
8. Ibid., p. 152.
9. Asher, pp. 104–06.
10. Kochanski, p. 154.
11. H. Raugh (ed.), *The British Army 1815–1914* (Routledge, London, 2006), p. 255.
12. Lehmann, p. 345.
13. A. Preston (ed.), *In Relief of Gordon, Lord Wolseley's Campaign Journal of the Gordon Relief Expedition* (Hutchinson, London, 1967), p. xxix.
14. Kochanski, *Sir Garnet Wolseley*, p. 157.
15. Lehmann, p. 347.
16. Kochanski, *Sir Garnet Wolseley*, p. 158.
17. J. Symons, *England's Pride – The Story of the Gordon Relief Expedition* (Hamish Hamilton, London, 1965), p. 91.
18. Maurice, p. 182.
19. Arthur (ed.), p. 136.
20. Symons, *England's Pride*, p. 130.
21. Lehmann, p. 361.
22. Preston (ed.), *In Relief of Gordon*, p. 75.
23. Ibid., p. 76.

24. Ibid., p. 72.
25. Ibid., p. 77.
26. Asher, p. 194.
27. Lehmann, p. 367.
28. WO 147/10 Entry Book of telegrams to and from War Office 29 January 1885.
29. Arthur (ed.), p. 162.
30. Ibid., p. 166.
31. Symons, *England's Pride*, p. 272.
32. WO147/8 Journal Entry of 17 February 1885.
33. Ibid., 19 February 1885.

**Chapter 6: Success and Frustration**

1. Symons, *England's Pride*, p. 272.
2. WO 147/39 Confidential Reports on the Nile Expedition 1884–5 By Officer who took part in the operations, Edited and arranged in the Intelligence Branch, War Office, 1886.
3. H. Bailes, 'Patterns of Thought in the Late Victorian Army', *Journal of Strategic Studies*, Vol. 4, No. 1 (1981), p. 40.
4. I. Beckett, 'Edward Stanhope at the War Office 1887–92', *Journal of Strategic Studies* (June 1982), p. 279.
5. Maurice, p. 227.
6. Beckett, 'Edward Stanhope at the War Office 1887–92', p. 291.
7. Kochanski, *Sir Garnet Wolseley*, p. 197.
8. Ibid., p. 199.
9. Ibid., p. 203.
10. Maurice, p. 275.
11. Lehmann, p. 384.
12. H. Kochanski, 'Field Marshal Viscount Wolseley as commander-in-chief, 1895–1900: A reassessment', *Journal of Strategic Studies*, Vol. 20, 2 (1997), p. 121.
13. Lehmann, p. 385.
14. B. Bond, 'The Retirement of the Duke of Cambridge', *Royal United Services Journal*, Vol. 106 (1961), p. 553.
15. T. Travers, *The Killing Ground* (Pen & Sword, Barnsley, 2003), p. 41.
16. R. Meinertzhagen, *Army Diary 1899–1926* (Oliver & Boyd, Stroud, 1960), p. 16.
17. Maurice, p. 315.
18. Ibid., p. 317.
19. E. Spiers, *The Late Victorian Army 1868–1902* (Manchester University Press, 1992), p. 306.
20. Lehmann, p. 390.

**Conclusion**

1. Kochanski, 'Field Marshal Viscount Wolseley as commander-in-chief, 1895–1900', p. 137.

# Bibliography

Note: Place of publication is London, unless specified.

**Primary Sources**

The Buller Papers, Devon Heritage Centre, Ref: 2065.
Wolseley's Private Journal of the Asante Expedition WO 147/3.
Wolseley's Private Journal kept during 1879 South Africa Campaigns WO147/7.
Wolseley's Private Journal of the Gordon Relief Expedition WO 147/8.
Entry Book of Telegrams to and from the WO WO147/10.
Confidential Report of the Nile Expedition WO 147/39.
Report of Committee WO 147/59.

**Secondary Sources**

Arthur, G. (ed.), *The Letters of Lord and Lady Wolseley 1870–1911* (Heinemann, 1922).
Asher, M., *Khartoum – The Ultimate Imperial Adventure* (Viking, 2005).
Beckett, I. (ed.), *Wolseley and Ashanti* (The History Press for the Army Records Society, Stroud, 2009).
Black, J., *War in the Nineteenth Century* (Polity, Cambridge, 2009).
Blunt, W., *The Secret History of the English Occupation of Egypt* (A.A. Knopf, New York, 1922).
Bond, B. (ed.), *Victorian Military Campaigns* (Tom Donovan Publishing, 1994).
Brackenbury, H., *The Ashanti War – A Narrative – Prepared from the Official Documents*, 2 vols (William Blackwood, Edinburgh, 1874).
Brice, C., *The Thinking Man's Soldier – The Life and Career of General Sir Henry Brackenbury, 1837–1914* (Helion, Solihull, 2012).
Brooks, R., *The Long Arm of Empire – Naval Brigades from the Crimea to the Boxer Rebellion* (Constable, 1999).
Butler, F., *The Life of Sir George Pomeroy-Colley* (John Murray, 1899).
Claridge, W.W., *A History of the Gold Coast and Ashanti*, 2 vols (John Murray, 1915).
Cope, W., *The History of the Rifle Brigade, Vol.2: 1816–1876* (Leonaur, Driffield, 2010).
Corvi, S. and Beckett, I. (eds), *Victoria's Generals* (Pen & Sword, Barnsley, 2009).
David, S., *Zulu – The Heroism and Tragedy of the Zulu War of 1879* (Viking, 2004).
Dodds, M. (ed.), *History of Ghana* (American Women's Association in Ghana, Accra, 1974).
Edgerton, R., *The Fall of the Asante Empire – The Hundred-Year War for Africa's Gold Coast* (The Free Press, New York, 1995).
Farwell, B., *Queen Victoria's Little Wars* (Allan Lane, 1973).
Farwell, B., *Eminent Victorian Soldiers – Seekers of Glory* (Viking, 1986).
Featherstone, D., *Tel-el-Kebir* (Osprey, Oxford, 1993).
Featherstone, D., *Khartoum 1885* (Osprey, Oxford, 1993).
Gordon, H., *The War Office* (Putnam, 1935).
Greaves, A., *Crossing the Buffalo – The Zulu War of 1879* (Weidenfeld & Nicolson, 2005).

Harding, M. (ed.), *The Victorian Soldier – Studies in the History of the British Army, 1816–1914* (National Army Museum Publication, 1993).

Harries-Jenkins, G., *The Army in Victorian Society* (Routledge, 1977).

Haythornthwaite, P., *The Colonial Wars Source Book* (Arms & Armour Press, 1995).

Heathcote, T., *The British Field Marshals, 1736–1997, A Biographical Dictionary* (Leo Cooper, Barnsley, 1999).

Hernon, I., *Britain's Forgotten Wars – Colonial Campaigns of the Nineteenth Century* (Sutton Publishing, Stroud, 2003).

Hernon, I., *The Sword and the Sketch Book – A Pictorial History of Queen Victoria's Wars* (Spellmount, Stroud, 2012).

Keegan, J. and Wheatcroft, A. (eds), *Who's Who in Military History* (Routledge, Abingdon, 1995).

Keown-Boyd, H., *A Good Dusting – The Sudan Campaigns 1883–1899* (Leo Cooper, 1986).

Knight, I., *Queen Victoria Enemies, Vol. 2, Northern Africa* (Osprey, Oxford, 2005).

Kochanski, H., *Sir Garnet Wolseley – Victorian Hero* (Hambledon Press, 1999).

Kofi Tieku, A., *History and Facts About Ashante Kingdom and Ghana*, Vol. 1 (Schrodinger's Publications, Accra, 2016).

Kwadwo, O., *An Outline of Asante History* (O. Kwadwo, Kumasi, 1994).

Kwadwo, O., *An Outline of Asante History*, 2 vols (O. Kwadwo, Kumasi, 2000).

Kwadwo, O., *A Handbook on Asante Culture* (O. Kwadwo, Kumasi, 2002).

Lehmann, J., *The Model Major-General, A Biography of Field Marshal Lord Wolseley* (Houghton Mifflin, Boston, USA, 1964).

Lloyd, A., *The Drums of Kumasi – The Story of the Ashanti Wars* (Panther, 1964).

Low, C. R., *A Memoir of Lieutenant-General Sir Garnet J Wolseley*, 2 vols (R. Bentley, 1878).

McNicholls, P., *Journey Through The Wilderness – Garnet Wolseley's Canadian Red River Expedition of 1870* (Helion, Warwick, 2019).

Manning, S., *Evelyn Wood V.C. – Pillar of Empire* (Pen & Sword, Barnsley, 2007).

Manning, S., *Soldiers of the Queen* (Spellmount, Stroud, 2009).

Manning, S., *The Martini-Henry Rifle* (Osprey, Oxford, 2013).

Manning, S., *Bayonet to Barrage, Weaponry on the Victorian Battlefield* (Pen & Sword, Barnsley, 2020).

Manning, S., *Britain at War with the Asante Nation, 1823–1900* (Pen & Sword, Barnsley, 2021).

Manning, S., *Britain Against the Xhosa and Zulu Peoples* (Pen & Sword, Barnsley, 2022).

Mansfield, P., *The British in Egypt* (Holt, Rinehart & Winston, New York, 1972).

Maurice, F., *The Life of Lord Wolseley* (Heinemann, 1924).

Maxwell, L., *The Ashanti Ring – Sir Garnet Wolseley's Campaigns 1870–1882* (Leo Cooper, 1985).

Meinertzhagen, R., *Army Diary 1899–1926* (Oliver & Boyd, Stroud, 1960).

Miller, S. (ed.), *Queen Victoria's Wars – British Military Campaigns, 1857–1902* (Cambridge University Press, 2021).

Morris, D., *Washing of the Spears – The Rise and Fall of the Zulu Nation* (Simon & Schuster, New York, 1965).

Preston, A. (ed.), *In Relief of Gordon, Lord Wolseley's Campaign Journal of the Khartoum Relief Expedition 1884–1885* (Hutchinson, 1967).

Preston, A. (ed.), *The South African Journal of Sir Garnet Wolseley, 1879–1880* (A.A. Balkema, Cape Town, 1973).

Raugh, H. (ed.), *The British Army 1815–1914* (Routledge, 2006).

Robinson, C., *Celebrities of the Army* (George Newnes, 1900).
Smith, P., *Victoria's Victories – Seven Classic Battles of the British Army 1849–1884* (Spellmount, Tunbridge Wells, 1987).
Spiers, E., *The Late Victorian Army 1868–1902* (Manchester University Press, 1992).
Spiers, E., *The Scottish Soldier and Empire, 1854–1902* (Edinburgh University Press, 2006).
Stanley, G., *Toil & Trouble – Military Expeditions to Red River* (Dundurn Press, Toronto, 1989).
Stanley, H., *Coomassie & Magala* (Sampson Low, Marton & Co., 1874).
Symons, J., *Buller's Campaigns* (Cresset Press, 1963).
Symons, J., *England's Pride: The Story of the Gordon Relief Expedition* (Hamish Hamilton, 1965).
Thomas, J. H., *A Full and Authentic Diary of the Ashanti Expedition* (William Emelow, Pembroke, 1875).
Travers, T., *The Killing Ground* (Pen & Sword, Barnsley, 2003).
Vandervort, B., *Wars of Imperial Conquest in Africa 1830–1914* (UCL Press, 1998).
Wheeler, O., *The War Office Past & Present* (Methuen, 1914).
Wilkenson-Latham, R., *The Sudan Campaigns 1881–98* (Osprey, Oxford, 1976).
Williams, C., *The Life of Lieut-General Sir Henry Evelyn Wood*, Vol. 1 (Sampson Low, Marston, 1892).
Wolseley, G., *Narrative of the War with China in 1860* (Longman, 1862).
Wolseley, G., *The Soldier's Pocket Book For Field Service* (4th Edition, Macmillan 1882).
Wolseley, G., *A Soldier's Life*, 2 vols (Archibald Constable, 1903).
Wood, E., *From Midshipman to Field Marshal*, 2 vols (Methuen, 1906).
Wood, E. (ed.), *British Battles on Land and Sea*, Vol. 2 (Cassell, 1915).
Wood, E., *Winnowed Memories* (Cassell, 1917).
Wright, W., *A Tidy Little War: The British Invasion of Egypt 1882* (The History Press, Stroud, 2009).
Wright, W., *A British Lion in Zululand – Sir Garnet Wolseley in South Africa* (Amberley, Stroud, 2017).

**Journals and Internet Resources**

Bailes, H., 'Patterns of Thought in the Late Victorian Army', *Journal of Strategic Studies*, Vol. 4, No.1 (1981), pp. 29–45.
Beckett, I., 'Edward Stanhope and the War Office, 1887–1892, *Journal of Strategic Studies*, Vol. 5, No. 2 (1982), pp. 278–307.
Beckett, I., *Wolseley, Garnet Joseph, First Viscount Wolseley (1833–1913)*, Oxford Dictionary of National Biography (2008) https://doi-org.uoeibrary.idm.ocic.org/10.1093/ref:odnb/36995.
Bond, B., 'The Retirement of the Duke of Cambridge', *Journal of the Royal United Service Institution*, Vol. 106 (1961), pp. 544–53.
Hansard – http://hansard.parliament.uk
Holt, E., 'Garnet Wolseley Soldier of Empire', *History Today*, Vol. 8, No. 10 (1958), pp. 706–13.
Kochanski, H., 'Field Marshal Viscount Wolseley as Commander-in-Chief, 1895–1900: A Reassessment', *Journal of Strategic Studies*, Vol. 20, No. 2 (1997), pp. 119–39.
McIntyre, W., 'British Policy in West Africa: The Ashanti Expedition of 1873–4', *The Historical Journal*, Vol.5, No.1 (1962), pp. 19–46
Manning, S., 'Learning the Trade: Use and Misuse of Intelligence during the British Colonial Campaigns of the 1870s', *Intelligence*, Vol. 22, No. 5 (October, 2007), pp. 664–60.

Queen Victoria's Journals – http://www.roya.uk/queen-victoria-journals.
Patterson, R., '"To Form a Correct Estimate of Their Nothingness when Compared with it": British Exhibitions of Military Technology in the Abyssinian and Ashanti Expeditions', *Journal of Imperial & Commonwealth History*, Vol. 44, No. 4 (Aug 2016), pp. 551–72.
Robinson, C., Major-General, 'The European Brigade under Sir Archibald Alison in the Ashanti War, 1873–4', *Royal United Services Institution Journal*, Vol. 63, pp. 15–38.
Tylden, G., 'Tel-El-Kebir, 13th September, 1882', *Journal of the Society of Army Research*, Vol. 31, No. 126 (1953), pp. 52–7.
Tylden, G., 'The Sekukuni Campaign of November to December, 1879', *Journal of the Society of Army Research* (1951), Vol. 31, No. 110, pp. 129–35.
Ukpabi, S. C., 'West Indian Troops and the Defence of British West Africa in the Nineteenth Century', *African Studies Review*, Vol. 17, No. I (1974), pp. 133–50.
Wolseley, G., 'Narrative of the Red River Expedition', *Blackwood's Magazine*, Vol. 109 (February 1871).
Wolseley, G., 'Our Autumn Manoeuvres', *Blackwood's Magazine*, Vol. 112, November 1872, pp. 627–44.
Wolseley, G., 'Long and Short Service', *Nineteenth Century*, Vol. IX (1881), pp. 558–72.
Wood, E., 'The Ashanti Expedition of 1873–4', *Journal of the United Services Institution*, Vol. XVIII (1875), pp. 331–57.

# Index